Amazing Facts
IV
Tantalizing Trivia

Thomas F. Shubnell, Ph.D.

ISBN 13- 978-1974264438

ISBN 10- 1974264432

Cover and interior design by TFS

Please ask your local library to carry my books.

We live in an interconnected world. Many are used to reading quickly, then going back and reading more background information later. I have included some links within the text of this book.

Links are easy enough to overlook while reading, but available for further in depth reading online. For eBook readers, the links are live for easy clicking.

Autohagiography

If you enjoy this, you will also love, Amazing Facts and Bite Sized Brain Food, Amazing Facts II Tons of Trivia, and Amazing Facts III Trivia Treasures. They are collections of thousands of amazing facts about the things you don't know, but want to know, and facts you think you know, but don't. Nestled in among the facts are bite sized tidbits of knowledge you can use to spice up any conversation.

"Bacon Orgazmia" a pandect of porcineology and a homage to the goodness and gallimaufry of all things bacon, including history, types, recipes, events, and more.

"Gracious Me . . . Is Nothing Sacred" is a non-sectarian and hilarious look at all religions from the beginning of time. From Atheism to Zen it truly proves that laughter is good for the soul.

Medical humor abounds in the best selling "Medical Humor - medical nonsense to tickle your funny bone. A great collection of medical funny stuff, including stories, jokes, and hilarious pictures and cartoons.

"Unelectum All" is a reader's digest of politics. It makes the case for change using politicians own words. It begins with early campaign promises and follows with political absurdities that unfold after elections.

A wacky book, "Men vs. Women, a Book of Lists" examines life from a different perspective and tells it all - the differences between the sexes are real and funny.

Even more fun can be found in "The Best of Terrible Tommy and Yucky Chucky," a collection of the best Terrible Tommy and Yucky Chucky jokes of all time.

More hilarious reading can be found in "Giggles, Gags, and Quips, Special Picks" a collection of the best jokes, pictures, billboards, stories, and cartoons.

Relationships can be funny, as shown in "Flowers, Foreplay, Facelifts, and Flatulence" a humorous romp through the four stages of relationships.

Also collect all the "Greatest Jokes of the Century" series of books. 25 wildly funny and hilarious compendiums of the greatest jokes, tidbits, stories, and trivia that are all sure to induce uncontrollable laughter.

"The Art of Installation and the Science of Implementation" is a serious project management primer, including tools and techniques for successful software implementation projects.

Don't forget to collect my Profound Thoughts, a 5 book series of great wisdom, aphorisms, and quotes from great minds.

All written by Thomas F. Shubnell and available online, your favorite bookstore, or as eBooks.

Table of Contents

Technology Facts

ALL ABOUT GOOGLE

The following Technology sections contain live links that can be used if you are reading an electronic version of this book. If you are reading a paper copy, enjoy the information and ignore the links. The information is interesting and informative on its own, whether you use it now or remember the next time you visit the web.

Six Great Google Tips - We all know Google is great for searches, but here are a few tips to make your online life simpler.

If you want to track a USPS, UPS, or FedEx package, no need to go to their site, just type in the tracking code to find out where your package is.

How about that flight? Just type in an airline flight number to get its arrival/departure status.

If you need a quick stock quote, just type in the stock symbol.

Are you looking for a movie? Type in movies followed by your city name.

Wondering if it will rain today? Type in weather followed by your zip code.

Last, don't forget to use the quote marks for names, like "chuck norris" or "liberty bell" to get the whole name. *If you want to buy my books, you don't need Google, just go to Amazon and type my surname (shubnell).*

Google Truth - You have probably heard that the Library of Congress is to archive every single public tweet ever made. There are about 55 million tweets sent every day.

Google also revealed how it is going to make the Twitter archive searchable for users. Google unveiled a replay feature that lets users search tweets posted at any given point in time right down to the minute.

Anyone wanting to know what people tweeted about on say the Haiti earthquake or the Oscars can type into the Google search box, select "show options" on the result page and then click 'updates'. A timeline will appear above the results allowing you to zoom in on tweets by the hour or minute.

Google says, "We think this is pretty significant because up until now the discussion has been about what is happening now and with today's replay button people will be able to go back and see what people were actually talking about around big events."

Currently the replay feature will only cover the last two months of tweets. Google said later this year it hopes to cover the entire archive all the way back to March 2006.

YouTube - YouTube has been open for business for five years. Last October, 2009, it stated that it was getting one billion hits a day. Now, Google owned YouTube gets over two billion hits a day on the site. The site said its traffic is more than double the traffic of the top three commercial TV stations combined.

YouTube is no longer just for quick and funny videos, it now has live sports (complete games), news, live music concerts and more. There are twenty four hours of new video content uploaded each minute. *The best part is that Billy Mays commercials are 'on demand' and not 'in your face'.*

Google Art - If you like ancient masterpieces, Google has a real treat for you. Google staff has been photographing art from various galleries around the world the pictures are available for free on the web. It is called the Google Art Project and it is spectacular. You can zoom in on pictures to great detail. It is like going to a museum with a magnifying glass. It is worth a look and a good link to share with children going to school. Here is the link http://www.googleartproject.com/

Google Faces - If you need to find some images for various occasions and find searching for images is too difficult. Google has a parameter in place for images in situations where you might need an image which describes a face.

Suppose I search for the term "happy" then the Google results page displays smileys, but I would like to use images of happy people. Even if I choose the term as "happy face" the results don't show images which contain people. For this there is a parameter "imgtype" which you can use with the URL. For this put in the URL as follows:

   http://images.google.co.in/images?q=happy&imgtype=face

Five More Great Google Tips -
Look for keywords that could be similar to the one you are using. "vizio ~ tutorial". (The tilde ~ is usually the left top key, next to the numeral one.) Google will search for similar keywords like guides, how tos, manuals etc.

Have a math problem, type "sqrt(100)" for the square root of 100.

How to find a site that your company has blocked - "cache:xyz.com".

Looking for a specific title - "intitle: papamurphys".

Looking for pictures, type in something like "shadows" then click on the 'images' word on the left of the results page. It will show all pictures, instead of web pages.

Google Earth - Most of you have heard of the Google Earth project that takes satellite pictures of the globe, but have you seen the pictures? Google Earth has software that can be downloaded to your PC to navigate anywhere on the globe and do close up and far away looks at many things.

Another Five Great Google Tips - Google is more helpful than many know. Here are a few more tips to make your life on the web easier. *Quotes are used for examples only.*

Need a map, type "map tampa fl".

Need a definition, "define beauty".

Lost your calculator and need to do some quick math, "15+15".

Shopping for a new PC, give it a price range, "PC $500..$700".

Looking for a zip code, "75214". This query also offers a map.

Two More Google Search Tips - Type "Google patents" in a search bar, and the first hit you get will take you to Google Patent Search. Google and the U.S. Patent and Trademark Office have struck an agreement, and you can now have access to more than 7 million patents, including drawings.

When searching for something and you only want current information, click on the 'search tools' on the left. It opens a list of other features, such as 'Past 24 hours', past week, etc.

Try one, then click the search button again and it refines your search to whatever time period you chose.

Google Realtime Search - For those news junkies, or tweet followers, or just those who want an up to the minute (or look back in time) look at breaking stories or topics, Google has a new tool.

You can access Google Realtime Search at its own address, www.google.com/realtime There is a link just under the search box "Learn more about realtime search" that has a video and some tips for using the new feature.

On the new homepage you will find some great tools to help you refine and understand your results. First, you can use geographic refinements to find updates and news near you, or in a region you specify. So if you are traveling to Las Vegas this summer, you can check out tweets from Vegasonians to get ideas for activities happening right where you are. You can check out other things, like earthquakes, etc. and follow the stories from real people in real time.

In addition, there is a conversations view, making it easy to follow a discussion on the real-time web. With the new "full conversation" feature, you can browse the entire conversation in a single glance. Tweets, or other conversations, are organized from oldest to newest and indented so you quickly see how the conversation developed.

There is also an update to Google Alerts, making it easy to stay informed about a topic of your choosing. You can create an alert specifically for "updates" to get an email the moment your topic appears, or you can set alerts to email you once per day or week. *The web may have much useless and useful information, but it also provides honesty and truth that is not available from politicians or the media. In the future, it will be difficult to rewrite history when it is available from the web, as it actually happened.*

Historypin - There is an interesting web site that allows you to add historical pictures to Google Street Maps. Now you can put yourself on the map. Go to http://www.historypin.com - Very Cool Stuff.

Google Transparency - A new feature from Google tells how many government requests it gets from around the world to remove content from services, or provide information about users of services and products, or shut down sites. It shows by country for six month increments. Sensitive government requests are not shown, due to national security concerns. Not surprisingly, the US seems to top the list for numbers of requests.

http://www.google.com/transparencyreport/governmentrequests/
Personally, I am tired of the 'transparency' word. What ever happened to plain old 'truth' and 'honesty'?

Google Voice - Users can register, sign up for a phone number in a local area code, and add multiple land line and cell-phone numbers to an account. When someone calls a Google Voice phone number, all the registered phones ring at the same time.

The service takes several telephony technologies and connects them to the Web. It is the voice equivalent of an e-mail address. Once you register a number you never have to worry about which phone you are using, even if you switch offices, homes, or cell phones. You can even press 4 to record a current call.

No matter which phone you use, there is one portal for all voice-mail messages. You can play them on the Web, save them as MP3 files, and even post a voice-mail message on a website. Conference calls are also easy. Answer an incoming call to add it to the current one.

Google Flights - This is very interesting. Go to Google and type in "flights" sans quotes and check prices from airlines, all in one place. This is sure to provide some competition from other sites that do the same. I would think Google has more sources. Anyway, good way to get fast comparisons and hopefully save a few bucks.

Five More Google Goodies - The quote marks are only used to show a sample.

To find the time anywhere, type time and the city name, "time Dallas".

To exclude something, type a dash in front of the word, "football - lions".

To find the current currency exchange rate, "usd euro".

To find the weather, "weather detroit".

To find a number, "phonebook: jones chicago".

Google Voice and Image Search - Two very cool new ways to make your life easier while searching. For Google Voice Search, click on the microphone icon to the right of the search box and start speaking. For Google Image Search, you can use a photo from the web, from your PC, or scan a photo in. To use this, you need to click on 'images' while on the Google page, then click on the little Camera icon on the right of the search bar. It will provide any information it can find, such as location, history, or whatever.

I used voice and it works as well or better than typing, and there were no mistyped words. Tried images and had interesting results. First used a photo of myself and it found many pictures with the same pose and coloring, but the people did not look similar and it did not find any pictures of me, although there are many on the web.

Next I tried a picture of a church and it found similar colored pictures and many buildings, but also showed pictures of beaches, people with camels, etc. Next, I tried a logo, using the IBM logo. It immediately came up with 'best guess' and guessed IBM logo. It then gave history, company facts, Wikipedia info, and a thousand other results.

Bottom line, Google voice is easy, fun, and works if you have a mic on your PC (most laptops and all phones (*duh*) have a mic built in). Google image is not yet ready for prime time, except in limited situations, such as finding info on famous locations, buildings, logos, etc. *Google Image is available now, and Voice is available. You will know when you can use it, by looking for the microphone icon in the search bar.*

Send Money in Gmail - If you are in the US or UK, you can exchange money with friends and family quickly and safely using Google Wallet. You can also do this directly from Gmail.

If it is your first time sending, receiving, or requesting money, you may need to verify your identity. Once you verify your identity, any money someone sends to you will automatically go into your Wallet Balance.

Receiving money, and transferring it to your bank account, is always free no matter which payment source the sender uses. Sending money is also free using a bank account or debit card, but has a 2.9% fee if you use a credit card. Most transactions are completed within 2 business days or less.

Google News is Cool - Why read twenty newspapers to get a glimpse of what is going on around the world? Google News watches more than 4,500 news sources worldwide and you can search about 200 years of articles. You can personalize news to your specific taste if you have a Google account and you can get alerts of topics that interest you. It also works on your Smartphone. Type *google news* in Google and it will take you to the site.

Seven Useful Google Tips - Are you trying to remember the name of a song you heard? Try typing, winner takes it* abba and Google will try to complete your search.

You can search by file type by typing filetype:ppt or filetype:excel or any other file type.

Putting two periods, .. between two numbers will search within that range, such as news 2013..2015.

If you are looking for a definition type, define: followed by the word you want defined.

In a restaurant and need to figure out tip, type in, tip calculator and Google will present an onscreen calculator for you. You set amount, tip percent and it does the work for you.

If you want listen to some music, type in, music by Cher or any other artist and add youtube at the end.

You can do the same for books, type in, books by and the author name, (of course I had to test this by typing in my own name).

Google Ocean View - If you think Google street view is cool, you will love street view/ocean. I like to use street view to see what a house, or building, or block looks like, so when I drive there I know what to look for.

Now we can do the same under the sea. Thinking of going somewhere warm to do some snorkeling? Try ocean view to see what types of fish you might encounter or take a tour of sunken ships. Street view/ocean has wonderful photography and all the features of street view, plus video. Caution, the views can be addicting.

Google Timer - You can set a timer for yourself for free. Type any time into Google, such as ten minutes timer. Adding the word timer after the time period sets the timer countdown and Google will play a sound when time is up. Great way to set a break time for yourself or reminder that coffee is done.

Using Google Voice - Users of Google's voice-control features such as OK Google are probably aware that the company stores the voice recordings it receives when they talk to it. Did you know it keeps a list of all the recordings the company has ever made of you. If you have or have ever had an Android phone with Google's "OK Google" voice-control system, the link below will show a list of every command you have ever given it, including a play button next to it. https://history.google.com/history/audio

Google also has a location history, showing any location the company has tracked you to, through apps such as Google Maps as well as simply using an Android phone. It can be found here https://maps.google.co.uk/locationhistory/b/0

Google - It is cataloging the history of words, and now pictures. The book section is already up to millions (including most of mine) and it is actively scanning books in libraries around the world and offering full text search. If someone could make use of the combined knowledge, we could be in for a unprecedented age of wisdom and invention. This is in addition to the pictures of all the major, and some minor roads in the world and satellite shots of the earth, and recreating the ruins of times gone by, and cataloging languages, not to mention the billions of web pages.

Google is using its money to be the "Webster on steroids" of our age. It is one company that is giving back (for free) knowledge. As mashups gain in strength and ease-of-use, I can see many Leonardos emerging to make sense of that knowledge and bring a true new age of wisdom.

One recent effort is scanning Life magazine's library. Not finished, but what they have is already great.

With the recent talk of the economy reminding many of the 1930s, that group of pictures is a bit depressing.

The picture collection is like a walk through living history. The fifties are all Disney and the sixties are all moon shot stuff, but the file is growing and will have more later. They are all free if you don't make money by using them. They are high quality and could make for some great framed prints for the wall. Here's the Life magazine link, but be careful, you could spend way too much time looking.
http://images.google.com/hosted/life

What Do You Love - Here is another fun Google feature. It is called What Do You Love, or WDYL. It is a Google search page, but shows results in categories. It has latest news, books, start a discussion group, pictures, dates for events, blogs, 3D, translation, maps, patents, and more. You can enter a name, word, topic, such as bacon, or anything you can search for in Google. Just another fun way to find out about those things you love. www.wdyl.com/

WORLD WIDE WEB AND INTERNET

Father of the Internet - Sir Tim Berners-Lee, born 1955, and inventor of the Web's software standards in 1989, tends to be fast-paced and nonlinear. He is currently director of the World Wide Web Consortium and a professor at M.I.T.

When asked if he were do it over again today, would he do anything differently, he admitted he might make one change. He would get rid of the double slash "//" after the "http:" in Web addresses.

He said the double slash, a programming convention at the time, turned out to not be really necessary. *Amazing to think the web is less than thirty years old and how much it has changed the world. In fact, the world wide web (WWW) was first mentioned in print in the New York Times in 1993.*

> The world wide web (WWW) was first mentioned in print in the New York Times in 1993.

Here's a tip, when typing in a site name, just type the name, such as 'shubsthoughts' then hold down the 'ctrl' key and hit 'enter'. Your web browser will fill in the rest for you and send you to the site.

Internet Immortality? - While recently browsing Forbes, found an interesting web site, postedforever.com. It allows you to post up to 16Gb of any documents, pictures, videos, family tree info, etc.

It promises to post the info on the site in a private 'room' for you where you can make any or all of the information public or private. It also promises, for a onetime fee, to keep the info "at least as long as civilization exists". Very interesting concept and worth a read. If you try it, click on the 'About Us' and 'FAQ'. For a sample, click on search and type in "lindstrom" the site owner's name.
https://postedforever.com/intro/index.html

Paying For It - Here is an interesting site. It is called daystopay. The site provides a calculator that helps you find out how many days you have to work to pay for things you want to buy. For instance, if you want to buy a new television and it takes 100 days to pay for it, is it still worth the price. Fun site, easy to use, and provides for some fun budget discussions.

This Book is Awesome - This is not the first time I have mentioned a book, but there is something in this book for everyone. 'The Book of Awesome' has a thousand awesome everyday things, like #335 Catching someone you love admiring you from across the room. It adds detailed explanations to each item.

Read some of the entries on the web site - or get the book http://1000awesomethings.com/

You've Got Mail - This phrase and other familiar phrases spoken by your computer including 'Welcome', 'File's done' and 'Goodbye' were voiced by Elwood Edwards. He said his wife worked for a company called Quantum Computer Services that became AOL and she volunteered his voice in 1989 to the then future CEO, Steve Case. He recorded the words on a cassette deck in his living room. The familiar voice made it into a movie of the same name and continues, even though Edwards has been retired for a few years.

Looking Back - Rrrewind provides a way to look back at social media's past, letting you browse the archives of the most popular items posted to sites like Delicious, Reddit, YouTube, Hulu, and more.

Using Rrrewind is pretty simple. Upon visiting the site you will be presented with the popular posts from yesterday, currently defaulting to Delicious. You can switch between different sites via the left hand menu, or visit the archives by clicking the link in the upper right hand corner.

Currently Rrrewind's archives date back to June 29th, 2009 for Delicious, but it varies depending on the site. If you're looking for old, popular social media, Rrrewind is a great place to find it.

Little Book, Little Price - Amazon has created a sweet spot for many would-be authors. It now offers Amazon Singles, which allows writers, thinkers, scientists, and others to submit original material of 5,000 - 30,000 words for publication. These relatively short works, beginning at about 30 pages, allow those folks who do not have enough information to fill a book, but more than might fit in a magazine, to get published.

Pricing is intended to fall between $.99 and $4.99. This niche fits nicely with the current short attention span of the internet generation, who want to finish a book on the commute to work or become an almost expert on the latest technology or scientific process. Many 'How To' books fit nicely into this length. *Taken to the extreme, I can visualize describing the history of the world on one page as we progress back to petroglyphs.*

Searching in a Kayak - Kayak.com is an interesting meta-search engine. Kayak itself sells nothing, but what it does do is find airline prices and information. That is something that had been limited to Priceline, Orbitz, etc., and the airline sites.

When you log onto Kayak.com, you are presented with a simple search form that asks where you wish to travel. You can search for one-way or round-trip trips, as well as multi-city itineraries. Clicking the "Search multiple sites" button starts the action.

The results page graphic shows airline websites being scanned for their up-to-the-moment information. Kayak has the ability to go to nearly all of the airline databases, extract their information and reformat it into something understandable. The animated display also shows you an interim status of specific airlines that are being scanned at that moment.

When Kayak is done, you are presented with an ordered list of flights that meet your search criteria. The default is to sort them by price, from the most economical to the very expensive, but can change the sequence as you desire. It has many other cool features and can also help with hotels, cars, etc. *A great alternative that is not beholding to any specific airline.*

Ways to Find Someone on the Web - There are a dwindling number of sites that provide name or phone number info for free. Seems we all need to make a living. There are a few interesting sites that provide more information about you than you might like to see.

Scam callers are an increasing problem but there are a few sites to report the information and you can use them to see if anyone else complained about a particular number. One site, identifycallers.com lets you post comments and read others comments.

Whitepages.com and yellowpages.com offer name to number and number to name lookups for people or businesses, just like paper.

Addictomatic.com/ is another site that offers a wealth of information, mainly from blogs, tweets, YouTube, Yahoo, Facebook, etc., but not personal info, such as address, phone.

Wayback Machine - If you are interested in what a particular web site used to look like, you can use the Wayback Machine website to help. It shows a calendar and you pick the date you wish to see what the site looked like. http://waybackmachine.org/

Some get around it and the pages are no longer available. For instance, I was looking up some info from the Obama campaign where he answered questions that were sent in. The pages have all been replaced with a page that sends you to the whitehouse.gov site. *Seems the answers from back then might not be the same today and we might be confused.*

Speed - We have become accustomed to speed for our internet play time that we get upset when things slow down. All Internet Service Providers (ISP) do not measure their speed equally.

ISPs are the big name companies, like Comcast, Verizon, AT&T, Sprint, etc., that offer you service and provide an on-ramp to the internet and email from your phone or wireless access for your laptop, or iPad. They tout claims of 3G (3rd generation cellular wireless), 4G (4th generation), etc., but the claims are not truly living up to the legal descriptions of those services. For instance, the original ITU-R requirements of data rates approximately up to 1 Gbits (1 gigabit = a billion bits per second) for 4G systems.

Average phone users get speeds of about 1Mbps (1 thousandth of a Gbits) and the minimum is 400Mbps.

Bottom line; do not believe any of the hype. All providers these days are good enough, unless you are a power user and download large amounts of data or play games with users around the world. Be happy that, for the most part, we no longer have to rely on dial-up service for our home PCs.

There are many sites to measure your internet speed. Just type in something like test my internet speed into Google and it will provide options. Most are free and take less than a minute.

Tiger Oil Memos - There is a number of absolutely wacky memos from irascible Edward 'Tiger Mike' Davis, CIO of Tiger Oil, written in the 1970s. Did some checking and he did exist and did have a terrible attitude toward his employees. If you think you have boss problems, they are minor, compared to this guy.

Sample: "I swear, but since I am the owner of this company, that is my privilege...There will be absolutely no swearing, by ANY employee, male or female, in this office, ever." "Anyone who lets their hair grow below their ears to where I can't see their ears means they don't wash. If they don't wash, they stink, and if they stink, I don't want the son-of-a-b**ch around me." "We do not pay starvation wages, and there are some people left in this world who want to work. I am not fond of hippies, long-hairs, dope fiends or alcoholics." *BTW, Tiger Oil went bankrupt. Not sure if it was related to Tiger Mike's memos. I think some should be framed for posterity.*

Facebook Statistics - It is amazing how Facebook has been growing by over a hundred million users each year for the past few years. Of course, along with that fame comes click scams and apps that steal your friend list with their email and phone numbers, ripe for the plucking. It is much more fun than scary, so enjoy, just be sure to review your security settings and do not click on anything that seems too good to be true. *See ya on Facebook. . .*

New Kind of Search Engine - This one doesn't just provide links, like Google. Wolfram/Alpha.com gives you meaningful data back. Type in a company name and get the stock quote, type in a calculation and it gives you the answer, type in a date and it gives you information about sunrise, day of year, etc. It gives scientific answers, chemistry answers, culture.

Internet Radio - Here is an interesting 'old is new' concept. Free music, sports, and news from around the world. It is called Ira, an Internet Radio Adapter that connects automatically to any wireless Internet network in about three minutes without the need of a computer. Just take it out of the box, plug it in, and connect it to your home stereo or speakers with the included audio cables. It features over 11,000 stations from just about every country in the world and includes On Demand (Podcast) programming for many stations so you can listen to your favorite shows when you want. It costs about $150 for the device, including the remote control and piggybacks on your internet connection for free.

Go ask Alice - There is an interesting site called simply Alice.com. It is a storeless shopping site where manufacturers display their household items directly. Coupons, if available, are subtracted from purchases and always free shipping. The idea is big savings by factory direct with multiple manufactures, like Tide, etc.

Manufacturers set their own prices and receive all of that revenue. The site makes money by giving the companies spending data, advertising space, and distributing samples for them to targeted customers. It allows price comparisons. An interesting concept to save money on the mundane items we use every day. *Sorry, not available in Alaska or Hawaii.*

I Don't Believe it - There is a new site, on the order of Snopes that allows you to find out if the web page you are reading is disputed by other sources and what the alternative points of view are.

As you browse <u>http://disputefinder.cs.berkeley.edu/</u> it looks for disputed claims. If it finds any then it highlights them. Clicking on a disputed claim brings up evidence for and against that claim found by other users of Dispute Finder. It allows you to mark new disputed claims and see what disputed claims have been marked by other users.

It is from Berkeley and beta, and somewhat biased from what I have seen so far, (You know how those damn academics are) but still might be fun to try. One example about Global Warming being a scam - it offers government data that shows the Earth's average surface temperature has increased by about 1.2 to 1.4°F in the last 100 years. *Take off your clothes, another thousand years or so and this place will be about eleven degrees hotter. For those that use Firefox, there is a Dispute Finder extension. I use it and it seems stable.*

How to Get Rid of Unwanted Catalogs - When you receive unwanted catalogs or other paper mail from specific sources, call the (usually toll-free) customer service number of the organization or business and request that your name be removed from their mailing list.

Other options are to make your request via e-mail from the company's website, or via letter or postcard.

Since the mailing label will help the company identify how you are listed in its files, have the label handy when you call, or tape it to the postcard if you make a written request. Sign and date your request. *Think of the cycle, they print the stuff, send it to the post office, which delivers it to our mailbox, and we take the paper from the mailbox, and deliver it to the garbage. What a waste. Literally!*

Amazon Pay Phrase - Amazon's payment technology, PayPhrase, lets customers buy from Amazon and affiliated merchants by using two or more words and a four-digit password. The technology accesses information stored in the customer's Amazon account to pay for purchases and to identify the shipping address. Like PayPal, PayPhrase is designed to work on Amazon's own site and on third-party sites that use the payment technology.

Amazon wants PayPhrase to compete directly with eBay's PayPal

Amazon wants PayPhrase to compete directly with eBay's PayPal and Google Checkout.

Analysts worry that the combination of a memorable phrase and a simple four-digit PIN may not be secure enough for financial transactions, even if Amazon promises to freeze an account when the wrong information is entered too many times. *More ways to spend money in the airways.*

Microsoft Maps - Microsoft is trying to get in on the Google action of taking pictures of streets, so you can actually see store fronts on the map as you move down the street. Just tried it and it has a ways to go before catching up with Google.

If you have not tried the Streetview when using the Google map, just click on the outline of a man on the view bar on the left side of the map and drag him the street you are looking at. You will see a photograph of the buildings. Google has also done many neighborhoods and I tried my own house and the pictures are reasonable.

To try it, look up your own address on Google maps. Type in your address and zoom in to your house. Then hold down the left mouse button and drag the little man to your street. It will turn the map into a photo. Click on the left or right arrows to move up and down your street.

Founding Fathers Papers - Thousands of unpublished documents from our nation's founders are in a free online resource. Collected over many years by the Founders Documentary Editions, these letters and other papers penned by important figures such as James Madison, John Adams, and Thomas Jefferson offer Americans of all ages and interests, a unique view of the early Republic.

Web Wills - A new service called My Webwill launched a new web based service. The Swedish Internet site offers to manage email and social networking accounts after death. My Webwill is testing in Sweden and the United States and plans to go live in Britain and Germany and more countries after that.

Users can set up a digital will with directions on what should happen to their email and social network accounts after they die. Currently, a Facebook profile, for example, can remain active long after its creator has passed away.

Some services, such as Legacy Locker Inc., Deathswitch, and Slightly Morbid, will send posthumous emails to friends and family. My Webwill will enter accounts and manage them according to a person's last wishes.

The basic service is free and includes the deactivation of 10 Internet accounts and the option to send up to five prepared e-mails written by you. A premium service paid service offers more detailed management of social networking profiles as well as unlimited posthumous e-mails and account deactivations. It offers a range of services, including posting prepared messages, changing profile pictures or updating status bars. Users can also pre-write emails that will be passed on to designated receivers such as friends or family.

In Sweden and Germany, My Webwill is automatically notified of a death by national authorities. In other countries clients will need to choose one or two people who notify My Webwill about the death and send a death certificate for the deceased.

Currently families have much difficulty shutting down sites and emails. For instance, Facebook's current policy is to move a deceased person's profile into a "Memorial State," removing contact information, status updates and group memberships once a death has been confirmed. The profile itself usually remains and confirmed friends can still find them through the search tool and write on the person's wall. *This whole business may sound morbid, but it makes sense as we spend more and more time online.*

Web Viewing Tip - Here is a tip that I use all the time. When viewing a web page that has small print, hold down the CTRL (control) key and move your scroll button on your mouse forward. It increases the size of print for easier viewing. It is temporary and only lasts for the page you are viewing. Moving your scroll button back reduces the size of print. It works in Internet Explorer and Firefox. If you do not have a scroll button, use the + for larger and - for smaller font size.

More Hoaxes Debunked - An image of an enormous cat being held in the arms of a bearded man began circulating around the internet in early 2000. The picture attracted attention, because it did not seem possible for a cat to be that large, but the chance that the cat was real could not be ruled out.

At some point an unknown prankster added a caption to the image, claiming it showed "Snowball," a monster cat owned by Rodger Degagne of Ottawa, Canada.

The photo attracted so much attention that it was eventually featured on television shows such as NBC's The Tonight Show with Jay Leno and ABC's Good Morning America, but both Snowball's story and picture were fake.

In May 2001 Cordell Hauglie, a resident of Edmonds, Washington, came forward to admit that he created the fake image by using photo manipulation software and had then e-mailed the image to a few friends as a joke, never intending that it would pass beyond those friends.

A few months later the picture had spread worldwide. Hauglie only realized what had happened when the picture started appearing on TV shows, in newspapers, and in magazines. To his amazement, he had unintentionally become an internet celebrity simply by sharing a joke with a few friends.

Internet Reading Tip - Have you tried reading some web pages with type so small that you have to strain your eyes? Here is a tip. Hold down the 'ctrl' key and move the scroll button on your mouse forward. To reduce, move the scroll back. It only works for the page you are reading and is temporary, until you change pages.

Facebook Faces - Did you know Facebook has a feature called 'Facial Recognition' that allows people to tag photos that may contain your face, without your permission? It has been around for a while and this feature is turned on automatically. If you like to be tagged in photos, enjoy. If not, to turn it off:
1 Go to the "Account" tab in the top right hand corner
2 Click on "Privacy settings"
3 Click "Customize settings"
4 Scroll down to "Things others share"
5 Click "Edit settings" next to "Suggest photos of me to friends"
6 Choose "Disable" or "Enable" from the drop down

Restaurant Coupons - There is an app that promises to be the one place to go to for local restaurant coupons. It is called bitehunter and will search the web and combine coupons from various sites and make them all available in one place. Excellent information, including menus with prices, reviews, links, and maps. Might be handy to look for local places even if no coupons are available. *While checking, I found a restaurant called 5napkinburgers (ten ounce juicy burgers) that I hope comes to Texas soon.*

Tips to Make Your Browsing Easier - Here are a few tips that might help while browsing the web to get around your screen a bit faster without using your mouse.

Go directly to the Address Bar - (to type in a new site)
   Firefox: Control (CTRL) + L
   Chrome/Safari/WebKit: Control + L
   Internet Explorer: Alt + D
   Opera: Control + L

Get to your browser search box - (to search for something)
  Firefox: Control (CTRL) + K
  Safari: Command + Option + F
  Internet Explorer: Control + E
  Opera: Control + E

An Internet Minute - You probably have heard the expression, 'A New York Minute' meaning fast. Here is an 'Internet Minute' as of 2016. I thought it might be interesting to show what happens on the internet, every minute of every day. You may not understand all of the terms, but a look at the numbers, shows an astounding amount of activity every minute.

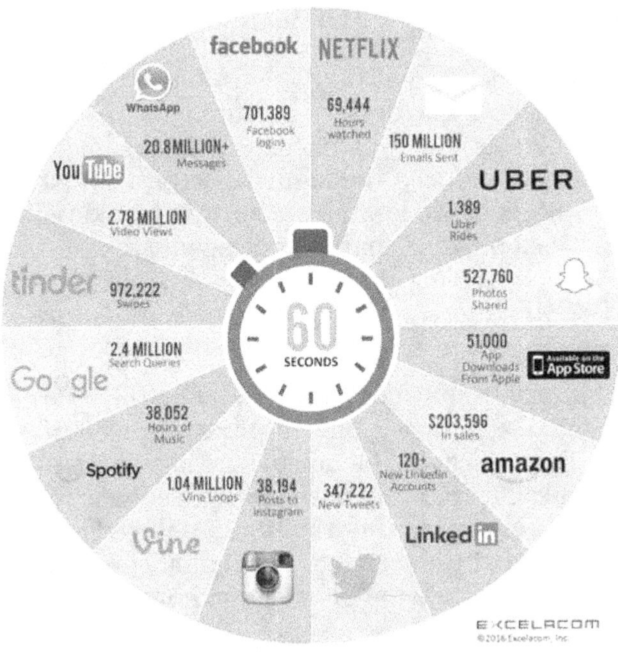

Yep, all this activity every minute of every day and some of the content is actually useful and interesting. Now, aren't you glad you only have to deal with my Friday Thoughts summary from all that activity.

Illusioneering - Here is a fun site that teaches science by way of magic tricks. /www.illusioneering.org/ The site is a brainchild of Peter McOwan and Matt Parker from Queen Mary, University of London. Its purpose is to help teachers and students better understand science with fun tricks using scientific principles. It also shows some common magic tricks and explains how they work. The site has downloadable explanations, videos, and more, including Penn and Teller's world's most expensive card trick. *Great for children, grandchildren, teachers, and the curious child in all of us.*

Computer Cookies - Cookies are used to save a user's information and relay this information between your computer and a website. This is used to authenticate a user, provide easier access to password controlled sites, or save various preferences of the user. Cookies are also used to track the sites you visit as well as what you buy online, and then can be read by companies to send direct ads to you, based on your visits. There are many other uses for cookies, but they are all for the web site owners and not users.

The reason the word cookie is used seems to come from a comparison to fortune cookies – the dessert common from fast-food Chinese inside which there is a slip of paper with a fortune. Early internet programmers likely noticed the similarities of a program that saves information within its code and the fortune cookie slips of paper. Cookies are placed on your computer and you are not told. *I have an aversion to anyone saving anything on my computer so I regularly delete cookies. All browsers have a delete cookies feature.*

Wiki - As you may or may not know, a wiki on the internet is a group of interconnected sites that is built from user interaction. Wikipedia, Encyclopedia Dramatica and Metapedia are all examples of this "wiki" model. WikiLeaks has recently been in the headlines for its collection of unclassified, classified information. Wikipedia is a brilliant collection of facts that are donated, then editable by anyone. The idea is that the masses will keep the information honest and correct.

In Hawaiian, "wiki wiki" means "quick." Creator Ward Cunningham decided that a "wiki" online would be a quick way to access and manipulate vast amounts of information.

Crowdmug - This is a bit scary. Want to know if a particular Bar or Restaurant is crowded before you go there? You can request a photo or video on Crowdmug and find out in minutes. You decide how much you are willing to pay and send in a request on your iPhone. If someone is at the place and accepts, they will take a picture for you. You can also take pictures and/or movies of your favorite place and upload them for free.

Crowdmug bills itself as the site to help you find out about a place before going there. It hopes to build a large library of photos for your viewing pleasure. The samples are quite well done and each place includes a map along with the photo. *I imagine some bars and restaurants might upload photos, just to be included in the database.*

Google Maps Amazon Style - Most of us are comfortable with using Google maps and clicking on the little man to get a street view. Google has been expanding that for the whole world and even began sending tricycles, to the Amazon to begin street maps there. Tricycles are used for stability and because there are no streets for automobiles. It also began hooking the same 360 degree cameras unto a boat to give us a water view of the Negro River. *So, the next time you plan to vacation in the Amazon, you will be able to get a street view before you leave.*

Google+ - Google+ (The Facebook/Linikedin alternative). One of the nice features is that you have circles of people, so you can set up family, friends, business, etc. When you make a comment, you decide which circle it is intended for and it is only viewable by that group.

You can set up a category of people that you follow, and comments can be sent to them independently or you can send to all groups. Below each comment box are icons to add pictures, links, video, location, and this makes it extremely easy to attach. Another feature is that you can add people to your circles so that they receive emails only and do not have to join Google+.

Google does it under water - Google launched a new service to allow Internet users to explore the depths of the world's oceans from the comfort of their homes on dry land. The "Ocean in Google Earth" feature allows users to virtually dive beneath the water surface, explore 3D underwater terrain and browse ocean-related content contributed by marine scientists.

Nearly four years after Google Earth enabled users to zoom in to view streets, and later explore galaxies in the sky, the latest version of the software allows virtual travelers to cross miles of unchartered territory underwater. Ocean in Google Earth was unveiled formally at the San Francisco Academy of Sciences.

Google Earth users can click icons on sea maps to see video of creatures that thrive in those locations and can virtually swim with the sharks, dolphins or turtles.

More Google wiz-bang technology - This scary bit of news recently hit the web. Google unveiled an upgrade to Google Maps that allows people to track the exact location of friends, foes, or family through their mobile devices or laptops. Google Latitude not only shows the location, but it can also be used to contact them via SMS, Google Talk, or Gmail. A beta version of Google Latitude has been around for a while and there are others, but Google is the biggie to bring it to the masses.

You can do things like find where your spouse is stuck in traffic or what bar your friend is at, or where the kids really go when they are out at night. Businesses can watch employees, anywhere in the world. *The good news is that it is opt-in for now, but I can see company paid-for phones not offering a choice. I can also see where it might be good for law enforcement and military use. This one was overlooked by George Orwell, but could be more devastating than anything he ever thought of, if used wrong.*

Unknown Phone Numbers - Have you ever received a call from a number you do not recognize? Usually these are companies trying to sell you something. There is a place to look up the number to see if it is a scam. Also, if your phone has the feature, you can block the number. One place to look is http://8oonotes.com/. It is a web site where you can look up these numbers to see if others are receiving calls.

You can also report the number. You do not need to leave your name or phone number. I received a call from 505-506-1046 and found it was a scam from a company based in Albuquerque, with Indian operators trying to sell credit card interest rate reductions. Worth the few minutes it takes to rid the airwaves of pushy sellers.

What You Like on Facebook - Many people innocently spend way too much time on Facebook and tell way too much about their personal lives. Now researchers have found a way to determine your personality by your Facebook friends and the things you like. It might be time to think about what you say electronically before your fingers hit the keyboard.

Researchers have created a website that combines the Facebook profiles of fans of companies and public figures with personality testing to create a sophisticated new marketing tool.

Barack Obama, Adam Sandler, and Family Guy all attract the same type of personality on Facebook, according to a website, http://www.likeaudience.com, which has been designed by two researchers at the University of Cambridge.

Sarah Palin appeals to a rather different personality type. Her followers are likely to be more traditional in mindset, disciplined, dutiful, and older than the average Obama fan. Unsurprisingly, her typical Facebook followers are not hockey-mums, but men. *Long before the internet or Facebook, my mother told me to be careful about the people I hung around with. How prescient she was.*

Facebook Address Book - If you use Facebook on your phone, it is likely that all of the addresses from your phone address book are now on Facebook. This would have happened sometime during the past few months when Facebook changed the software.

Luckily, there is a way to fix it.
1. Visit facebook.com from a PC and log in

2. In the top-right corner of the screen, click on Account and then Edit Friends

3. In the menu on the left side of the screen, click on Contacts

4. Here, you will see your contacts in Address Book are listed along with their phone numbers

5. On the right side of the screen, click on the "this page" link

6. Follow the instructions on this page. You will have to disable contact-sync in Facebook's mobile app if it's enabled. Click the Remove button

Some people like phone numbers on Facebook, but I do not. If you don't care one way or another, but my name is on your list, at least please delete it. Thanks.

Internet is Growing - If you ate a doughnut a second for the rest of your weight you would not grow as fast as the internet.

There was more data transmitted over the Internet during 2010 than the entire history of the Internet through 2009.

There are currently (2017) 8.4 billion connected devices around the world, Intel expects that number to increase to 50 billion by 2020.

Wow - 300 hours of YouTube videos are uploaded each minute. The average number of mobile YouTube video views per day is 1 billion. 500 million tweets sent per day. Over 100 million hours of video was watched on Facebook Daily and 350 million photos are uploaded every day. LinkedIn boasts more than 450 million user profiles. Also, think about the billions of spams sent each day and billions of emails.

It used to be that the internet added the equivalent of the entire Library of Congress every fifteen minutes and now it does so in less than half that time, and 24 hours a day. I like to think I am doing my share by adding these postings, just to keep the world from taking itself too seriously.

Bad Guys Release Bad Guy - A Mexican member of online hacker group Anonymous was released by the Zetas drug cartel ahead of a threat by the Web group to expose details of the crime ring's activities. The kidnapped man was released ahead of a deadline set by Anonymous, after which it planned to divulge the Zetas' links to politicians and others.

The US released a video in which a masked individual claiming to be part of Anonymous had threatened to make information public about the Zetas in retaliation for the kidnapping of one of his associates. *Isn't technology great!*

Who is Watching You - Millions of people have iPhones and Androids with video and still cameras. Google Earth is constantly scanning the globe from satellite and you can actually zoom into a view of your own home. I found one site where you can compare pictures from today, side-by-side with the same location from many years ago.

There are many thousands of cameras in public places around the world. Earthcam has locations of cameras that you can watch what is going on in full detail, live, up-to-the-minute color, and in full screen. Get a view from the Statue of Liberty, or Trafalgar Square. Check out the ski conditions in Switzerland. How about a live view of Hong Kong, or Melbourne? There is even a camera to watch the penguins in Sarasota, Florida.

Dallas has hundreds of traffic cameras that you can click on and watch traffic and weather. If you know someone it going to work on I75, you can actually watch them drive all the way to work, using the many traffic cameras. You can even set up a list of personal cameras that you want to watch. If a spouse or friend calls and says there is an accident, you can check the cameras and tell them what happened. Of course, if they have their iPad, they can look it up themselves while they are at a dead standstill.

Be careful if you call and tell your boss you are stuck in traffic, he or she might just check the cameras to make sure you are telling the truth.

Planning a trip, check the weather and traffic cams set up in the city you are going to and get a close up look at weather and traffic conditions.

Tie these together with Google Streetview and you can look up pictures of the building, neighborhood, or house you are looking for. If you are going on vacation almost anywhere in the world, let your family back home know where you will be and they can watch you on a local camera. Of course, you can just stream your own video from your phone.

It is fun, interesting, distracting, and a bit scary at the same time. *Big brother, big sister, and their nieces and nephews, cousins, and neighbors are all watching. Smile, you are on camera!*

Obituaries - There is a web site that shows obituaries for the whole country. www.legacy.com/NS/ You can look up hundreds of newspapers from the US and abroad. You can look up by time period. You can even set up a reminder for the name you are searching, so that when a person dies, you can receive a notice. It has funeral home locators, and many more features.

This sounds a bit morbid, but I know some folks are interested in relatives that live far away and may not have any other way of finding out.

Before I write about stuff, I usually like to try it, so I did. Here is the answer that came back from my search, "We're sorry, there are no obituary search results for 'shubnell'." *Don't know why they were sorry, I was delighted.*

Sony's New Camera - What makes it interesting for $500 is that it has web access to send your photos instantly from the camera to the web. The only thing that doesn't seem to have web access these days is the toilet. We have shower screens to check email in the shower, TV screens behind the mirror so you can get your fix while you shave or put on your makeup.

Refrigerators and ovens have built in screens, cars have direct access, phones can do everything. Next, they will probably put GPS, phone, and email in rifle stocks so you can find out where you are and tell the world what you just shot, send a picture, and call your friends to help you drag the poor critter back to the truck - all in real time.

Which? is on first - Speaking of names, here is one with a question mark as part of the name. Which? is England's equivalent to Consumer Reports, plus it has many 'how to' articles and not one ad in sight. When you are about to buy something and check Consumer Reports, check out Which?, also. *It compares products so you can tell which is which on Which? What?*

Internet Privacy - The U.S. Department of Homeland Security released a draft to develop a voluntary identification system and set up a website to gather input from experts and Internet users about how it should be structured.

From the web site - *"The Nation faces sophisticated threats against the sensitive and confidential data of our citizens, industries and government. Securing identities in transactions and creating a trusted online environment has become a critical national priority, and the President's Cyberspace Policy Review called for development of a strategy to address this issue."*

"The technology that has brought many benefits to our society and has empowered us to do so much has also empowered those who are driven to cause harm," said White House cyber czar Howard Schmidt in a blog that outlined the need for better security online.

The plan, he said, envisions a future in which people would be able to get a secure identifier - such as a smart identity card or a digital certificate - from a variety of service providers.

Customers could then use the card or identifier to prove who they are as they make their online transactions.

The draft plan is part of an administration effort to promote cyber-security among society as a whole. Lawmakers have introduced a number of bills aimed at furthering those goals.

When You Were Born - Check this site out and put in the year of your birth to discover some interesting things that happened that year. whathappenedinmybirthyear.com/

Audio Books - There is a web site, LibriVox, that makes audio books from public domain books and they are free to download. The range is wide, from Aesop to Emile Zola.

Nice to have when you are driving, or just seeking a pleasant diversion. Also, great if you have someone in the family that does not see as well as they used to. I sampled "The Importance of Being Ernest" and it was read by a cast, just as if it were being acted on stage. *Good stuff.*

Phone Radio - Here is an interesting twist, an application for the iPhone that plays radio.

Public Radio Exchange (PRX) developed the free Public Radio Player for the iPhone and now millions of downloads. The other application it has developed is for the show 'This American Life'. Since we already have video on the phone, seems logical to add radio as another battery burner. Caution, it has many ads built into broadcasts.

Google Ads - Google has a web site that allows you to opt in or opt out of having specific ads shown as you wander around the web http://google.com/ads/preferences. To see ads that are more related to your interests, you can edit the interest categories, which are based on sites you have recently visited.

Your interests are associated with an advertising cookie that is stored in your browser.

------------------------¶

Internet Cookies - Speaking of cookies, unlike the tasty morsels of real cookies, internet cookies are dropped in your computer from almost every site that you visit.

Sometimes there are good cookies, like those that let you log in to sites without always typing your password, but usually the cookies track where you have been so the web owner knows you have been there before. Anyone with a bit of coding knowledge can look at all your cookies and track where you have gone on the web.

I find cookies to be an invasion of my privacy, and luckily there is a way to get rid of those pesky space hogs on my disk.

If you use Internet Explorer, go to the top line and click on 'Tools' then click on 'Internet Options', then click on 'Browsing History'. You are then shown options to delete temporary files, history, cookies, etc. Click on the boxes next to those items you wish to delete and click 'delete'. You may be surprised that it will take a few minutes if you have never deleted the files before. If you use Firefox, go to 'Tools', 'Options', 'Privacy' to do the same thing.

Both Internet Explorer and Firefox, also have a check box option to 'Delete browsing history on exit' and it will clean out your cookies and history each time you exit the program. This does not clean up all the temporary files, but it does help preserve your privacy. *It's like cleaning your computer and protecting your privacy at the same time.*

Find Feature - Did you know that most web browsers, such as Internet Explorer, Firefox, Chrome, and Crazy Browser, etc have a great, but little used feature. It is the "find" feature, usually located under the "view' button on the top of the page next to "file."

Click on "view" then click on "find" or " find on this page" and type in the word or phrase you are looking for. It moves to that part of the web page you are on and highlights the text for you. Holding down the CTRL button and typing the letter F does the same thing on most sites. It also works in apps like Word, or Excel.

This is great when looking for a person's name or other specific word in long web pages and it saves a bunch of extra reading when you are looking for something specific.

World Front Pages - There is a web page of newspaper front pages from around the world.

A great way to see the real big stories beyond your hometown. You can sort by region of the country or international, etc. *Sure opens your perspective about what the rest of the world thinks is important.*

http://www.newseum.org/todaysfrontpages/

Search Me - Want to find out what is going around the web about you, go to searchme.com Type in your name or the name of someone you know. *You might be surprised at what information they are collecting about you.*

Google This - Another week and another mammoth undertaking by Google. The Internet search giant said it had begun digitizing millions of pages from New York Magazine, Popular Mechanics, Popular Science, Ebony and other publications. "Thus far, we've digitized more than a million articles from titles ranging from Men's Health, Baseball Digest and Runner's World to local publications like Atlanta Magazine and Indianapolis Monthly, with many more to come," Google said.

It said the magazines are being scanned in full-color and made available through Google Book Search. "Users will be able to search and read an increasing number of magazines online in full color, each cover, article and advertisement appearing exactly as it did in print," Google said.

A search on books.google.com will now not only bring up links to relevant books, but also to magazine articles related to the query. Users can also use advanced search on Google Book Search to search through magazines only. Entire issues of magazines can be scrolled through using the "next page" or "back" buttons.

-----------¶
Internet Birthday - The World Wide Web turned 20 on March 13, 2009. Cern chose the date to mark the 20th anniversary of the day when one of its employees, Tim Berners-Lee, first proposed a

"universal linked information system" that would over the next few years develop into what we now know as the worldwide web. It was originally designed as a way of improving information management within Cern, a large organization employing several thousand people who all needed to communicate, share information, equipment and software. Berners-Lee specified a number of clear, practical system requirements. One was remote access from computers running different operating systems.

During March, 2017 He said, "It is 28 years since I submitted my original proposal for the worldwide web. I imagined the web as an open platform that would allow everyone, everywhere to share information, access opportunities, and collaborate across geographic and cultural boundaries. In many ways, the web has lived up to this vision, though it has been a recurring battle to keep it open, but over the past 12 months, I've become increasingly worried about three new trends, which I believe we must tackle in order for the web to fulfill its true potential as a tool that serves all of humanity.

1) We've lost control of our personal data.

2) It's too easy for misinformation to spread on the web.

3) Political advertising online needs transparency and understanding."

Another Google Tip - When you look at Google results, check the left side of the page and click on "show search tools" button. A list of options about time will appear. These are very handy if you are just looking for some news or other items that are current or maybe even older. Since web pages seem to live on forever, it is a quick way to get information that is timely for the subject.

Another Google Search Tip - Use a minus sign right before a word to eliminate it from your search results. For example, if you are looking for cowboys, but not the team, you would type "cowboys -dallas -football" without the quotes. This trick goes a long way toward eliminating information that you are not interested in reading. In addition, try typing inurl:2008 or whatever year you like, at the end of the words and it will come back with results for that year only, example: computers inurl:2008.

If you want to see the results for different years, you can type: computers view:timeline and it will come back with this on the top of the page. You can then click on any of the years and only the results for those years will be displayed.

BTW use quotes if you want to find a particular phrase or string of words. If I used my name without the quotes it would find many extraneous things for first name and surname name. By using the quotes around both names, I limit the search to one person.

Google This - Google's success as an Internet search and advertising king has placed it in the cross hairs of regulators worried the firm will trample free market competition.

Google acknowledged that it has been contacted by the US Federal Trade Commission regarding potential legal conflicts caused by chief executive Eric Schmidt and director Arthur Levinson being on the Apple board.

US state attorneys have also begun inquiries into the settlement that would allow Google to create the world's largest digital library and online bookstore. *24 of my books are included in the settlement, and it seems fair to me.*

Growing ranks of politically-influential enemies are also trying to aggravate Google's situation. Microsoft is aching to come from behind and dethrone Google as king of the online search advertising market which held 72.4 percent of the US Internet search market as compared to the 16.4 percent share for Yahoo, and 5.5 percent for Microsoft.

Crap Email Hack - We all get way too much marketing stuff in our inbox. One way to reduce it is to filter for the word unsubscribe and send the mail straight to trash. If you want to keep some of the materials, set up a folder for marketing and send the emails there. That way you can keep the info, but it is not mixed with important emails.

Twitter and the Stock Market - The mood on Twitter predicts what's going to happen in the stock market with 87 percent accuracy. Researchers from Indiana University analyzed the tweets of 2.7 million Twitter users, dividing them into six categories of emotions. They were surprised to find that the higher percentage of "calm" tweets on a given day, the higher the Dow Jones Industrial Average was in the following two to six days. This method yielded a 87.6 percent rate of accuracy.

E-Books - Amazon's Kindle might be getting new competitors in the market for electronic-book devices. Verizon is considering entering the e-book market that Kindle doesn't focus on, like college textbooks.

Amazon uses Sprint Nextel Corp.'s wireless network to provide access to a store with 100,000 books. (*soon to include some of mine*)

So far, Kindle's main competitor has been Sony Corp.'s Reader. It has the same type of screen, but lacks wireless access.

AT&T, the second largest wireless carrier after Verizon Wireless, has also been talking to e-reader manufacturers and its network is more similar to ones used overseas, that could support international e-book readers, where Kindle can download books only in the U.S.

National Museum of Funeral History - Here is a place to go for a few chuckles. It's motto "Any Day Above Ground is a Good One." The Museum is in Houston, Texas and opened in 1992. You can view exhibits that include a Civil War embalming display and a replica of a turn-of-the-century casket factory. It also has a collection of fantasy coffins designed by artist Kane Quaye. The collection includes a casket shaped like a chicken, a Mercedes-Benz, a shallot, and an outboard motor, all based on the dreams and last wishes of his clients. *Sounds like a fun place.*

Bigger Ads on the Net - Twenty seven publishers with a reach of about 109 million unique visitors per month have agreed to try one of three new online ad formats. The publishers are all members of the online publishers association.

* The Fixed Panel, which looks naturally embedded into the page layout and scrolls to the top and bottom of the page as a user scrolls.

* The XXL Box, which has page-turn functionality with video capability.

* The Pushdown, which opens to display the advertisement and then rolls up to the top of the page.

The formats they have agreed on all have one trait in common: they are much bigger and more attention-grabbing than the banner, which is despised by publishers, advertisers, and readers alike. *The reason banner ads are despised is because they are too damn intrusive and, contrary to public opinion, bigger is not always better, especially when it comes to ads.*

The Wayback Machine - It is a 150 billion page web archive of web pages as they were before they changed. Think of it as a perpetual inventory of web pages, showing what each page looked like at any one point in time. It has documents, videos, audio, and many interesting things to pleasantly waste your time for days.

It serves about 500 queries per second from over 5Petabytes (5 million gigabytes) of archived web data. The cluster of computers and the Modular Datacenter acts as a single massive computer.

It has movies, TV shows, cartoons, pictures, music, archived web pages from the past, famous family genealogies, and thousands of documents scanned from the Library of Congress. This site is interesting, fun, and a place to add to your favorites and go back often. Oh, and the vast majority is available to download for free.

The http://www.archive.org/index.php is a tribute to the Rocky and Bullwinkle Show's "Waybac Machine" which in turn was a reference to the Univac Sherman and Peabody live on.

Free Faxes - Time to get rid of that old fax machine collecting dust in your home office. Now there is a way to go online and send and receive faxes for free.

Do you need to send faxes just once in a while? Ditch the fax machine and the trips to Kinko's, and use free-to-try online services such as Qipit and FaxZero.

Qipit lets you send up to five faxes each week for free. You can upload JPEG images or even send them directly from a camera phone. Free faxes include a header banner that mentions Qipit.

FaxZero limits you to two faxes of three pages each day, and its transmissions include a FaxZero-branded coversheet. Instead of sending images, FaxZero takes PDFs and Word documents.

You can even cancel your dedicated incoming fax line and have people send physical faxes to you online. eFax Free handles everything, digitizing faxes and routing them to your e-mail account. You get a free phone number that is connected to eFax and is always listening for incoming calls.

eFax Free has a few limitations, however. You don't get to pick an area code for the incoming number, and you can't receive more than 100 pages each month. Plus, you have to read faxes in an eFax application, in its proprietary .efx format.

Lost Cursor - Have you ever been looking at a page on the screen and forgot where the cursor was. Here is a trick, hit the CTRL (Control) key on the right or left bottom row of your keyboard and a big circle shows up where the cursor is. If it doesn't work, go to the control panel, click on mouse, then mouse pointer options, then click on the box that says "show location of pointer when I press the CTRL key'.

How to Find Stuff on a Web Page - You are looking for a specific name on a web page that is way too long and has too much information. Here is a trick. Hold down the "ctrl' (control) key on the lower left or right of your keyboard and hit the "f" key. Then type in the word or name that you are looking for. Your browser will find the word and highlight it for you (look at the very top or very bottom of the page to see it). *Just one more cool trick to make your web travels easier.*

Copies of Antique Manuscripts -A remarkable archive of antique manuscripts which opens a window on to the experiences, hopes, fears and interests of people who lived during the 15th to 18th centuries has been put online.

The University of Cambridge Scriptorium Project features thousands of pages taken from twenty different handwritten "miscellanies", some of which date back as far as the Wars of the Roses.

The books were used to record snippets of information that people had read, been told, or overheard, at a time when paper was a scarce and expensive commodity.

The collection includes a notebook in which Edward VI wrote down various Biblical passages and a miscellany kept by William Rawley, chaplain to Francis Bacon, in which he recorded Bacon's sayings and a number of his (rather bad) jokes.

Perhaps more significantly, however, it features copious amounts of material reflecting the day-to-day lives of other people. Recipes, accounts, sonnets, quotations, prayers, sermons, legal tips and medical instructions were all added to the compendia as they were passed down through the generations.

Over a period of decades, their owners recorded everything from poems by Shakespeare and Milton, to plague remedies, laundry lists, or, in one case, the contents of their fish pond. As a result, the books provide an insight into sections of the population of whom we would know far less without them, not least the women of the era.

The website also includes a complete and interactive online course in deciphering medieval and early modern handwriting as well as further resources for manuscript studies.

"The idea is to enable other researchers to decipher their own manuscripts even if they have not encountered early modern handwriting before," Dr. Beadle added. "Hopefully this project will help to open up the literature, history, theology and philosophy of this period to a new generation of students and scholars all over the world." http://scriptorium.english.cam.ac.uk/manuscripts/

British Papers go Online - The British Library has announced a project to make 40 million pages from its newspaper archive available online. It has more than 300 years of information, including coverage of the Crimean and Boer Wars. The plan is to complete the digitization of more than 4 million pages within the first two years. With journalism standards as they are today, the world will get a totally different view of reality, if it depends only on newspapers.

Get the WiFi passwords at various places by checking the comments section of their FourSquare accounts.

You are welcome.

Handy Uses for the Windows Key - Do you use that 'Windows Key' on the lower right or left of your keyboard? It has many uses. For instance, if you just hit it, it brings up your programs from the start button. If you hold it down and hit m it takes you to your desktop. Hold it down and hit e and it opens up the filesscreen. Hold it down and hit f and you go directly to the search screen.

Deepweb and Darknet - These two words are often spoken by the news media and we hear them on some TV shows, but they are never explained.

The Deepweb refers to part of the Internet, specifically the world wide web (anything that starts www) that is not indexed by search engines, and can't be accessed by Google.

The Darknet refers to non-www networks, where users may need separate software to access them. For example, Silk Road and many illicit markets are hosted on Darknet networks like I2P and Tor.

American Radio History Magazines - The web site has searchable scanned copies of hundreds of old magazines about the radio industry, popular electronics, audio engineering, regulations, yearbooks, etc. It also has magazines from specific radio stations, television, engineering, and more. Great site to look at old magazines from the 1940s forward. It is like going up to your grandparents attic and sitting for hours reading old magazines (ads included). http://www.americanradiohistory.com/index.htm

----

Global Internet Speeds - The US is still slipping behind the rest of the world when it comes to download speeds, with an average of 10 Mbps it ranks just 55th worldwide.

For coverage, US subscribers get an LTE signal 81 percent of the time, or seventh best in the world. By comparison, Romania offers only 61 percent coverage for its LTE network, but has speeds as fast as 33 Mbps.

The global average for download speeds on LTE is 13.5 Mbps. Singapore offers the fastest networks, with downloads as fast as 40 Mbps. During 2015, America's average download speed was a paltry 9 Mbps.

Top 5 fastest countries average speeds:
    New Zealand, 36 Mbps
    Singapore, 33 Mbps
    Romania, 30 Mbps
    South Korea, 29 Mbps
    Denmark, 26 Mbps.

TECHNOLOGY

Hack My Car - More than 100 drivers in Texas found their cars disabled or the horns honking out of control after a hacker used a web-based vehicle-immobilization system normally used to get the attention of consumers delinquent in their auto payments.

Police arrested a 20-year-old former Texas Auto Center employee who was laid off and allegedly sought revenge.

"We started having a rash of up to a hundred customers at one time complaining. Some customers complained of the horns going off in the middle of the night. The only option they had was to remove the battery."

The dealership used a system called Webtech Plus as an alternative to repossessing vehicles that have not been paid for. The system lets car dealers install a small black box under vehicle dashboards that responds to commands issued through a central website, and relayed over a wireless pager network. The dealer can disable a car's ignition system or trigger the horn to begin honking, as a reminder that a payment is due. The system will not stop a running vehicle. *Honk if you love technology. Who says there is no big brother.*

Telephone - OK, it's time to think about that home phone you are paying for. The number of people in the US who have eliminated their home landline phones in favor of cell phones doubled between 2006 and 2009, according to a government report. Twenty five percent of US households have no landline.

In December 2009, AT&T proposed that the government develop a plan and set a date to eliminate all telephone line service for the country. Interesting to see something that was once so vital to our comfort and convenience be made redundant. Some may remember the beginning of phones in the home and 'party' lines. Amazing that in one generation an amazing technology can come and go. *I have a feeling many things we have seen the birth of will die before we do. Technology is advancing at such a rapid pace, it is difficult to keep up. Of course it helps if you love technology, like I do. . . almost as much as potato chips and bacon.*

Tree Saver - Leave it to the Japanese to be this creative. Oriental Company has come up with a machine by the name of 'White Goat'. It is an innovative machine that converts wasted office paper into toilet paper in about 30 minutes. After you put about 40 sheeets of paper into the machine will then shred the paper, dissolve it in water, thin the paper out, and then dry it into toilet paper sheets.

The company claims it costs $0.11 to churn out one toilet roll and it will save up to 60 trees a year. The machine is expected to hit the market in Japan at a price of about $100,000.

Windows Number Tip - Those little icons along the bottom of your screen that you use for everyday program shortcuts are handy. Normally you use the mouse to click on the icon to open the program. There is an easier way to open them without using a mouse. Each program to the right of the Start button is assigned its own numerical shortcut, with the first program being "1," the second being "2," and so on up to the 10th shortcut, which is "0."

Press the Windows key, plus the number of the program you want to open and it will launch. For example, if the first icon is for email, hold down the windows key (on the lower left of most keyboards) and press the number 1. Your email will open.

You can rearrange the icons and move the most used to the left position to make it easier to remember.

Retro PC - Thanks to my nephew, I was browsing the December 2000 edition of Popular Science online when I came across this super fast (for the time) PC. Wow, only 17 years ago, $1,799 would pay for 128MB memory and a large 15GB hard drive.

These days memory is measured in GB and storage in Terabytes, with prices down into the low hundreds of dollars. Current watches and phones have more memory and storage than the old devices.

Am voting for a personal wearable eye device so I can watch 100 inch, or larger, fully immersive 4D TV with at least 8k resolution and omnidirectional sound. Of course for the big game it will need to be full wall TV picture and wall speakers. Am also thinking wearable/implantable phone/PC devices with stretchable screens so we can keep our pockets empty. Wouldn't it also be nice to have a ceiling that glows with natural light instead of bulbs. Ah, the mind wanders.

New Mini Computers - The drive is on for TVs to get larger and computers to get smaller. During 2014 Intel introduced Edison, a computer the size of a postage stamp. During 2015 it introduced a new model called Curie, which is so small that it could be built into a button on a shirt.

Curie is based on the Quark SE core, Key Features
• A low-power, 32-bit Intel® Quark™ SE SoC
• 384kB Flash memory, 80kB SRAM
• A low-power integrated DSP sensor hub with a proprietary pattern matching accelerator
• Bluetooth* Low Energy
• 6-axis combo sensor with accelerometer and gyroscope
• Battery charging circuitry.

It is for both the wearable fitness market and biometric and security applications, with additional tie ins to other brands like Fossil (watches) and Oakley (glasses). *Unlike TVs, when it comes to computers, smaller is better.*

Whether Weather - The National Weather Service boosted its computing power by more than tenfold, which officials hope will translate to better weather forecasts.

The National Oceanic and Atmospheric Administration's two supercomputers will more than triple in computational ability to 5,000 trillion calculations per second.

NOAA chief Kathryn Sullivan, in a press release, said the computer boost, "Will lead to more timely, accurate, and reliable forecasts." *It would be nice if some of the climaticogasmic scientists would upgrade their capabilities to predict, rather than just forecast.*

News Summary - If you want to find out news for a specific period, search [month][year] or just [year] in Wikipedia to see the major world news during that time period. If you use year, it will display events by month and day. Try it for the year you were born. Also, use the year or month of someone else's birth, print it out, and include the info in a birthday card. Should provide for some interesting conversations.

Gotta Go? - There is an app for that. When you really <u>Gotta Go</u>, Flush Toilet Finder is an app for smartphones that helps you find free public restrooms.

The app on Android and iOS is handy if you are in a strange city and you do not know where you can go or if you are shopping, and an emergency hits.

Open the app and it searches the area around you. Its database covers over 100,000 public restrooms around the world and the database is constantly expanding. When you find the one you want, you can get directions via Google or Apple Maps. Flush also lists if a restroom has a fee, requires a key, or if it provides disabled access.

Robot Reporters - Quarterly business earnings reports are dull and boring to read. That makes them ripe for automation. The Associated Press has been using an automated system to write its stories and few readers noticed. AP publishes more than 3,000 such stories every quarter and that number is poised to grow.

> The Wordsmith platform generates millions of articles per week for other companies, such as Allstate, Comcast, and Yahoo, whose fantasy football reports are automated.

AP says the automated system is now logging in fewer errors than the human-produced equivalents from years past. Of the estimated 3,000 such reports each quarter, about one hundred will have an added human touch, either by updating the original story or doing a separate follow-up piece.

The giveaway is that there is no byline and at the end of the article we see, "This story was generated by Automated Insights."

Sound Mirrors - Mirrors can actually reflect sound as well as light. Mirrors that reflect sound waves are known as "acoustic mirrors," and were used in Britain during World War I to detect certain sound waves coming from enemy aircraft from 8 to 15 miles away. This was before the development of radar.

Several were built around the coast of Britain, and are still standing today. They are located on both the north and south shores of England. They are also called listening stones.

Concrete acoustic mirrors were built on the south and northeast coasts of England between about 1916 and the 1930s. The 'listening ears' were intended to provide early warning of incoming enemy aircraft.

They did work, but the development of faster aircraft made them less useful, as an incoming aircraft would be within sight by the time it had been located. Increasing ambient noise made the mirrors harder to use successfully, and then radar rendered acoustic detection redundant.

There is also an example of one that is a parabolic sound mirror carved into boulders to dramatically magnify the sound of a nearby stream for listeners. It is inspired by satellite dishes, the seating in choir lofts where curved walls reflect sound and the antique hand-held sound magnifiers used in the days before hearing aids.

I Know What You Are Thinking - Intel Corp. has introduced software that analyzes functional MRI scans to determine what parts of a person's brain are being activated as he or she thinks. It has 90 percent accuracy in guesses about which of two words a person was thinking about. Eventually, the technology could help the severely physically disabled to communicate.

The system works best when a person is first scanned while thinking of dozens of different concrete nouns - words like "bear" or "hammer." When test subjects are then asked to pick one of two new terms and think about it, the software uses the earlier results as a baseline to deter mine what the person is thinking. *Very cool stuff.*

Amazon May Print your Product - Amazon plans to create and patent 3D-printing delivery trucks. The patent, called 'Providing

Services Related to Item Delivery via 3D Manufacturing on Demand', describes an effort to deliver 3D printed items manufactured on a truck to customers.

3D printing is a process, which three dimensional objects can be printed on demand.

The 3D printing trucks will double as delivery trucks. The patent lays out a sequential series of steps in regard to how this process will likely happen: first, a customer places an order, the 3D printable order is sent to the delivery truck closest to the customer, and the item is produced en-route and delivered once complete.

The patent also covers subtractive printing, which is the process of taking a block of material, usually metal and removing pieces in order to obtain the desired shape.

LED, Lumen, CFL, and CRI - We are now faced with many choices for light bulbs. Prices vary widely for not much difference in light. Here a few things to know about the choices.

Incandescent bulb watts - lumens
60 - 800
75 - 1,100
100 - 1,600
150 - 2,600

First, lumens are the new watts. Watts are power and lumens are light. An old incandescent 60 watts is about 800 lumens of light. The wattage does not matter and most of the comparisons regarding electricity costs are measured over years, so not very consequential in a monthly or annual budget. A 60W incandescent lamp may push 800 lumens, while a CFL only needs 15W and an LED only needs 10W to produce the same lumens. (A 10W incandescent is a night light.) The thing to remember is how bright you want your light to be. Look at lumens below to get the correct amount of light from your new bulbs.

Heat might not seem important, but with a number of lights burning, it adds up, especially during the summer. One heat test - halogen bulb, a type of incandescent bulb, measured 327 degrees. A Cree LED downlight was measured 107 degrees and a Philips Par38 CFL measured 167 degrees. LEDs produce 3.4 BTUs/hour, compared to 85 for incandescent bulbs.

Bugs don't fly toward many LEDs, because bugs are attracted to ultraviolet light and most LEDs do not give off this type of light.

LED are rated to last 50,000 hours, while CFLs are rated for 10,000 hours and incandescents are rated for about 1,000 hours.

LED bulbs turn on as quickly as incandescent bulbs and faster than CFLs. LEDs produce roughly the same amount of useful light, but much of that light is focused in one direction. LEDs typically shine up, rather than in all directions like incandescent bulbs. Newer LEDs can be omnidirectional, look for that word on the package.

Some LEDs do not dim well and tend to buzz or sputter when the dimming is at half. Check the package to make sure the bulb will work with a dimmer.

A new term to further confuse us is CRI, because of the number of different light types. It did not make any difference in the past as all lights were the same. CRI is color rendering index. The higher the CRI, the better the color rendering ability. Light sources with a CRI of 90 or higher are excellent at color rendering and should be used for tasks requiring the most accurate color discrimination. CRI is independent of color temperature, but I won't even go there. Too much information.

When considering lighting, I usually think of CFL as meaning 'crap for light'. They take longer to turn on (it typically takes 30 seconds to 3 minutes to complete), need more energy to turn on, contain mercury, may leak UV radiation, do not work well in cold conditions, produce artificial fluorescent color, and are less efficient than LEDs.

Although initial price is still much higher, the price of LEDs is coming down quickly. LEDs are down to twenty five percent of they used to cost.

Bottom Line, let your old bulbs burn out before you rush out to buy new "energy savers" the price will likely be cheaper when you are ready to replace. Also remember, higher lumens are brighter and higher CRI provides better color discrimination.

History of CDs - Compact discs, or CDs, were one of the defining technologies of the 1990's and 2000's. They successfully killed cassette tapes, and are likely the last physical audio technology that we will ever have, as digital formats now dominate the music industry.

CD's were actually invented during 1974, nearly a decade before they even became available to the public market.

The inventors were the Dutch company Philips and the Japanese company Sony. In the mid 70's, both companies independently began working on technologies that could imprint digital sound onto a small plastic disc. The two companies joined forces to develop the technology as fast as possible. The first album ever recorded on CD was ABBA's The Visitors in 1981.

Cell Phone History - First cell phone 1973 large commercial mobile phone, first flip type mobile phone, 1G system, Nordic Mobile Telephone was introduced in 1981, first 2g second generation cell phone 1991, digital vs. analog first phone to phone text 1993, 1994 Simon Smartphone could fax had stylus, touch screen color screen (never became a success).

In 1999, the Japanese firm NTT Docomo released the first Smartphones to achieve mass adoption within a country, 2001 first 3g phone, 2007 first touch screen Smartphone, 2009 first 4g phones. 5G phone development has begun and in test markets as of 2017.

2g, 3g, etc., is for generation, and LTE is for Long Term Evolution (a specific type of 4g).

Origins of Apple Words - Steve Jobs came back from working on a commune-type All-One farm in Oregon and announced to his partners that he had a name for their company, Apple Computer.

Jef Raskin, an Apple employee who first started the project, picked "Macintosh" because the McIntosh was his favorite apple. The spelling was changed to avoid copyright infringement. Steve Jobs said the product was "insanely great".

The slogan, "Think Different" was dreamed up by an art director, Craig Tanimoto.

TBWA ad agency came up with the 'i' prefix to infer internet. It also connoted individual, imaginative, and more.

App Store was pure Jobs and meant both applications and a contraction of Apple.

Smart Phone Hack - When going out of town, or to a large mall, finding your car when you come back can be a hassle. Take out your phone and take a picture of any landmark, especially if the lot is color coded, or numbered/lettered close to where your car is parked. Might save a bunch of time wandering around looking for your car.

Hoverboards and Batteries - Lithium-ion batteries serve as the power source for everything from Smartphones, laptops, hover boards, to electric cars, such as the Tesla. They are rechargeable and have four to six times the energy of standard nickel-cadmium batteries.

Lithium-ion batteries in those technologies are made by experienced and highly reliable manufacturers. They know how to construct them in a way that balances the amount of power produced with the amount of power consumed by the device during operation.

This type of battery has three primary parts: Two electrodes, an anode made of graphite, and a cathode made of lithium cobalt oxide or a similar metal oxide. Between is a thin, but porous polyethylene separator that keeps the two apart.

The electric current flows between the anode and the cathode via a liquid, called the electrolyte. If the anode and cathode are not engineered correctly for the power draw or the separator is imperfect, a short circuit can result. When that happens, the electrolyte heats up, the cathode and anode become unstable, and the two react violently with the electrolyte. The temperature may cause the battery to eject its hot internal contents, which catch fire or explode when they come in contact with oxygen in the atmosphere.

Hoverboard manufacturers had many less-than-expert battery suppliers using possible defective materials or improper engineering of parts. Hoverboards pose additional risks. They draw energy from batteries much faster than cellphones and laptops do, which strains the electrodes and raises the internal heat. They are also subject to more mechanical abuse.

Robot Progression - According to a research study by Tractica, annual shipments of consumer robots - a category that includes robotic vacuums, lawn mowers, and pool cleaners as well as social robots - will increase from 6.6 million units in 2015 to 31.2 million units worldwide by 2020 with a cumulative total of nearly 100 million consumer robots shipped during that period.

The fastest growth will occur in robotic personal assistants, a category that is nascent today. According to the report, "the next 5 years will set the stage for how these robots could fundamentally transform our homes and daily lives."

China, Japan, and South Korea are responsible for 40% of all new robot installations. China has more than 25% of all annual installations. The world market for robots grew 17% during 2015 and has had steady growth since 2009. Indications are that this growth rate will continue.

It used to be that the largest market for robotics was the United States. By 2014 China took over as the single largest market. During the past two years it had 50% annual growth in terms of new robot installations. China still has much below average installations of robots per capita. The maturity of a market is typically compared by number of robots installed per 10,000 workers in the manufacturing industry. Mature industries, such as automotive, will typically have 1 robot for every 10 workers.

South Korea has the most robots for manufacturing with 478 robots per 10,000 workers. Japan is second with 314 per 10,000 workers. Germany is at 292, USA is at 164. The world average is 87. China is currently at 36. Even with twice as many robots sold, China would still be below average in its use of robots.

Screen Resolution Evolution

It seems appropriate to recap where we are with TVs and how we got here.

First, 3D TV is dead. Curved screens remain a hard sell. 4K TV now common, but may be usurped by 8K TV. 8K may suffer the same fate unless TV and movie producers begin to crank out content capable of utilizing the new standards. In times past, we always waited for hardware to catch up to our needs, now we are waiting for content to catch up to hardware.

Sharp released its first 8K TV in 2015. The 85-inch LV-85001 costs $133,000. Samsung showed its 110-inch 8K TV in January, 2016. It also announced that a 11K TV is being developed for the 2018 Pyeongchang Winter Olympics. LG also showed off a 98-inch 8K TV in January, 2016. All of this advancement comes amid a current dearth of 4K content. These advances may still prove to be more resilient than the 3D revolution that never happened.

HDR, High Dynamic Range is a standard for adding more colors to TV. It is found on most 4G TVs, but is also finding its way on current 1080p TVs. It is brilliant to the eye and shows better than more pixels, as in 4K. The difference is also seen in a greater difference between black and white.

Advances in hardware and software continue to outrun battery capacity and bandwidth speed. Although bandwidth is less of an issue in Europe and other countries as the US continues to lag, mostly due to politics, not capability.

How we began the race comes from early television. For the first half-century of television, resolution was measured in lines per screen rather than pixels. TV resolution in the 1930s and 1940s had 240 to 819 lines per screen, improving upon previous resolutions. The new resolution used a display method known as progressive scanning, where each line of an image is displayed in sequence, in contrast to the traditional analog method where first odd and then even lines are drawn alternately.

In 1953, analog color TV had 525 lines, establishing the NTSC color standard. Europe followed up in the 1960s by introducing the 625-line standards. However, bandwidth barriers limited widespread adoption of analog HDTV.

In 1977, the Apple II introduced color CRT display to home computers by adapting the NTSC color signal. The Apple II achieved a resolution of 280 pixels horizontally by 192 pixels vertically. By the 1980s, home computer makers began using pixels (picture elements) as a unit of measure.

IBM introduced a VGA standard display of 640x480 in 1987. Since then, demand for digital videos and video games has driven resolution to greater and greater density. Desktop monitors are now a standard resolution of 2560x1600. Mobile devices range lower from 240x320 for the smallest devices.

During the 1990s, plasma TVs and LCD TVs moved toward thinner and lighter TVs. During 1996, digital was officially mandated by the US FCC as a new standard for future DTV/HDTV broadcasting. By 2006, LCDs became more popular due to better daytime viewing and lower prices. LCDs created colored images by selectively blocking and filtering a white LED backlight rather than directly producing light.

HDTV uses a resolution of 1920x1080p, equivalent to 2,073,600 pixels per frame, and known as 1080p. The 4K Ultra HDTV uses 3840x2160p, known as 2160p. This amounts to four times the amount of pixels and twice the resolution of HDTV, hence 4K. The newer 8K increases this eight times to 7680x4320.

OLED improved color by directly producing colored light, allowing for greater contrast. OLED TVs are also extremely thin, measuring in fractions of an inch.

When the iPhone 4 was released, Steve Jobs claimed that the human eye cannot detect smartphone resolution beyond 300 pixels per inch (Apple's limit at the time). However, many others have proven the eye can actually detect at least 900 or greater PPI.

Incidentally, it is the relationship of HD, 4K, 8K, etc., to screen size that makes the difference. Phone screens are small, so HD, 4K, etc., are a waste, as our eyes cannot perceive the difference. Distance between our eyes and the screen is also a factor, that is why many TV manufacturers show the optimal distance for viewing.

As TV sets grow, it takes more pixels to see the same clarity of picture that are needed on a smaller screen. *The arguments of not being able to tell the difference between HD, 4K, and 8K are relative to size and distance from the screen. However, 8K is likely beyond the average household to notice any perceptible difference vs. 4K.*

Artificial Voice - Artificial voices have been around since the 1700s and have made much progress, but have been very limited until now. There is a new service hoping to help some of the millions of voice impaired people. A company, VocaliD has been set up to allow volunteers to donate their voice to help someone speak.

To create a voice, the company takes the shape of the vocal tract from a voice donor, and the source from a recipient, who has given something as limited as a vowel. After taking that short recording from the recipient the team selects a donor with a similar 'filter' and uses a computer algorithm to layer one over the other. The process takes about ten to fifteen hours after recordings from both donor and recipient have been completed.

It provides unique voices for those who rely on computerized devices, because they are unable to speak. The technology builds on speech science theory and creates a hybrid voice that preserves the clarity of the donor's recordings while conveying as much of the recipient's vocal identity as possible.

Some things from the FAQ on the site - A banked voice would make it possible to re-create your voice should you ever lose it in the future.

Your voice may also spark new discoveries and innovations in speech technologies, biometrics, and health diagnostics. Becoming a speech donor is simple, rewarding and even educational. All you need to record is an Internet connection, a microphone, a quiet place, and a computer or smartphone running the Chrome browser. You will be asked to read or repeat short sentences that, together, cover all the combinations of sounds that occur in the language. It takes a few hours, but you can record at your leisure and do not need to complete all at one sitting. https://www.vocalid.co/voicebank

----

Energy and Power - Energy is measured in Joules. Power is measured in Watts. Energy is how far you can run. Power is how fast you can run.

When it comes to batteries, Elon Musk says, "It's really rare that there's a big breakthrough, because there are so many constraints. You can easily improve, say, the power, but then it would make the energy worse."

Current electric cars have batteries that provide less power and less energy. This is why the Nissan Leaf has a range of only 84 miles (one-third that of the Tesla Model S) and takes three times as long to get to 60 miles per hour.

Musk's Tesla Gigafactory, built outside Reno, Nevada, will be the second-largest building in the world by volume. It opened in 2016 and will be complete during 2020. His plan is to build enough batteries to reduce the price and improve the power and energy of batteries, so electric cars can go faster and farther. (The latest edition of the Model S received a score of 103 from Consumer Reports, which was a problem only in that Consumer Reports ratings are typically scored out of 100. The magazine had to revise its scale in response to the record-breaking result.)

In addition, the plant will produce large batteries that store energy in homes and even larger batteries that do the same for utilities and businesses. One of its goals is to make home and business solar power more practical. It also produces a line of solar roof shingles. Current prices are already half what other battery manufacturers charge. Musk says, "The issue with existing batteries is that they suck. They are expensive. They are unreliable. They are stinky. Ugly. Bad in every way." His new battery plans are on the path to fix those problems.

In addition to CEO of Tesla Motors and Space X, Musk is also the chairman of solar energy provider SolarCity.

More Power - During July 2017, Tesla Inc. won an Australian contract to install the world's biggest grid-scale battery that will serve as emergency back-up power for South Australia. Tesla must deliver the 100-MW battery within 100 days of the contract being signed or it will be free.

The battery, designed to light up 30,000 homes if there is a blackout, will be built on a wind farm operated by France's Neoen. It overtakes an 80 megawatt-hour facility in California, also built using Tesla batteries.

Garbage Technology - This tickled me, so thought I would share. Seems Peru is mixing hi-tech and low-tech to solve an age old problem of garbage.

Officials in Lima are strapping GoPro cameras and GPS trackers to vultures to help map the area's illegal dumping problem. With about twenty percent of the Peruvian capital's garbage ending up in places other than one of its four landfills, officials hope the project brings more attention to the issue.

More Hi-Tech-Low-Tech - Dutch police are using eagles to solve the problem of unauthorized drone flights in restricted areas such as airports and over crowds. Dennis Janus said, "We use the birds' age-old hunting instinct to intercept and neutralize drones."

Police released video footage of the tests, which shows an eagle in flight firmly grasping the drone with its talons before landing a few metres (yards) away. The eagles are trained by 'Guard from Above', which describes itself as the "first company in the world that uses birds of prey to intercept drones."

Cell Phone Usage - During January, 2009, just 10% of the US population had smartphones, resulting in network traffic that mostly involved texts and voice, and some modest picture messaging.

By 2016, 88% of the US population owned smartphones.

Wordology

WORDOLOGY

Affronts and Aspersions - An affront is an insult, indignity, or something offensive. As a verb, it means to insult or offend. Affront comes from comes from French affronter "to face, to brave, to confront". It can be used in a sentence as, "These laws are an affront to our free speech."

Aspersion comes from aspergere "to sprinkle on, spatter" based on add- "(up) to, on" and sparger "to strew, scatter." An aspersion means a spattering or sprinkling, especially of holy water. It also means that which bespatters or besmirches someone's character, slander, defamation of character. People usually use the term 'cast aspersions', as in spatter someone with metaphorical mud.

Incidentally, Asperger's syndrome is named for Hans Asperger and totally unrelated to the word or word root above.

Armageddon and Apocalypse - These two words are often used interchangeably to refer to the end of the world, usually in a Biblical sense. They are actually very different. Armageddon refers to a place, while the Apocalypse is the reading of a series of events.

There is only one mention of Armageddon in the Bible, in Revelation 16:16. The verse is: "And He gathered them together into a place called in the Hebrew tongue Armageddon." The word Armageddon comes from the Hebrew words har (mountain), and Megiddo (Megiddon), which was the name of a city. Today, the once-great city is little more than ruins, located about 95 kilometers (60 miles) outside of Jerusalem.

Apokalypsis is a Greek word that means 'something uncovered'. Apocalypse refers to the uncovering of a vision for the future, such as in the Book of Revelation and the Revelation of John. Most beliefs about the apocalypse are pieced together from different texts throughout the Bible, meaning that the apocalypse is actually presenting guidelines for interpreting a series of events in the world around us.

The religious apocalypse is a way of interpreting events. The general belief is that we are not going to be able to change what is going on around us.

The secular apocalypse is meant to be a way of examining the world around us. The difference is that we can theoretically do something about the secular apocalypse. We can pay attention to the effects of wars, conflict, and crisis. While the religious apocalypse is meant to give hope, the secular one is meant to make mankind aware of what we are doing to the world around us, so we can change.

Cattywampus and Caterwaul - Cattywampus or catawampus means not lined up, askew, awry, not straight. Perhaps related to Scots wampish to wiggle, twist or swerve about. In use, "The picture frame is cattywampus on the wall."

Caterwaul verb: to make a harsh cry or to protest or complain noisily, a shrill howl or wailing noise. In use, "They caterwauled against the walls of Jericho."

Hogmanay - Hogmanay is the Scots word for the last day of the year and is synonymous with the celebration of the New Year in the Scottish style. The celebrating begins on the last day of the year and lasts through the night until the morning of New Year's Day or January 2, a Scottish Bank Holiday.

Prosopagnosia - After the holidays are about over and we met many new friends, it seems this disease might fit the discussion. People with Prosopagnosia, about two percent of the population, find it difficult or impossible to remember faces, even their own. Some contort their own face when standing in front of a mirror in a crowded restroom so they can determine which is theirs. They are not technically face blind, but their brains cannot memorize what they see. Many Prosopagnosics are ostracized by people who are offended that they are not recognized. There is no therapy or cure, so most learn to cope with it by using secondary clues such as clothing, gait, hair color, body shape, and voice to recognize friends, family, and co-workers.

BASE is an acronym for Buildings, Antennas, Spans and Earth. Base jumps and other non-harnessed jumps are illegal in all US national parks.

Color Names - Am sure many of you woke up this morning with the same burning question on your mind, where did the common colors get their names.

Pink - In English, pink used to refer exclusively to a flower called a pink, a dianthus which has pale red petals with fringed edges. Pink, as a verb means to cut or tear jaggedly, as with pinking shears and has been in use in the English language since the early 14th century.

Orange - When oranges (the fruit) were exported from India, the word for them was exported too. Sanskrit narangah, or "orange tree," was borrowed into Persian as narang, "orange (fruit)," which was borrowed into Arabic as naranj, into Italian as arancia, into French as orange, and eventually into English as orange. The color of the fruit was so striking that English speakers eventually began referring to the color by this word as well. Before oranges were imported in the 1500s, the English word for the color orange was geoluhread (yellow-red).

Vigorish - The US football Super Bowl always begets bets and vigorish is part of betting. It is also known as vig, juice, the cut, rake, or the take and it is the amount charged by a bookmaker or bookie, for taking a bet from a gambler. In the United States, it also means the interest on a shark's loan. The term is also used in other forms of gambling, banking, auctions, and casino games. The term originates from the Russian word for winnings, vyigrysh.

Bookmakers charge vigorish to make money on their wagers regardless of the outcome. To minimize their risk, some bookmakers do not want to have an interest in either side winning in any event. They seek equal betting on both outcomes of the event to minimize risk. The bookmaker adjusts the odds to encourage both sides to bet. Vigorish is usually factored in proportionally to the true odds. A common amount of vig is about two percent.

Speakeasy - A speakeasy, also called a blind pig is an establishment that illegally sells alcoholic beverages. The phrase 'speak easy shop', denoting a place where unlicensed liquor sales were made, appeared in a British naval memoir written in 1844. The phrase, 'speak softly shop', meaning a "smuggler's house," appeared in a British slang dictionary published in 1823.

According to an 1889 US newspaper, "Unlicensed saloons in Pennsylvania are known as speak-easies." They were so called because of the practice of speaking quietly about such a place in public or when inside it, so as not to alert the police or neighbors. The term is reported to have originated with saloon owner Kate Hester, who ran an unlicensed bar in the 1880s in the Pittsburgh area town of McKeesport, Pennsylvania.

The terms 'blind pig' and 'blind tiger' originated in the United States during the 19th century. These terms were applied to lower-class establishments that sold alcoholic beverages illegally, and the terms are still in use today. The operator of a saloon or bar would charge customers to see an attraction, such as an animal and then serve a complimentary alcoholic beverage, thus circumventing the law. These words came before US Prohibition (1920 - 1933).

Red Handed - This expression has its origins in Scotland. Given the context it was often used in the earliest references, the phrase 'red hand' or 'redhand' probably came about referring to people caught with blood on their hands. The first known documented instance of "red hand" is in the Scottish Acts of Parliament of James I, written in 1432: "That the offender be taken reid hand, may be persewed, and put to the knawledge of ane Assise, befoir the Barron or Landeslord of the land or ground, quhidder the offender be his tennent, unto quhom the wrang is done or not... And uthers not taken reid hand, to be alwaies persewed..."

The first documented instance of the expression morphing from 'red hand' to 'red handed' was in the early 19th century work Ivanhoe, written by Sir Walter Scott: "I did but tie one fellow, who was taken redhanded and in the fact, to the horns of a wild stag."

It later showed up in 'Guy Livingstone' written by George Alfred Lawrence and published in 1857: "We were collared on the instant. The fact of the property being found in our possession constituted a 'flagrans delictum' – we were caught red-handed."

Rum - It was originally called rumbullion. Richard Ligon in 1651 said, "Rumbullion alias Kill-Devill . . . is made of suggar cane distilled, a hott, hellish and terrible liquor . . . will overpower the senses with a single whiff."

The world rumbullion formerly existed as either Royal Navy jargon for "an uproar" or Creole slang for "stem stew" It was shortened to rum years later, but its reviews did not get any better. In 1654 a General

Court Order was issued in Connecticut to seize and destroy "whatsoever Barbados liquors, commonly called rum, Kill Devill, or the like." Demon rum was first coined by Timothy Arthur in his 1854 temperance play "Ten Nights in a Barroom," and it wasn't long before the phrase came to describe all forms of evil alcohol.

More Drinking Terminology - *Bootleg* comes from the late 19th century smugglers' practice of concealing bottles in their boots. In football, "bootleg" means the quarterback fakes a hand-off and runs while concealing the ball, ostensibly on his leg.

Touching glasses, as in *toasting*, comes from ancient Greeks, who clanked their cups in order to purposefully spill some alcohol, which was an offering to the gods. It also follows a medieval custom of clinking goblets together in order to frighten the demons out of the spirits, because it sounded like church bells.

Shot glasses serve two functions: to measure liquor for a cocktail or to consume straight liquor in a quick manner. The first printed use of the term "shot glass" occurred in the 1940s in a news story discussing ways to regulate the size of a shot of liquor in the restaurants and bars of New York City, US. Before it was called a shot glass, it was referred to as a jigger or pony. A *jigger* is a measuring glass of varying volume, while *pony* means one US liquid ounce.

The *cocktail glass* pre-dates the drink for which it is named. It was developed as a way to keep chilled drinks from being warmed by a drinker's hands. During the early 20th century the *martini glass*, which is wider and less rounded, became distinct from the cocktail glass.

The earliest reference to a *corkscrew* was in 1681 where it was called a 'steel worm used for the drawing of corks out of bottles'. The term 'steel worm' was derived by gunsmiths, who had crafted similar tools by the same name for cleaning the barrel of a musket.

Blotto and blackout are British slang from the early 1900s. To blot can mean both to soak up a liquid and to erase something, which is what happens to your memory when you blackout.

Three sheets to the wind comes from sailing terminology. If all three sheets (on a three-sail rig) are released and allowed to go slack, the sail will flap about sloppily, the boat will lose speed, and control. Another theory comes from the Dutch windmill industry. The mills generally had four blades that were just frames. When a miller wanted to grind grain he would put material over the frames of the blades, so that the wind would propel them. If the miller only put three sheets on before it started spinning, it would be lopsided. As the unbalanced blades spun it would cause the entire mill to sway back and forth, much like a drunken person.

The first documented use of *hangover* or hang-over was in 1894, and it meant a survival or a thing left over from before. The term was also associated with the 1929 US stock market crash often written about as if it were a hangover from the wild 1920s.

The verbal short form of *'86'* to mean to dismiss or quash, to bar entry or further service to, and even to kill. According to the Oxford English Dictionary, the first verifiable use of 86 for 'refuse service' dates to a 1944 book about John Barrymore, a movie star of the 1920s and infamous for his drinking. "There was a bar in the Belasco building, but Barrymore was known there as an 'eighty-six'. An 'eighty-six', in the language of western dispensers, means do not serve him." There are many other theories, but this seems to be the most accepted.

Mangle - I am sure you heard someone say this or that is all mangled. A mangle is a device that used to be used for drying clothes. Sometimes it is also called a wringer. A mangle iron is used to press clothes and usually has steam coming from inside the roller.

mangle wringer

The word mangle was coined in the early 20th century after many of the first industrial ironers had crushed and dismembered those who got too close to the feeder end or chain drives of the machines.

By Hook or By Crook - This was first used during the 14th century, it refers to peasants pulling down branches for firewood using either a bill-hook (long handle saw with curved blade) or a shepherd's crook (walking staff with curved handle). It is an old phrase that describes any means possible, but it has no relation to criminals.

Kilts - Regardless of what we learned in *Braveheart*, the kilt didn't appear until about 300 years after Wallace. The version we are familiar with today did not appear until the 18th century.

The word kilt is of Scandinavian origin. Middle English (as a verb in the sense 'tuck up around the body'): Danish kilte (op) 'tuck (up)' and Old Norse kilting 'a skirt.' The noun dates from the mid 18th century.

The kilt made its first appearance in the 16th century, but it was very different from the modern version. Now referred to as the great kilt or belted plaid, it was a full-body garment that covered both upper and lower halves. The upper half of the kilt could be draped over the shoulder like a cloak or worn over the head like a hood. This was the only type of kilt used for a few hundred years.

Sometime during the early 18th century, Englishman Thomas Rawlinson decided that the standard kilt was too cumbersome to wear while working, so he came up with the small kilt. It was just the lower half of the great kilt and resembled the kilt we all know today. He went into business with Scottish chief Ian MacDonell, who liked Rawlinson's idea and also started wearing the small kilt. Because they were influential, all of their employees started wearing the small kilt and its popularity spread throughout Scotland.

Donut and Doughnut - This issue has plagued food writers for decades, especially because there is one dictionary-approved spelling and one that is used by a popular chain. A doughnut gets its name because it is a combination of the words dough and nut. It is literally a nut (ball) of dough.

The shortened donut spelling came into popular usage about 1900 and is used mostly in the US, but gaining popularity around the English speaking world. Writers outside the US still favor doughnut. Donut appears about a third of the time in published US writing.

Think of donut as a cousin of the words lite and tonite. They are supposed to be spelled light and tonight, but marketers and advertisers choose otherwise.

Orchid - Take a look at certain orchids' roots, and you will probably notice that they look like testicles. If not, you have set yourself apart from multiple generations of language-makers that simply could not help but name the whole plant family after this observation.

The contemporary word for the flower, introduced in 1845, comes from the Greek orchis, which literally translates as testicle. Speakers of Middle English in the 1300s came up with a phonologically different word inspired by the same exact dirty thought. They called the flower ballockwort from ballocks, or testicles, which itself evolved from beallucas, the Old English word for balls.

Stave Off - To 'stave off' means to keep at bay, fight off, or defend against. In its original, noun form, around 1400, the Oxford English Dictionary says, a "stave" was a thin strip of wood that was curved to make a cask or barrel. Staves was originally the plural of staff, a long rod or walking stick. So by extension, many kinds of sticks or rods, including the staffs of a lance or other weapon, were known as staves.

By the 1600s, stave evolved to mean drive off or beat with a staff or stave. The use was meant literally, as in to stave off an attack on the castle, possibly using lances or other weapons with staves. The common use today has become figurative, as in to stave off a cold.

Trivia - The word trivia originates from the Latin word trivium (plural trivia), where "tri" stands for triple and "via" means way. Basically, the word means a place where three ways meet. This word gained prominence in Rome, where people would often chin wag with others at a trivium.

The word trivalis in Classical Latin meant an appropriate street corner and commonplace. In medieval times, the word gained broader meaning and came to refer grammar, rhetoric, and logic. Much of what you read here can be referred to as trivia.

SUV vs. Crossover - A crossover is based on a car's platform, while an SUV uses the chassis of a truck. The result is that crossovers use "unibody" architecture, meaning the body and frame are one piece, while SUVs use a "body on frame" design, meaning the body is built separate from the frame.

SUV is often applied to both crossovers and SUVs. In the past, that was even more common. Before, SUV brought up negative associations with large size and poor gas mileage. That is when many automakers started using the term "crossover" to describe a vehicle that was "crossing over" from the practicality of an SUV to the drivability and fuel efficiency of a car.

Many vehicles, such as the Explorer, Highlander, Grand Cherokee, Nissan Pathfinder, Lexus RX, and Acura MDX are technically crossovers.

The Chevrolet Tahoe, Ford Expedition, and Mercedes G-Class are all SUVs in the original sense of the term.

If you are unsure whether a vehicle uses a car-based unibody design or body-on-frame construction, it is safe to use the term SUV. That acronym is still used to describe nearly anything with available all-wheel drive and raised ground clearance.

Assent vs. Consent - In English, consent and assent are often used interchangeably, but there is a subtle difference. To assent is to agree with a statement made by an equal. For instance, in the Supreme Court, one justice writes the opinion of the majority, to which other justices assent. Those that disagree are said to dissent, that is to disagree.

To consent implies a power relationship where the consent is granted by the party with more power. To consent is to give permission, which could have been withheld. *Bottom line, consent is to give permission while assent equals agreement.*

Short Shrift - A shrift is a penance (a prescribed penalty) imposed by a priest in a confession in order to provide absolution. During the 17th century, criminals were sent to the scaffold immediately after sentencing and only had time for a 'short shrift' before being hanged.

The first known use of short shrift was in 1594. Shakespeare was the first to write it down, in Richard III. RATCLIFF: Dispatch, my lord; the duke would be at dinner: Make a short shrift; he longs to see your head.

It does not appear again in print until 1814, Scott's Lord of the Isles: "Short were his shrift in that debate. If Lorn encounter'd Bruce!"

The original meaning has little relation to the modern sense of short shrift, which usually has negative connotations. One usually does not want to be given short shrift or little consideration in dealing with a person or matter.

Theologians and confessors viewed the sacrament of penance as a prescription that cured a moral illness. In early medieval times penances were long and arduous and had to be performed before absolution. Lengthy pilgrimages and even lifelong exile were not uncommon. However, less demanding penances could be given in extreme situations.

Wallet vs. Billfold - The word 'wallet' has been in use since the late 14th century to refer to a bag or a knapsack for carrying articles.

A billfold is a type of wallet carried by a man that folds over. Billfold is one of those practical words that describe the function, as folding bills. It is like the kitchen cupboard, which was originally a wall attached board used to store cups and plates.

Americans call their paper money, bills even though they are really Federal Reserve Notes. Other English speaking countries call them notes.

Although billfold and wallet are used interchangeably, it is now more common to use wallet. Technically, a wallet is the type women usually carry in their purse. It has a long section where they can put money without folding it.

Wallets were developed after the introduction of paper currency to the West in the 1600s. The first paper currency was introduced in the New World by the Massachusetts Bay Colony in 1690. Prior to the introduction of paper currency, coin purses, usually simple drawstring leather pouches, were used for storing coins. Early wallets were made primarily of cow or horse leather and included a small pouch for printed calling cards.

During the 1800s, in addition to money or currency, a wallet would also be used for carrying dried meat, victuals, treasures, and "things not to be exposed". Wallets originally were used by early industrial Americans. It was considered semi-civilized in 19th century America to carry a wallet attached to the belt.

Incidentally, 'share of wallet' is a marketing measurement for the proportion of money the customer spends on a product brand in preference to the competing brands.

Bottom line, all billfolds are wallets, but not all wallets are billfolds.

Metonymy and Synecdoche - Metonymy, pronounced 'mi-tonn-ə-mee' is a figure of speech in which a thing or concept is called by the name of something associated in meaning with that thing or concept, rather than by its own name. The words "metonymy" and "metonym" come from the Greek: metōnymía, 'a change of name'.

Metonymy and related figures of speech are common in everyday talk and writing. Synecdoche is a specific type of metonymy. Synecdoche refers to a thing by the name of one of its parts. For example, calling a car "a wheel" is a synecdoche. A part of a car, the wheel stands for the whole car.

One of the main purposes of using a metonymy is to add flavor to the writing. The name of a sports team can be used in place of its individual members.

Other examples: "Wall Street" is often used metonymously to describe the US financial and corporate sector, and "Hollywood" used as a metonym for the US film industry. The national capital is often used to represent the government or monarchy of a country, such as "Washington" for United States government or "Downing Street" for the Government of the United Kingdom.

Other metonymys - Crown. (For the power of a king), The White House. (the American administration), Dish. (To refer an entire plate of food), and finally, the old adage, 'the pen is mightier than the sword' - [Pen (For the written word) Sword - (For military force)]

Six Common Acronyms - CVS (Pharmacy) is now just called CVS, but when it first opened, the letters stood for Consumer Value Store.

The ZIP in ZIP Code stands for Zone Improvement Plan.

GEICO used to stand for "Government Employees Insurance Company."

The fashion retailer H&M is for Hennes & Mauritz.

The Smart Car was a collaboration between Swatch and Mercedes Benz and originally called the Swatch and Mercedes Art Car.

Today TCBY stands for The Country's Best Yogurt, but used to be called 'This Can't Be Yogurt'.

Other Words for Underwear - *Knickers* is actually a standard word for underwear, mainly in Britain. "Knickers" derives from "knickerbockers," or "loose-fitting short pants gathered at the knee." Because the city's early Dutch settlers wore those pants, "New Yorkers" became known as "Knickerbockers." The Knickerbockers, more commonly "The Knicks" is the name of New York's NBA team.

In the 1500s, a *corselet* was something a soldier might wear, a piece of armor for the torso. The word comes from the French word for body. Several centuries later, the same word emerged and shortened to *corset*, to describe a combination of girdle and brassiere.

Drawers does not refer to where you store them, as in a chest of drawers. The word drawers has been used since the 16th century to refer to garments such as stockings, underpants, and pants. It comes from the verb draw used in the sense of pull, likely because you pull them up your legs.

The *union suit* gets its name by uniting the upper and lower pieces of underwear in one garment. Two-piece *long johns* are more common these days, and do not require a seat flap. Long johns are reputedly named after the late-19th-century heavyweight boxer John L. Sullivan, who wore a similar-looking garment in the ring. This explanation is uncertain and the true origin is unknown.

Singlet usually describes a sleeveless undershirt. It also refers to the one-piece suit a wrestler wears. It has only one thickness of cloth. A *doublet* is not underwear, but a lined jacket worn by men during the Renaissance.

Discreet vs. Discrete - This pair of homophones (words that sound alike, but are different in meaning, spelling, or both) can be confusing. Discreet implies the showing of reserve in behavior or speech. Discrete means distinct, separate, unrelated.

Both words derive from the same Latin word discretus meaning "separated." Until the 1700s, these words were each spelled many different ways including discrete, discreet, dyscrete, discreete, etc.

Eventually discrete and discreet came to be differentiated in spelling as well as in meaning. Discreet has yielded the noun discretion, but discrete's noun form is discreteness. For most of English history, discreet was more frequently used, but today discrete is much more frequently used than discreet; it has seen a dramatic rise since the 1940s.

Tip, if you mean 'separate', make the e's separated by the "t", use "discrete."

Kits and Caboodles - Kit has been in use as far back as the late 1200s and originally meant a round wooden tub, jug, tankard, or wooden container. Later it came to mean a knapsack as for a soldier, which contained all his needed items. Caboodle was first seen during the mid-1800s and from the earlier word boodle, meaning a collection of people among other meanings. Together they roughly mean all the people and all their things, the whole lot.

Kit and caboodle was first seen in print in 1884 in New York's Syracuse Sunday Standard: "More audiences have been disappointed by him and by the whole kit-and-caboodle of his rivals."

Whiskey Name Origins - *Four Roses* Co-founder Paul Jones Jr. trademarked the Four Roses name in 1888. The story is that Paul Jones Jr. and his father, Paul Jones Sr., had opened a grocery and warehouse in Atlanta and the younger Paul became interested in distilling. At the time, he was also courting a local lady, and asked for her hand in marriage. They agreed that, at a grand ball they were to attend, if she were to accept his proposal of marriage, she would wear a corsage of four red roses. She wore the corsage and the two were married.

Knob Creek is produced at the Jim Beam distillery in Clermont, Kentucky, US. It is named for the creek that ran behind Abraham Lincoln's childhood Kentucky home. The late Booker Noe, Jim Beam's sixth generation master distiller, chose the name because he thought it reflected his values in making whiskey.

The rye whiskey brand name *Whistlepig* comes from the 'single oddest piece of social interaction' that founder Raj Bhakta had ever experienced. Bhakta was hiking outside of Denver, Colorado, US. "Out of the blue popped a guy with a thick French accent and a big shock of white hair," says Raj. "He got very close into my personal space and asked 'Could it be? A whistlepig?' I had no idea what he was talking about or what he was looking at. When I didn't understand, he snapped in my face and repeated himself. When I still didn't understand, he flicked his wrist and took off."

The *Wild Turkey* name dates back to the 1940s, "Thomas McCarthy, an executive from the company that made the whiskey at the time, took all the New York business folks on a big turkey hunt every year." The trip's festivities would include hunting and whiskey. That year, he pulled 101 proof bourbon for the guests. The next year, they asked him to bring the same bourbon. He pulled a sample, and the brand's name was born.

Origin of Con Man - The perpetrator of a confidence trick is often referred to as a confidence or con man, con-artist, or a grifter. The first known usage of the term 'confidence man' in English was in 1849 by the New York City press, during the trial of William Thompson. Thompson chatted with strangers until he asked if they had the confidence to lend him their watches. If they did, he would walk off with the watch. He was captured when a victim recognized him on the street.

Difference between Burka, Hijab, Niqab - The burka is the most concealing of all Islamic veils. It is a one-piece veil that covers the face and body, often leaving just a mesh screen to see through.

The word hijab describes the act of covering up generally, but is often used to describe the headscarves worn by Muslim women. These scarves come in many styles and colors. The type most commonly worn in the West covers the head and neck, but leaves the face clear.

Burka and niqab are often incorrectly used interchangeably. While a burqa covers the whole body from the top of the head to the ground, a niqab is a veil for the face that leaves the area around the eyes clear, but may be worn with a separate eye veil. It is worn with an accompanying headscarf. The half niqab is a simple length of fabric with elastic or ties, worn around the face. It typically leaves the eyes and part of the forehead visible.

A full niqab completely covers the face. It consists of an upper band that is tied around the forehead, together with a long wide piece of fabric which covers the face, leaving an opening for the eyes.

In Iran, the wearing of niqab is not common and is only worn by certain ethnic minorities. On 8 October 2009, Egypt's top Islamic school banned the wearing of the niqab in classrooms and dormitories of all its affiliate schools and educational institutes. In Syria in the summer of 2010, students wearing the niqab were prohibited from registering for university classes. The niqab is outlawed in Azerbaijan, Tunisia, and Turkey, and banned in Cameroon, Chad, Congo, Netherlands, Yugoslavia, France, Belgium, Norway (Schools and some municipalities), Canada (selected bans), and Italy (selected municipalities).

Other coverings: The *al-amira* is a two-piece veil. It consists of a close fitting cap and a tube-like scarf. The *shayla* is a long, rectangular scarf popular in the Gulf region. It is wrapped around the head and tucked or pinned in place at the shoulders. The *khimar* is a long, cape-like veil that hangs down to just above the waist. It covers the hair, neck, and shoulders completely, but leaves the face clear. The *chador,* worn by many Iranian women when outside the house, is a full-body cloak. It is often accompanied by a smaller headscarf underneath.

Plaid vs. Tartan - Tartan is the specific pattern unique to each Scottish clan or region. The term plaid comes from the Gaelic word, plaide, which referred to the actual blanket or outer layer the Scots wore during harsh weather. The terms are now often used interchangeably, even though they are different. There are many plaid designs that are not tartan. *All tartans are plaid, but not all plaids are tartans.*

Origin of Bloody Mary - This drink is believed by many to be the perfect hangover cure. A Bloody Mary is made up of vodka, tomato juice, cayenne pepper and Tabasco or Worcester Sauce.

The drink is said to have been named after the Catholic Queen Mary I (1516-58), nicknamed Bloody Mary due to her relentless pursuit of Protestant dissenters, of whom nearly 300 were burned at the stake. The tomato juice is thought to resemble the blood she spilled.

Every Day vs. Everyday - Every Day means each day. Everyday means commonplace, ordinary, typical.

Here are some examples for using every day and everyday correctly: Jane takes her dog out for a walk every day. It is important to floss every day.

Jack did not take very good care of his everyday shoes.

An "everyday occurrence" does not necessarily mean it occurs every day. It only means it is an ordinary, commonplace occurrence. It is not something unusual. Everyday is an adjective, so it describes an attribute of the occurrence.

If something occurs daily, you say it "occurs every day" or that it is a daily occurrence. Since "every day" is an adverb, it cannot be used as an adjective to describe the occurrence.

Eschatology - It is a sub-field of a variety of disciplines including Theology, Philosophy, and Physics that deals with the end of the World or end of time.

Cemetery and Graveyard - Graveyard and cemetery do not mean the same thing. From about the 7th century, the process of burial was in the hands of the Church (the organization), and burying the dead was only allowed on the lands near a church (the building), the churchyard.

The part of the churchyard used for burial is called a graveyard. As the population of Europe started to grow, the capacity of graveyards was no longer sufficient. By the end of the 18th century, the unsustainability of church burials became apparent, and completely new places, independent of graveyards, were devised. These new places were called cemeteries.

Cemetery comes from Old French cimetiere, which meant graveyard. The French word originally comes from Greek koimeterion, meaning 'a sleeping place'.

Bottom line, a graveyard is a type of cemetery, but a cemetery is not a graveyard.

More Wordology - *Disinterested* means unbiased and does not mean uninterested. Correct: "The dispute should be resolved by a disinterested judge." / Why are you so uninterested in my story?

Enervate means to sap or to weaken and does not mean to energize. Correct: That was an enervating rush hour commute. / That was an energizing cappuccino.

Hung means suspended and does not mean suspended from the neck until dead. Correct: I hung the picture on my wall. / The prisoner was hanged.

Escalumps - People who stand on the left while riding escalators, hindering others from passing.

Victorian Words - The Victorians had much influence on common terms - The avoidance of plain terms for bodily parts commonly is associated with the prudery of our Victorian ancestors, though many of the evasions predate Queen Victoria's ascension to the throne in 1837.

Interesting word thought - If womb is pronounced woomb and tomb is pronounced toomb, why isn't bomb pronounced boomb?

People started saying darn instead of damn, employed dashes (d – –) instead of the harsher word, to perspire instead of sweat, to have stomachaches instead of bellyaches, to wear unmentionables instead of trousers and breeches, to use nude rather than naked when referring to human figures in painting and sculpture, and to be laid to rest, not buried in a cemetery.

The taboo on breast was so strong that it was replaced by bosom in many contexts during the following century. Decorative breast knots on dresses became bosom knots, breast pins became bosom pins, and even English farmers were known to refer to the breast, or forward part of the moldboard of a plow, as its bosom.

Most likely, the reluctance to say breast also explains why William Congreve's line in The Mourning Bride, "Music has charms to soothe a savage breast," is often misquoted as "Music has charms to soothe a savage beast."

Mondegreens, Malapropisms, and Eggcorns - A *mondegreen* is a word or phrase resulting from a misinterpretation of another word or phrase that we hear. Mondegreens sound like the original wording, but often change the meaning of the word or phrase entirely. The term mondegreen is usually applied to misheard song lyrics or lines of poetry, but can also refer to other types of speech. For example, someone might hear the sarcastic saying "Thank you, Captain Obvious" as "Thank you, Katherine Obvious."

A *malapropism* is the use of an incorrect word in place of a word with a similar sound, resulting in a nonsense, or humorous utterance. Yogi Berra was a master of this, saying things, such as "Texas has a lot of electrical votes," rather than "electoral votes". Another example is "dance the flamingo" instead of "dance the flamenco."

Eggcorns are an idiosyncratic substitution of a word or phrase for a word or words that sound similar or identical in the speaker's dialect. The new phrase introduces a meaning that is different from the original, but plausible in the same context, such as "old-timers' disease" for "Alzheimer's disease" or "mating name" instead of "maiden name."

If a person stubbornly sticks to a mispronunciation after being corrected, that person has committed a mumpsimus.

Old Chestnut - An 'old chestnut' is another way of saying a joke is old or stale. The origin appears to be eating roasted chestnuts at the fireside while listening to old stories.

The Broken Sword, was a melodrama by William Dimond (1816) in which one of the characters, Captain Xavier, is forever telling the same jokes, over and over, with slight variations. As he repeats a certain joke involving a cork tree, he is corrected. The man says, "A chestnut. I have heard you tell the joke twenty-seven times, and I am sure it was a chestnut."

Wordology, Eke - If we see the word 'eke' these days, it is usually when we 'eke out' a living, but it comes from an old verb meaning to add, supplement, or grow. It is the same word that gave us 'eke-name' for 'additional name', which later changed from an 'eke-name' to 'nickname'.

Just Deserts - The 'desert' from the phrase 'just deserts' is not the hot, dry, and sandy kind, nor the after dinner kind. It comes from an Old French word for 'deserve', and it was used in English from the 13th century to mean "that which is deserved." When you get your just deserts, you get what you deserve.

NAMING BABIES

Up until 1993, France had a list of official names that new parents were required to pick from. After 1993, they were allowed to pick almost anything they wanted. However, one that caught the attention of the court was a girl named Nutella. The court ruled that the name would lead to the child being teased and was not in the best interest of the girl. When the parents failed to appear in court, the judge ruled that the girl's name be changed to Ella.

Belgium has a list of approved baby names.

Denmark has a list of 7,000 approved names.

Italian law says a name cannot be chosen "when the child's name is likely to limit social interaction and create insecurity."

In Japan, only official kanji may be used in babies' given names. The purpose is to make sure all names can be easily read and written by the Japanese. The Japanese also restrict names that might be deemed inappropriate.

Malays cannot name their children after animals, insects, fruits, vegetables, or colors.

In Morocco, there is a list of approved names that appropriately reflect 'Moroccan identity'. You can name a baby 'Sara' (Arabic version) but not 'Sarah' (Hebrew version).

Norway has an official list of acceptable Norwegian names and parents may be fined and go to jail if they choose to use a name not on the list.

In Sweden, "First names shall not be approved if they can cause offense or can be supposed to cause discomfort for the one using it, or names which for some obvious reason are not suitable as a first name."

During 2013, New Zealand released a report with all the names it has banned. A name may be rejected if it is thought to "cause offense to a reasonable person," is "unreasonably long" or "resemble an official title and rank." New Zealand has an agency that signs off on baby names.

In the Mexican state of Sonora, government officials pulled 61 names from the baby registry that were banned for being "derogatory, pejorative, discriminatory, or lacking in meaning".

The German government rules state that a name must clearly identify the person as male or female, and it cannot be offensive. No surname names are allowed in Germany, or are names of objects or products.

Iceland has a list of 1,712 male names and 1,853 female names. The lists exist to avoid embarrassment for the children, and are based on meeting certain rules of grammar.

The UK deed poll service has restrictions on name changes. It must have both a first and last name, and it cannot be vulgar, promote racial or religious hate, or the use of controlled drugs. A name cannot ridicule people or government departments.

Portuguese authorities ban nicknames from birth certificates. Tomás would be OK, but Tom is not allowed. Portugal has an 80-page document outlining names which are acceptable and which are not. Children's names must be traditionally Portuguese, a full name, and not unisex.

Spain bans names that can be unisex.

China babies are required to be named based on the ability of computer scanners to read those names on national identification cards. The government recommends giving children names that are easily readable, and encourages simplified characters over traditional Chinese characters. Numbers and non-Chinese symbols and characters are not allowed.

Saudi Arabia released a list of names that were banned including western names and names with royal connotations like Prince.

Hungary, Lithuania, and Poland also have laws dealing with children naming conventions.

The US has fewer naming laws than most countries and is rooted in the Due Process Clause of the Fourteenth Amendment and the Free Speech Clause of the First Amendment, but a few restrictions do exist. Restrictions vary by state, but most are for the sake of practicality, such as several states limit the number of characters, due to the limitations of software used for official record keeping. Some states ban the use of numerals, pictograms, or anything other than the 26 characters in the alphabet. A few states ban the use of obscenity.

WHAT'S IN A NAME

Cutty Sark - "Cutty Sark" is a brand of whisky, and before that it was the name of a legendary sailing ship. Originally, it referred to ladies' underwear. Cutty sark comes from the now outdated words cutty (short) and sark (shirt). The term first appeared in an 18th century Scottish poem where it described a skimpy nightgown worn by a seductive, but dangerous witch.

Incidentally, since the 1960s, American writers have increasingly used whiskey as the accepted spelling for aged grain spirits made in the US and whisky for aged grain spirits made outside the US. However, some prominent American brands, such as George Dickel, Maker's Mark, and Old Forester use the 'whisky' spelling on their labels, and the Standards of Identity for Distilled Spirits, the legal regulations for spirit in the US, also use the 'whisky' spelling throughout.

Whisky/ey is an umbrella term for a type of spirit distilled from a mash of fermented grains. Within the broad category of whisky/ey are sub-categories, including bourbon, rye, Tennessee, Scotch, Irish, and Canadian style whiskies. Whisky usually denotes Scotch whisky and Scotch-inspired liquors, and whiskey denotes the Irish and American liquors.

A way to remember - Countries that have E's in their names (UnitEd StatEs and IrEland) tend to spell it whiskEy (plural whiskeys). Countries without E's in their names (Canada, Scotland, and Japan) spell it whisky (plural whiskies)

Birdseye - The namesake of Birds Eye Frozen Foods was the company's founder, Clarence Birdseye, who introduced the concept of flash freezing to the world. He developed his technique after seeing food freezing in action in the Arctic, and noting how much better frozen fish tasted if it had been frozen immediately after been caught. He helped pioneer flash freezing as a frozen food standard and helped develop in-store freezer cases and refrigerated boxcars that allowed his frozen foods to travel in comfort.

Birdseye's food was the first frozen food sold commercially in the United States. On March 6, 1930, Birds Eye frozen foods were put on sale at Davidson's Market in Springfield, Massachusetts, the first product of its kind.

Stonewall Jackson - Thomas Jonathan 'Stonewall' Jackson was buried in a Lexington, Virginia cemetery that now bears his name, but he was so famous at the time of his death that his amputated left arm was taken away to its own separate grave.

Just after dark on May 2, 1863, Jackson launched a devastating attack against Union forces at Chancellorsville. Returning to his own lines with several staff, Jackson decided to conduct more reconnaissance in the area. As he and his staff rode through the woods near Confederate lines, a North Carolina regiment opened fire. Jackson was struck by three bullets, two of them shattering his left arm. He was evacuated from the area and given medical treatment, but his arm could not be saved and was amputated. Pneumonia set in, and on May 10, 1863, he died. Jackson's body was sent to Lexington without the arm.

Thinking that the limb of so great a soldier was too precious to simply throw on the regular body part pile, Jackson's unofficial company chaplain wrapped the arm in a blanket and took it to his family cemetery. The reverend gave the limb a standard Christian burial and placed a marker above the site.

Supposedly Stonewall Jackson's arm was dug up and reburied numerous times in the ensuing years and there is no evidence that it still resides in its original burial space. The simple gravestone remains to remember one of the oddest instances of hero worship in the history of battle.

Joaquin Phoenix - Joaquin Rafael Bottom/Leaf Phoenix was one of five children, all with equally interesting names, including River (1970–1993), Rain, Liberty, Summer, and a half-sister Jodean.

After Joaquin's parents, John Lee and Arlyn Bottom, married in 1969, they joined a religious cult and traveled around South America. They became disenchanted with the cult and moved back to the US in 1978, and changed their last name to Phoenix to symbolize new beginning.

About this same time, a young Joaquin began calling himself "Leaf," desiring to have a similar nature-related name as those of his siblings. Leaf was the name he used as a child actor until, at age 15; he changed it back to Joaquin.

Ouija Board - The Ouija board was created as a parlor game around 1890 by designer Elijah Bond, who patented it in 1891, then sold the patent to William Fuld in 1901. Fuld popularized the game and promoted it as a novelty. He sold the business in 1966 to Parker Brothers, which was acquired by Hasbro, which now owns it, along with Monopoly, Risk, Trivial Pursuit, etc. Ouija is a combination of two words: 'oui' and 'ja' which mean 'yes' in French and German respectively.

One of the first mentions of the automatic writing method used in the Ouija board is found in China around 1100 AD. The method was known as fuji, spirit writing or automatic writing using a suspended sieve or tray to guide a stick which writes Chinese characters in sand or incense ashes.

Despite being a trademark, "Ouija" is also used to refer to any kind of 'talking' board that used automatic writing. Shortly after it was introduced, Pearl Curran, a popular 20th-century spiritualist began using the Ouija board during WWI as a tool for her divination. Some people thought it was kind of ancient mystical device used to communicate with the dead. It has also been associated with devil worship or spirituality, despite Hasbro's insistence that it is just a board game. The 'automatic' writing is simply done by the ideomotor effect, people moving the indicator unconsciously.

Paranormal and supernatural beliefs associated with Ouija have been harshly criticized by the scientific community, since they are characterized as pseudoscience. There is a 'museum' of talking boards on the web.

----

eBay - When it was first created, eBay was called AuctionWeb. The original look for the site was very similar to Craigslist. AuctionWeb was one of four sites Pierre Omidyar ran under his eBay Internet, a domain he purchased before coming up with AuctionWeb. He originally wanted to call this "EchoBay," but the domain was already taken by a Canadian mining company, so he shortened it.

The other things you could find under the eBay umbrella were a page on the Ebola virus, a small travel agent site, and a personal shopper site. Within seven months of launching AuctionWeb, revenues coming in were out earning Omidyar's day job at General Magic, so he quit to devote himself full time to his side project.

About a year and a half later, general users and many in the press had been calling it "eBay," instead of AuctionWeb, so he switched the name. In September of 1997, he also switched the look of the site to be much more graphically based.

When eBay went public with a suggested price of $18 per share (but surged to $53.50 on the first day), the 30 employees of the company at the time did a conga line around the office. The biggest recipients of that public offering were Omidyar, who today is worth about $8.7 billion, and the first CEO of the company, Meg Whitman, who has a net worth of just under $2 billion today.

The section eBay 'Deals' is a part of eBay where it highlights the best deals at a given time on eBay, saving you the effort of sifting through to look for them. It also breaks up the deals in various categories, such as Technology Deals, Fashion Deals, Home Deals, etc.

Bugs Bunny - Looney Tunes wanted to add a rabbit to their lineup and animator Ben "Bugs" Hardaway had a sketch of the proposed bunny. When the drawing was finished, he labeled it as "Bug's Bunny," his nickname and bunny.

Later the studio was looking for a name, saw the caption at the bottom, so just eliminated the apostrophe from bug's and the new name was born.

QUOTES

Ten Steven Wright Quotes - This is one funny guy that makes us think. Here are a few:

1. I'd kill for a Nobel Peace Prize.

2. Borrow money from pessimists - they don't expect it back.

3. Half the people you know are below average.

4. All those who believe in psychokinesis, raise my hand.

5. The early bird may get the worm, but the second mouse gets the cheese.

6. I almost had a psychic girlfriend, but she left me before we met.

7. OK, so what's the speed of dark?

8. Hard work pays off in the future; laziness pays off now.

9. I intend to live forever. . . so far, so good.

10. If your car could travel at the speed of light, would your headlights work?

Yogi Berra Quotes - Here a just a few of his many famous quotes:

- You can observe a lot by just watching.

- He hits from both sides of the plate. He's amphibious.

- Take it with a grin of salt.

- Baseball is 90% mental and the other half is physical.

- You wouldn't have won if we'd beaten you.

- It gets late early out here.

- You've got to be very careful if you don't know where you are going, because you might not get there.

- I'm not going to buy my kids an encyclopedia. Let them walk to school like I did.

- If the people don't want to come out to the ballpark, nobody's going to stop them.

- If the world were perfect, it wouldn't be.

- I never said most of the things I said.

- If you ask me anything I don't know, I'm not going to answer.

- When you come to a fork in the road, take it.

- It ain't over till it's over.

- It's like déjà vu all over again.

- No one goes there nowadays, it's too crowded.

- A nickel ain't worth a dime anymore.

- Always go to other people's funerals, otherwise they won't come to yours.

- We made too many wrong mistakes.

- Congratulations. I knew the record would stand until it was broken.

- You better cut the pizza in four pieces, because I'm not hungry enough to eat six.

- I usually take a two-hour nap from one to four.

- Never answer an anonymous letter.

- I'm lucky. Usually you're dead to get your own museum, but I'm still alive to see mine.

- Slump? I ain't in no slump... I just ain't hitting.

- The future ain't what it used to be.

- We have deep depth.

- Pair up in threes.

- Why buy good luggage, you only use it when you travel.

- It was impossible to get a conversation going, everybody was talking too much.

- So I'm ugly. I never saw anyone hit with his face.

- The towels were so thick there I could hardly close my suitcase.

- Little League baseball is a very good thing because it keeps the parents off the streets.

Quotes - Some folks on the web made pictures for some of my quotes.

Books are like bacon for the mind.
Thomas F. Shubnell

If you never get to your goal of setting goals, you will never get to anything.
– Thomas F. Shubnell

Laughter is the lubrication to soothe your soul.
Thomas F. Shubnell

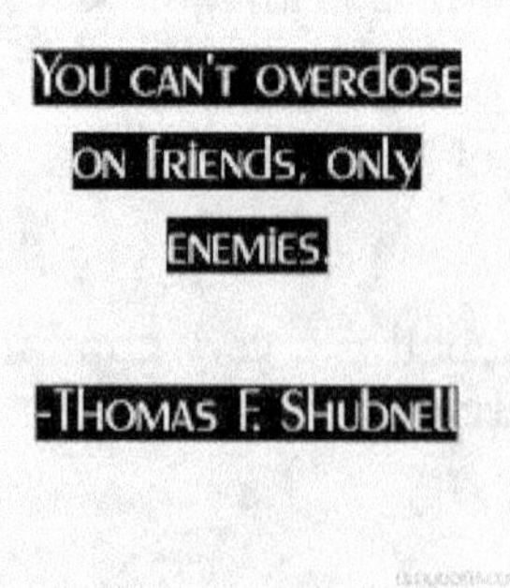

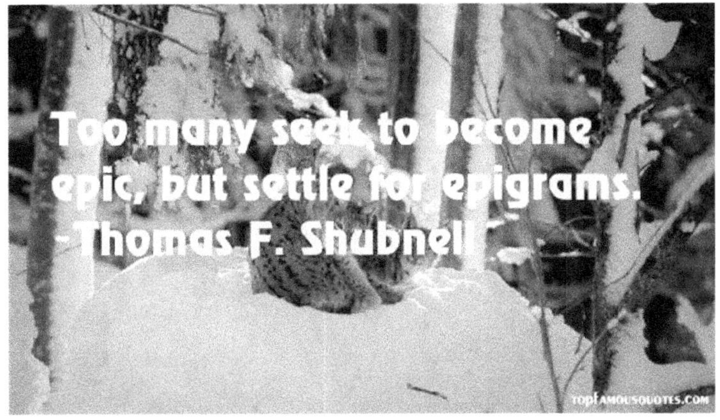

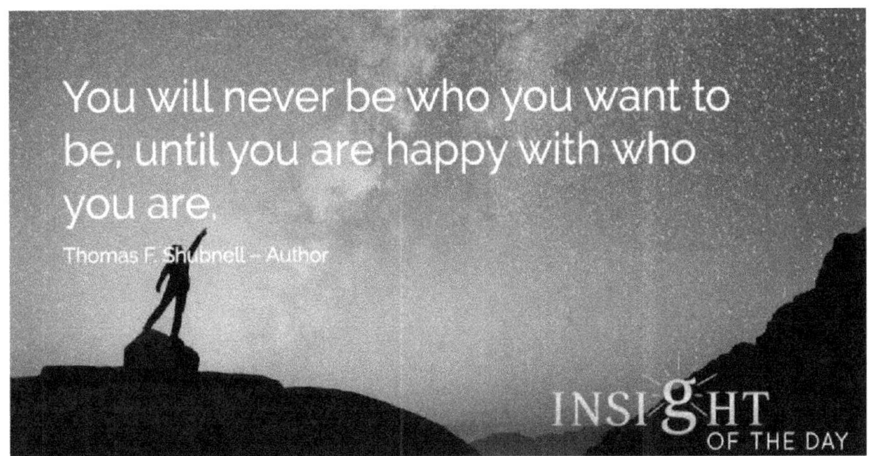

You will never be who you want to be, until you are happy with who you are.
Thomas F. Shubnell – Author

INSIgHT
OF THE DAY

Unread books are like
unopened doors.
~Thomas F. Shubnell
topfamousquotes.com

Medicine and Healthcare

HEALTH INFORMATION

Robert Liston MD - He was a Scottish speed surgeon during the 1800s. In one case, he amputated a leg in less than 2.5 minutes (the patient died afterward from gangrene). He amputated, in error the fingers of his young assistant (who died afterward from gangrene). He also slashed through the coat tails of a distinguished surgical spectator, who was so terrified that the knife had pierced his vitals he dropped dead from fright. *It was the only operation in history with a 300 percent mortality.*

Recipes and Rx - Retail prescription drugs in the US are over $200 billion annually. The origin of the Rx symbol comes from medieval time as an abbreviation for a form of the Late Latin word recipere meaning 'to take' or the imperative form of recipe, meaning 'take'.

A man is 35% more likely to be diagnosed with prostate cancer than a woman is to be diagnosed with breast cancer.

By the late 1500s it came to mean medical prescription. This meaning lasted until the mid-1700s, when it was also applied to food preparation.

Physicians typically begin their directive with the command recipe, abbreviated to Rx. Other abbreviations used in the medical field for charting are "dx" (diagnosis), "sx" (signs and symptoms), and "hx" (history). *Incidentally, females in the US fill almost fifty percent more prescriptions per capita than males.*

Handshakes and Health - A new study in the British Medical journal Lancet suggests the strength of a person's hand-grip could predict the risk of heart attacks and strokes and is a stronger predictor of death than blood pressure checks.

The international study, involving almost 140,000 adults in 17 countries during four years found weak grip strength is linked with shorter survival and a greater risk of having a heart attack or stroke. It also found that grip strength is a stronger predictor of death than systolic blood pressure. Grip strength was assessed using a handgrip dynamometer. Reduced muscular strength, which can be measured by grip strength, has been consistently linked with early death, disability, and illness.

Honey vs. HFCS - High-fructose corn syrup has recently been touted as the bad kind of sweeteners, while honey has sailed by on its natural and healthy origins. According to a recently-released study, it turns out that sugar is sugar, no matter what you eat.

Both honey and HFCS contain similar ratios of fructose and glucose; the largest difference between the two is the origin. Because their compositions are similar, they cause the same effects in people who ingest large quantities of either.

Full Fat vs. Low Fat - You are better off getting the full-fat versions of your favorite cookies, chips, and other snacks. Low-fat foods have been found to have five times the amount of sugar that their full-fat counterparts do, largely because manufacturers were under pressure to keep the products' taste and texture as similar as possible.

Since higher levels of sugar over time in the body lead to an increased chance for diabetes, heart disease, and more, it turns out that low-fat is likely the worst option you can choose if you are trying to watch your health.

Expired Sun Screen - Spring is time to get organized for yard work. One thing to keep in mind as we brave the season is sunscreen. According to the Mayo Clinic, most sunscreen works at full strength for about three years. So, if you are not sure how old those tubes and sprays are, toss them and replenish.

Incidentally, an SPF 15 product blocks about 94% of UVB rays; an SPF 30 product blocks 97% of UVB rays; and an SPF 45 product blocks about 98% of rays. Most experts tell us to save our money and do not pay for SPF above 30.

US to Drop Warning Against Cholesterol - Every five years, the United States government updates a set of Dietary Guidelines intended to help its citizens make healthier food choices. These guidelines also help inform how companies package and market their products. The 2015 edition of the DGAC says that, "cholesterol is not considered a nutrient of concern for over consumption."

The DGAC is now more concerned that Vitamin D, Vitamin E, potassium, calcium, and fiber are under-consumed in the US. It is placing a greater emphasis on pushing people toward healthy choices like nutrient-dense vegetables.

The human body makes far more cholesterol than it takes in. The liver adjusts its cholesterol production to account for what we eat, and will get rid of any cholesterol it does not need. Eating much cholesterol has little to no effect on what is in your blood.

Physicians Changing Attitudes - Doctors have always encountered the problem of how to best tell their patient of a terminal sentence. Recently, medical professions have been more upfront about tragic news such as this. Physicians used to think that by not telling a person they were dying, it would boost their moral and increase their hope.

During 1961 only 10% believed it was correct to tell a patient of a fatal diagnosis. This changed after studies were done that revealed nearly 90% of patients said they would like to know the truth of their prognosis.

By 1979, physicians had completely reversed their beliefs and a survey revealed that 97% felt full disclosure was the correct course to take.

Aspirin Origin - On March 6, 1899 acetylsalicylic acid, was patented by The Friedrich Bayer & Co. under the trade name Aspirin at the Imperial patent office in Berlin. For over a century, it is still one of the most effective, versatile, and commonly used medications in the world.

Its active ingredient, salicin, had been used for many centuries to alleviate pain and fever. Hippocrates is known to have used it, and it had been used in modern medicine since the 19th century. As effective as it was, willow bark and salicin were used sparingly, because the taste was so bad, its use caused a severe upset stomach, and in extreme cases could even damage a stomach.

This changed when Bayer chemist Felix Hoffman created a form of the drug that was just as effective, but much better tasting and drastically easier on the stomach. Three years after Hoffman's death in 1949, another scientist at Bayer, Arthur Eichengrün came forward claiming responsibility for Hoffman's work.

Eichengrün, who was imprisoned in the Theresienstadt concentration camp during World War II, maintained he was denied his due because he was Jewish.

Either Hoffman or Eichengrün also perfected another medication around the same time as Aspirin. Heroin was believed to have even greater potential. It was created to be a non-addictive alternative to morphine for such ailments as labor pains and curing heavy coughs.

When Aspirin was first recommended to Heinrich Dreser, head of the pharmacological laboratory at Bayer, he rejected it, supposedly stating "The product has no value." Once Heroin quickly began to fall as people realized how addictive it was, he revisited his decision regarding Aspirin and it quickly became Bayer's best selling product. After World War I, Bayer had to give up its trademark on Aspirin as part of the Treaty of Versailles in 1919.

Aspirin sales slumped with the introduction of other over-the-counter pain relievers such as ibuprofen and acetaminophen, but sales rebounded when clinical trials showed that a small daily dose of Aspirin could lower the risk of heart attack and stroke. Today, approximately 40 billion Aspirin tablets are consumed annually.

Stroma Procedure - There is a laser treatment, pioneered by California-based Stroma Medical and it is currently available in several countries. It is undergoing human testing in Costa Rica that turns brown eyes blue. The Strōma laser disrupts the brown layer of pigment, causing the body to initiate a natural and gradual tissue-removal process. Once the tissue is removed, the patient's natural blue eye is revealed. The procedure is totally non-invasive and takes about 20 seconds to perform, but takes two to four weeks to see final results. Current cost is about US $5,000.

HEALTH AND HAPPINESS

Science Advice, Ten Things to Make You Happier - These may seem more common sense than science, but scientists have been paid big money to research the topic and feed back the obvious.

Exercise more - It can help you to relax, increase your brain power, and improve your body image, even if you do not lose any weight.

Sleep more - Sleep-deprived people fail to recall pleasant memories, yet recall gloomy memories.

Move closer to work - People never get accustomed to their daily slog to work because sometimes the traffic is awful and sometimes it is not. Over time the negative outweighs the positive.

Spend time with friends and family - Friends and family reinforce positive feelings and increase happiness. Not staying in touch with friends and family is one of the top five regrets of the dying.

Help others - Volunteering is rewarding in terms of higher life satisfaction. Performing a kind act produces the single most reliable momentary increase in well-being of any exercise.

Get outside - Studies found that spending 20 minutes outside in good weather not only boosted positive mood, substantially increased happiness, broadened thinking, and improved working memory.

Plan a trip - The act of planning a vacation and the positive anticipation actually can increase happiness for up to eight weeks, while after taking the vacation, happiness drops quickly.

Meditate - It has long been known to help us be calm, improve focus, increase clarity and attention span. It is also useful for improving happiness. Brain scans show it is the single most effective way to live a happier live.

Be grateful - Simple things like keeping a journal of things you are grateful for, sharing three good things that happen with friend or family, and going out of your way to show gratitude when others help you all contribute to increased happiness. A study asked people to write three letters of gratitude over a 3 week period. Results indicated that writing letters of gratitude increased participants' happiness and life satisfaction, while decreasing depressive symptoms.

Practice smiling - Saved the best for last. Smiling (and backing it up with positive thoughts) improves mood, reduces stress, and increases happiness.

Happiness is Physical and Emotional - Japanese researchers have mapped, using MRI where happiness emerges in the brain. The study, published in Scientific Reports, paves the way for objectively measuring happiness and provides insights on a neurologically based way of being happy.

A team at Kyoto University has found an answer from a neurological perspective. Overall happiness, according to their study, is a combination of happy emotions and satisfaction of life coming together in the precuneus, a region in the medial parietal lobe.

People feel emotions in different ways, for instance, some people feel happiness more intensely than others when they receive compliments. Psychologists have found that emotional factors like these and satisfaction of life together constitutes the subjective experience of being happy. The neural mechanism behind how happiness emerges, however, remained unclear. Understanding that mechanism will be a huge asset for quantifying levels of happiness.

Their analysis revealed that those who scored higher on the happiness surveys had more grey matter mass in the precuneus. In other words, people who feel happiness more intensely, feel sadness less intensely, and are more able to find meaning in life.

"Several studies have shown that meditation increases grey matter mass in the precuneus. This new insight on where happiness happens in the brain will be useful for developing happiness programs based on scientific research."

Six Ways to be Happy - A recent study found: "When participants physically discarded a representation of their thoughts, they mentally discarded them as well, using them less in forming judgments than did participants who retained a representation of their thoughts." If you have pervasive negative thoughts, write them down on a piece of paper, and physically throw them away, or burn them. This strategy can be employed as a quick way to clear your head of negativity.

Another just-released study found that the human imagination is powerful to a scary and exciting degree. This is the first set of experiments to definitively establish that the sensory signals generated by one's imagination are strong enough to change one's real-world perception of a different sensory modality. Exercising your imagination will generate creative ideas, motivate you, and make you happier if you use it well. Happiness is a perspective, and using your imagination is an effective way to alter your perspective in a positive way.

Experiences have been shown to make us happier than material possessions. A study from Cornell says, "Consumers spend more time thinking about material purchases they didn't choose than they spend when they buy an experience." When it comes to spending money, experiences are almost always a better value than possessions. Material possessions tend to make us happy initially and quickly wane, but the happiness gained from experiences can last a lifetime. If you want to be happier in the long term, consider taking a trip instead of buying a new TV.

A few studies show that you can be much happier by giving, such as being a volunteer, pay for the person behind you at the tool booth, cook a surprise meal for someone, or give someone an unexpected gift. We are incredibly powerful in our ability to make someone else's day with very little effort on our part.

One study found that toddlers before the age of two years old exhibit greater happiness when giving treats to others than receiving treats themselves. Another study by a Harvard scholar found that happiness can be bought, so long as you are spending the money on someone else. Giving brings real happiness results. If you truly want to maximize your happiness, find ways to give to others.

Matthieu Ricard, a Buddhist monk, is sometimes called the happiest man in the world. "There is a possibility for change because all emotions are fleeting. That is the ground for mind training. Mind training is on the idea that two opposite mental factors can't happen at the same time. You cannot in the same gesture shake a hand and strike a blow. There are natural antidotes to emotions that are destructive to our well-being."

Ricard says that mind transformation is achieved through meditation on unconditional compassion and loving kindness. "Some of [the monks] who came to the labs did 20-40 thousand hours of meditation. When the monks were tested for happiness using tests that measure brain activity for happiness, it was found that the monks were four standard deviations from the norm in favor of happiness; in other words, they were off-the-charts happy. If you want to multiply your happiness results, meditate on compassion and loving kindness.

The monks' theory on opposite mental factors holds true. They spend so much time thinking of positive things, that negativity and angst are pushed out of their mind, and they become very happy.

Perhaps the most surprising and 21st century relevant happiness factor is focus. A study found that people's minds wandered 47% of the time on average and it had a more negative impact on their happiness than what they were doing. There is a direct connection between focus and happiness. Focusing your skills and energy on fewer areas is a simple formula that brings big results.

The more you focus on what matters, the more your life becomes as you desire, and the happier you will be. True happiness is not being a slave to a piece of technology. It is deciding what is most important in this moment and focusing all of your energy on it. *So, if you want to be happy, toss out negativity, think good things, do good things, give to others, imagine being happy, and focus on being happy.*

----

7 Habits of happy people:
1. They ignore nonsense
2. They talk less
3. They learn new skills
4. They help less fortunate
5. They laugh
6. They wake up early
7. They have no entitlement

Animal and Insect Facts

FUN CREATURE FACTS

Five Anti Ant Actions - Warm weather is the time ants are really having fun with us, but here are a few household things to keep them away for a while. These are all cheaper than the commercial insecticides.

Put some vinegar in a spray bottle. Spray around the areas they show up, like all your door jams. Vinegar leaves behind a natural ant repellent and the smell dissipates quickly.

Draw a wide line of chalk on the ground, ants will not cross over it, nor will a number of other little creatures. if you see a few ants, draw a circle around them and watch how effective it is.

Black Pepper is another natural safe item to use if the other methods are not available, try sprinkling some pepper around. They hate that. Sprinkle some by their nest to keep them from feeding the queen. Course ground pepper is less effective.

Cayenne Pepper has the same abilities as regular pepper and it also keeps the squirrels away if you mix it with a bit of Vaseline and put it on your fence. Of course you need to replace after a heavy rain.

Cinnamon is also good to bug the bugs and it smells great.

Rabbits and Hares - Rabbits and hares are often confused with one another. Rabbits and hares do not breed with one another in their natural habitats. Jackrabbits are a type of hare.

From the moment they are born, rabbits and hares are easily distinguished. Baby rabbits, called kittens, are born blind and furless. They are unable to move around much on their own and are weak. Baby hares, called leverets are born with their fur and their eyes open. A baby hare explores its new world shortly after birth.

Rabbits are more social and when they are in the wild they prefer to share their burrows with other members of their colony. They sleep in their burrows during the day, hiding from potential predators. If mother rabbit needs to leave her kittens, she will cover them up with fur and leaves to keep them warm and safe.

Each group of rabbits tends to have a dominant male that gets to mate with the majority of the females. Rabbits prefer softer foods, such as grass and vegetables. Rabbits have been domesticated while hares have not.

Hares are generally larger, lithe, wiry, and have larger back legs and paws. Their ears are longer, and stick straight up from the head. Usually, a hare's ears will have black markings. Additionally, hares usually change color according to season; they are grayish brown in spring, summer, and fall, and turn white in the winter. A hare's skull is slightly different in shape to a rabbit's skull.

Hares prefer to live alone, coming together only to mate (with little contention among males over mating rights), and usually make their homes in nests among tall grasses rather than dig a burrow. They also are not afraid to leave their leverets just hours after the babies are born. Baby hares are well equipped to living without their mothers at just an hour old. Hares are more likely to choose harder foods like bark and twigs.

Sheep Burps - *I first thought this was a hoax, but it is from a reputable scientific organization, and I verified it with other publications.* Australian scientists are looking for ways to reduce harmful methane emissions from the country's woolly flocks.

Twelve percent of Australia's total greenhouse gas emissions originate with agriculture, and some 70 percent of that amount is blamed on livestock, with most of it coming from burps, study leader John Goopy said.

With sheep, almost all of the methane produced comes out of their mouths. "There is not very much passed out the animal's anus at all," said Goopy, from the New South Wales Department of Industry and Investment.

> The male gypsy moth can 'smell' the virgin female gypsy moth from 1.8 miles away.

Scientists measure the sheep's methane emissions by herding them into a specially designed booth shortly after they eat and then calculating the amount of gas belched. They hope to find whether there is a genetic link between the sheep that produce the least methane, which could be exploited to breed low-emissions sheep.

Sheep produce about seven kilograms (15 lb) of methane a year while other cattle produce ten times that amount. Cows, sheep, goats, camels, buffaloes, and termites release methane.

"Of the 200 sheep so far tested, about half produced much more than average while the other half belched considerably less methane." *(Hmmm, real science here)*

Methane has about 17 to 21 times the environmental warming capacity of carbon dioxide. However, methane lasts only 12 years in the atmosphere vs. CO2, which lasts 100 years in the atmosphere. Wikipedia says the main greenhouse gases in the Earth's atmosphere are water vapor, carbon dioxide, methane, nitrous oxide, and ozone.

Let's sum this up - most of 70% of 12% comes from all livestock, of which sheep are some part of, and half of them produce more burps than the other half, so let's change nature and breed out the burping half. - We will deal with farting cows later.

And these people actually get paid by the government for these kinds of studies. Of course, half get paid more and half get paid less than average.

Did You Know - Spider silk is very light weight. The circumference of Earth, 25,000 miles of a single fiber would weigh about 16 ounces.

English Gorillas - Chessington Zoo in London has issued an apology to guests after giving the gorillas a Christmas treat of Brussels sprouts. The seasonal sprouts are highly nutritious, but the gorilla farts caused horror among people around them.

Gorilla keeper Michael Rozzi said, "We feed the gorillas Brussels Sprouts during the winter, because they are packed with vitamin C and have great nutritional benefits. Unfortunately, an embarrassing side effect is that it can cause bouts of flatulence in humans and animals alike. However, I don't think any of us were prepared for a smell that strong."

Wombat Wonders - Did you know that Wombats were once as big as rhinos, thousands of years ago? Now they are just up to four feet and weigh about eighty pounds when adults.

In the Genes - A team at the University of Edinburgh concludes stud fees, the price paid for a stallion to father a racehorse, do not reflect the winning potential of his genes. In fact, a high price tag is a poor predictor of future prize-winning potential.

The researchers compared the stud fees, winnings and lifetime earnings of over 4,000 horses used for racing and breeding since 1922. Only ten per cent of a horse's winnings can be attributed to parentage, according to a study published in the journal Biology Letters.

The majority, up to ninety per cent of a horse's lifetime winnings, rest on how the horse is reared, trained, and ridden, not to its genetic inheritance. *Some comfort to horse breeders is that the stables that can afford vast stud fees can also give the horse the best riders, care, and trainers.*

Jack Russell Terrier - Jack Russell was a real guy. John Russell was born in Dartmouth, England in 1795, and was a hunting enthusiast. While he was studying to become a clergyman at Oxford, he met a milkman who had a white terrier bitch named Trump who seemed to be the perfect dog for fox hunting. After convincing the milkman to sell him the dog, Russell began breeding Trump to develop a line of terriers with the stamina to hunt foxes all day and the courage to go after game that had slipped into holes.

Russell actually has two dogs named after him. The Jack Russell terrier and the Parson Russell terrier, a similar breed with longer legs, which also takes its name from Russell. It is recognized as a separate breed.

Lhasa Apso - The Lhasa Apso was originally bred as a watchdog for Tibetan palaces and monasteries. It was difficult for an intruder to sneak past the watchful, yipping dogs. The "Lhasa" in the name comes from the city of Lhasa, Tibet's longtime capital. Apso is a Tibetan word meaning "bearded," so the breed's name signifies that it is a longhaired dog that originated in Tibet.

Cocker Spaniel - Spaniels have been around as far back as the 14th century, and these popular pets had their start as gun dogs. English hunters prized the dogs' particularly skilled tracking of woodcocks, so the dogs became known as 'cockers'.

Weimaraner - The beautiful gray dogs with the expressive eyes have likely only been around since the 19th century. According to tradition, that is when Grand Duke Karl August of Weimar began to selectively breed hunting dogs that were fast, had strong noses, would not back down from large game like wolves or wildcats, and were smart.

Karl August's breed allegedly became fashionable among his fellow Weimar noblemen, and the breed gained popularity as a bird-hunting dog as well.

Labrador Retriever - These dogs originated in the region of Canada that is now the province of Newfoundland and Labrador. Local fishermen perfected a breed they called the St. John's water dog, which were prodigious swimmers that would jump in the water and haul fishing nets back to shore.

In the early 19th century the Earl of Malmesbury began bringing the dogs to his English estate and trained them to retrieve the ducks he hunted. The Earl referred to his pack of pooches as his 'Labrador dogs' in reference to their home region, and the name stuck as their popularity grew.

A Penny for Your. . . Birdbath - Prevent algae from growing in a birdbath by tossing a few pre-1982 pennies into the water. The copper keeps the organisms from multiplying so fast.

Fall Fruit Fly Trap - As it cools and we begin to open our windows, those pesky fruit flies sometimes sneak in. Here is a trick to get rid of them. Pour some apple cider vinegar into a bowl or cup and add a few drops of dishwashing soap. The smell of the apple cider draws them and the soap breaks the surface tension of the water so they sink. Takes about a day to get rid of them. Pour it all down the drain when finished.

Oyster Herpes - Is nothing free from the effects of global warming? This is true - National Geographic has found that a new strain of herpes in oysters.

The new strain, which is named Ostreid herpesvirus 1 μvar, was first detected in 2008 among breeding Pacific oysters in France. Since then, the virus has wiped out 20 to 100 percent of oysters in the

French beds, and appears to have spread to United Kingdom waters. They say it infects the shellfish during breeding season.

Although reasons behind the recent emergence of herpes in oyster beds across Europe are still a mystery, many researchers have not been surprised to find a correlation with global warming. *Hmmm!*

Smart Birds - Researchers have found that rooks, a member of the crow family, are capable of using and making tools, modifying them to make them work and using two tools in a sequence. The rooks quickly learned to drop a stone to collapse a platform and acquire a piece of food, and subsequently showed the ability to choose the right size and shape of stone without any training.

Not only could they use stones to solve the task, but they were flexible in their tool choice, using and modifying sticks to achieve the same goal. When the correct tool was out of reach, they used another tool to get it, demonstrating the ability to use tools sequentially. They also bent a straight piece of wire to make the hook to reach food.

Cat Lovers Unite - Did you know the Jaguarundi, a unique type of cat that lives along the Texas border with Mexico is endangered?

WildEarth Guardian, a non-profit environmental organization, recently filed a lawsuit in Houston federal court against Ken Salazar, Secretary of the US Department of the Interior, demanding that he put a conservation and survival plan together for the animal. The organization says the cat has been listed as endangered since 1976, but has no survival plan.

According to the US Fish and Wildlife Service, the cats are larger than a domestic cat and have small ears, long, narrow bodies with short legs and flattened heads and tails. They generally look more like a weasel than a cat. They make their homes in the dense thorny mesquite, cacti, and thickets of southern Texas.

WildEarth argues that humans are making it tough on the jaguarundi. Farmers are clearing away their habitat to make room for more vegetables and crops and the border fence between the United States and Mexico is limiting their access to other jaguarundis to mate with. *Seems to me they have done well enough for over 40 years without a plan, maybe they should be taken off the endangered list.*

Magnificent Eagles - A bald eagle's nest grows with each year of use. They usually start with one of the taller trees in a given area, with a network of strong supporting branches. While the nest may start out only a couple of feet wide, after a few years of use, the nest can grow to more than six feet wide and ten feet deep. The male usually brings nest material to the nest site where the female will arrange it to suit her. Softer material, such as grasses and leaves, will be used to line the center of the nest.

Copulation usually occurs at the nest. The male will simply mount the female to make contact. The whole thing lasts just seconds. After copulation the pair might perch next to each other for a half hour or so, sometimes preening themselves and each other.

Bald eagles generally lay two eggs, although one or three are not that uncommon.

The eggs are laid about two days apart and will normally hatch in the same order as they were laid, with approximately the same intervals between hatchings as there were between layings. The eggs are bluish-white, about 3 inches in length, and roughly oval-shaped. Through time, the eggs will discolor until they appear to be more of a mottled, or dirty, white.

Incubation lasts 34 to 36 days with both the male and female birds incubating. Females will incubate the eggs about 60 percent of the time. During incubation, the male will bring food for the female, many times to one of the supporting branches of the nest and she will usually come off the eggs to eat, with the male taking her place on the nest.

To Be a Bee - A queen bee is selectively bred in a special "queen cell" in the hive and fed royal jelly by worker bees to induce her to become sexually mature. A virgin queen that survives to adulthood without being killed by her rivals will take a mating flight with a dozen or so male drones. During mating, their genitals explode and snap off inside the queen. The snapped-off penis acts as a genital plug to prevent other drones from fertilizing the queen. *Ouch!*

Man vs. Horse - Each year, for the past thirty years there is a race in Wales that pits men vs. horses. About 50 horses with riders compete against hundreds of runners for the $1,450 prize (£1,000).

The event began in June 1980 following a chat over a pint in the Neuadd Arms Hotel. The landlord overheard two men discussing the relative merits of men and horses. He decided it would improve business at his hotel and decided to put it to the test.

The 22 mile long Man vs. Horse Marathon race starts in the town center and is run over hilly farm tracks, footpaths, forestry roads, and open moorland on the edge of the Brecon Beacons in Wales.

The 2015 race was held June 12 and Sly Dai, ridden by Llinos Jones, completed the course in two hours and seven minutes. The nearest human came in 10 minutes later. Men have won the race two times. *Can a man run faster than a horse? Of course, I can prove it.*

Do Not Make Your Bed - I am sure many have been reading about the new fascination with and outbreaks of bed bugs (dust mites). Here is some good news for ridding your bed of these ugly little creatures, although I am not sure it really is good science.

Failing to make your bed in the morning may actually help keep you healthy scientists believe, because research suggests that while an unmade bed may look bad it is also unappealing to house dust mites.

A Kingston University study discovered the bugs cannot survive in the dry conditions found in an unmade bed. The minute bugs feed on scales of human skin and produce allergens which are easily inhaled during sleep. The warm, damp conditions created in an occupied bed are ideal for the creatures, but they are less likely to thrive when moisture is in shorter supply. The scientists developed a computer model to track how changes in the home can reduce numbers of dust mites in beds.

Mites need humid conditions to thrive and cannot survive in very dry conditions. Something as simple as leaving a bed unmade during the day can remove moisture from the sheets and mattress so the mites will dehydrate and eventually die.

The average life cycle for a male house dust mite is 10 to 19 days. A mated female house dust mite can live for 70 days, laying 60 to 100 eggs in the last 5 weeks of her life.

A good idea is to always wash sheets and pillowcases in hot water, even though you wash your others things in cold water. Another way is to use high heat in your dryer.

PS - It is commonly believed that the accumulated detritus from dust mites can add significantly to the weight of mattresses and pillows, but there is no scientific evidence for these claims. Also, a 1996 study from the British Medical Journal has shown that polyester fiber pillows contained more than 8 times the total weight of fine dust than feather pillows. *Sleep tight tonight, don't let the bedbugs bite.*

Crocks, Gators, and Plovers - Crocs and gators keep their mouths open as a way to avoid overheating. Keeping cool may be the primary purpose, but for some species there is a secondary gain from the behavior. For crocodiles living in the range of the Egyptian plover, or 'crocodile bird', sitting around with their mouth open means they get free teeth cleaning from the small birds. The plover acts as both a dental hygienist and a warning system for danger.

PawNation writes, "The plover comes along and, using its sharp little beak like a toothpick, removes the bits of meat from between the crocodile's teeth. This feeds the plover and removes parasites from the croc's mouth. The plover serves as a security alarm system for the crocodile. If, while in the croc's mouth, the plover senses danger from an oncoming animal, it screams and flies away. This behavior alerts the crocodile to the imminent danger, so it can slide into the water and out of harm's way."

Ant Life Facts - Spring is here and the ants have become active. The life of an ant starts from an egg. If the egg is fertilized, the progeny will be female; if not, it will be male. All females, except the queen are workers who feed the babies, take out the trash, forage for food and supplies, and defend the nest.

Males have one job, to mate with the queen. Males can deliver 5 to 6 million sperm, which the queen can store and use for the rest of her life. The queen can produce a few thousand eggs a day and up to a million or more during her lifetime. She also decides which eggs to fertilize.

Queen ants can live for up to 30 years, and workers live from 1 to 3 years. Males, however may survive for just a few weeks.

Incidentally, there is an estimated 22,000 species of ants. Also, all male ants have a grandfather, but no father, and their grandfather had only a grandfather, but no father.

Double Meaning Animals - We do not often think of the question of which came first, the chicken or the egg, and we ignore how many times we *egg* someone on by calling them *chicken*. Here are a few more ways we use animals in discussions.

I was *fishing* for how to begin this.

Am not trying to be a *leech* or to *sponge* off of you.

Sometimes we *hound* someone for no good reason.

Too often we *wolf* down food or just plain *pig* out.

We feel playful and *horse* around or *monkey* around.

When we get caught, it is time to *pony* up.

Children often *ape* their parents and too often *parrot* what they say.

When someone *gooses* you, it is time to *duck* out, but most often they just did it for a *lark*.

You probably think it is time for me to *clam* up, but I am not done yet.

There are a few more *squirreled* away, just to *badger* you a bit more.

Luckily there were no *moles* in the crowd to give away my secrets.

Am still *crowing* that I managed to finished this.

Cows Face One Way - Cows always face north or south while eating. A team of scientists reviewed thousands of Google Earth's satellite images of cows and found that cows will stand along the Earth's magnetic poles, facing north and south whenever they are grazing or resting. The pattern remained consistent regardless of other factors, and nobody is quite sure why. It appears that it may have a purpose because of the consistency with which it was observed among cows across six continents. However, some research has shown that wind and sunlight can cause herd animals such as cows to change their alignment, depending on the conditions.

Humans and Wallabies Share DNA - A tammar wallaby is a small or mid-sized macropod found in Australia and New Guinea. They belong to the same taxonomic family as kangaroos. One of them, Mathilda, became the first kangaroo to have her genetic code mapped.

The Australian researchers were shocked when they compared her code with a human's. They had expected the comparison to be a mismatch, but it turned out that the genomes of the two species were more than just similar. Apart from a few differences, the genes were identical, and many of them were arranged in the same order. Both species hold large pieces of genetic information about the other.

It made more sense when the researchers also discovered that people and these bouncy marsupials had a common ancestor that lived at least 150 million years ago. Mice separated from humans only 70 million years ago, but scientists feel that kangaroos can provide more answers about human evolution when it comes to why some DNA remained the same for eons while other DNA changed. By comparing different genomes from species, unknown genes can be identified, and Matilda revealed 14 new genes never before seen in kangaroos, which might possibly also be present in humans.

Blue Bears - Many have heard of black bears, brown bears, cinnamon bears, and white bears, but there are also blue bears. The Tibetan bear or Tibetan blue bear is a subspecies of the brown bear found in the eastern Tibetan plateau, western China, Nepal.

It is also known as the Himalayan blue bear and Himalayan snow bear and is one of the rarest subspecies of bear in the world and rarely sighted in the wild. The blue bear is known in the west only through a small number of fur and bone samples. It was first classified in 1854.

Tibetan blue bears are black with a tinge of blue gray. They often have a beige or white collar and chest. It is common for their face to be a reddish yellow.

Ten Fascinating Frog Facts -

* The name frog comes from the Old-English 'frogga', which means, to jump. There are over 5,000 varieties of frogs.

* From a taxonomic perspective, all members of Anura are frogs, but only members of the family Bufonidae are considered toads.

* Frog usually refers to species that are aquatic or semi-aquatic with smooth and/or moist skins, and the term 'toad' generally refers to species that tend to be terrestrial with dry, warty skin.

* A group of adult frogs is referred to as an Army of frogs and also a colony or a knot.

Touching frogs will not give you warts, that's just a myth.

* Frogs legs are considered a delicacy in China, Greece, New Orleans,US, and France.

* Frogs will only eat something that moves; in nature that would be insects or spiders. Tadpoles are vegetarian.

* Amphibians, such as frogs, always return to water to breed. However, there is a midwife frog where the male carries the frogspawn around on his body. When he senses the time is ripe, he swims out into the water and the tiny tadpoles emerge from their egg-jelly and swim away.

* Frogs, can change their color to suit their background; not as spectacularly as chameleons, but enough to save them from a casual predator.

* Ranidaphobia means fear of frogs.

Frogs and Toads - Toads have dry and pebbly skin, and frogs have moist and smooth skin. Frogs like water and toads prefer land.

Toads and frogs lay their eggs in water, because their babies start off as tadpoles. The difference is that frog eggs are laid in bunches or clusters, and they have a jelly-like substance around them. Toads lay their eggs in lines or strands, on leaves of plants that live in the water. A baby toad is a tadpole or toadlet.

Frogs have slim bodies and long legs, and jump to get around. Toads have short forelimbs and hop or walk. Toads have big glands behind their eyes, called paratoid glands, which produce poison.

> The frog name sequence is polliwog, tadpole, froglet.

There are three names for baby frogs, depending on which segment of the life cycle they are in. After 21 days of being an embryo, a baby frog is called a polliwog, has a long tail and lives in water. It becomes a tadpole when it sprouts legs. As a froglet, it has almost matured into an adult that breathes with lungs, but still has a bit of a tail.

Frogs do not actually drink water with their mouths; they drink it through their skin. A frog's skin absorbs water when it is in the water so its body gets all of the hydration that it needs.

True toads do not have teeth and the skin on the head is typically ossified to the skull. Toad's skin lets out a bitter taste and smell that burns the eyes and nostrils of its predators, much like a skunk does. True toads belong to the family Bufonidae, which consists of 50 genera and nearly 600 species, native to all continents except Antarctica and Australia. Toads belong to the order Anura, and are actually a subset of frogs. In popular use, toad seems to be used to refer to any frog that has a dry warty skin and short legs.

Frogs:
Need to live near water

> *All toads are frogs, but not all frogs are toads and neither frogs nor toads will give you warts.*

Have smooth, moist skin that makes them look slimy.
Have a narrow body
Have higher, rounder, bulgier eyes
Have longer hind legs
Take long high jumps
Have many predators
Hibernate in the winter.

Toads:
Do not need to live near water to survive
Have rough, dry, bumpy skin
Have a wider body
Have lower, football shaped eyes
Have shorter, less powerful hind legs
Do not have many predators
Will run or take small hops rather than jump.

Trivia, Facts, and Myths

Origin of Credit Cards - In 1949, Frank McNamara, an executive at the Hamilton Credit Corporation, was embarrassed to find himself short of cash when it came time to pay for a dinner with clients at a New York restaurant. Charge accounts were already common, allowing customers to add up a tab at certain establishments and pay it later, but those accounts were only for each specific business. McNamara had the idea of making a card which could be used at multiple unconnected upscale New York restaurants. Diners Club would pay the restaurant, and the diner would pay Diners Club, plus interest. Diners Club's had 20,000 members in its first year, who could use it to pay for services at 28 restaurants and two hotels.

Quick Number Fact - Forty is the only number whose letters are in alphabetical order.

Old Folks Wisdom - Never stand between a fire hydrant and a dog.

Never sleep with a woman whose problems are worse than your own.

Women are like cow pies, the older they are, the easier they are to pick up.

Age is a relative thing - think about dead fish and good wine.

Never skimp on spending money on a good pair of shoes and a decent bed. If you are not in one, you are in the other.

Always leave a party while you are still having fun.

Size Matters - The largest oil tanker ships displace about 520,000 tons when fully loaded, which is 10 times the 52,310 tons 883 feet length of the Titanic. The largest ship (and largest oil tanker) ever built is the Seawise Giant, 1,500 feet (458.46m) length and displacement 657,019 tonnes (724,239 tons).

Air Traffic Control Towers - Air traffic control towers always have windows that slope toward the tower at the base. Many people assume they are designed that way to prevent the sun's reflection or glare from blinding incoming pilots.

The benefit is not for those outside the tower, but those inside it. Ordinarily, we see reflections in glass all the time, for example from computer monitors or car windows, but air traffic controllers must not have any distracting reflections as they monitor flights. By tilting the glass away, any light from inside the tower (such as video screens, lights, etc.) are reflected up onto the ceiling, which is painted black. That way, the glow from a wristwatch across the room will not be mistaken for an incoming UFO.

Good to Know Costco - You can go to Costco and buy alcohol without a membership. Also, you can fill prescriptions and get shots at their pharmacy, eat at the food court, get your eyes checked, and use a Costco gift card bought for you by a member.

Oxford University Press Guidelines - The news is that Oxford University Press has issued guidelines instructing authors of children's books to avoid references to pigs, sausage, or anything else that might be construed as porcine for fear of offending Muslims. *It has no specific policies issued instructing authors not to offend Christians.*

1965 Inventions Plus - The Kennedy half dollar came out that year and contained 60% copper. An uncirculated one is worth about four dollars today. The artificial sweetener Aspartame came out during 1965. It came under attack as causing cancer, but the claims were debunked and it is now considered safe. Astroturf hit the ground in 1965 and is still around. Kevlar was invented that year and is still protecting us from the bad guys. Basic, the computer programming language was developed during 1965. The 'Big Bang' theory was developed during 1965 and the Nobel Prize in science was awarded its discoverer. Some say the internet was developed during 1965, but it was really conceived, much like its current form during 1968.

On Palm Sunday, April, 1965 fifty one tornadoes hit around the Southern US, causing tremendous damage. Medicare was created by Lyndon Johnson. The Maple Leaf became the official Flag symbol for Canada. The Gateway arch in St. Louis was completed. Warren Buffet takes over Berkshire Hathaway and the stock price was $18 per share. *No, the pencil was invented in Switzerland in 1565, not 1965.*

Prices in 1950 - Here are some prices from that year.

Car: $1,750
Gasoline: 27 cents/gal
House: $14,500
Bread: 14 cents/loaf
Milk: 82 cents/gal
Postage Stamp: 3 cents
Stock Market: 235
Average Annual Salary: $3,800.

Mary Poppins - Walt Disney sure knew how to save a buck. Dick Van Dyke played Bert, and also played Old Mr. Dawes the banker. Julie Andrews also provided her own whistling accompaniment when Mary Poppins sings with the robin during 'Spoonful of Sugar' and was also one of the Pearly ladies in "Supercalifragilisticexpialidocious." David Tomlinson as Mr. Banks, was also the voice of Mary's umbrella when it talked and one of the jockeys in the animated horse race scene. In addition, he dubbed the voice for Admiral Boom's first mate.

Another Poppins tidbit - When the children look surprised at all of the stuff Mary Poppins pulls out of her carpet bag, it was genuine. They could not see what was being fed to the bag from under the table, so when she pulled hat stands and huge potted plants out of that regular-sized bag, the children were completely stunned.

Elizabeth Bacon Custer, wife of General George Custer is one of the few women buried at the US Military Academy at West Point, New York.

George Washington spent about seven percent of his annual salary on liquor.

War Statistics - More than 8,100 US troops are still listed as missing in action from the Korean War, less than 600,000 of the 16 million Americans who served in World War II were alive during 2016, and the last World War I veteran (a British citizen) died during 2012.

Ngrams - Google has digested over thirty million books to date, including a number of my books and has come up with an interesting way to plot the usage of words over time. Ngrams are line charts that show the usage of words over time. Try some neologisms, like 'went missing', which is relatively new to American English or laser, etc., to track when they came into everyday use. You can also pick two words to compare and you get to decide the time-line.

It does not filter out any words, including four letter words. It also has proper names. Think about interesting words and see how they relate to each other. There is a timeline on the bottom that lets you click to read the books used in the analysis. It is a fun way to pass some time and may be a site to bookmark so you can go back when a new word intrigues you, like extoplasm. Google ngrams.

Incidentally, the US Library of Congress has about thirty-seven million books.

Prescient Predictions From the Past - That time of year when the predictors pontificate about the future. The Ladies Home Journal from December 1900 contained an article, "What May Happen in the Next Hundred Years." Here are a few of the surprisingly accurate predictions from a hundred years ago:

There will probably be from 350,000,000 to 500,000,000 people in America and its possessions by the lapse of another century *(309 million as of 2009)*. Nicaragua will ask for admission to our Union after the completion of the great canal. Mexico will be next.

The American will be taller by from one to two inches. His increase of stature will result from better health, due to vast reforms in medicine, sanitation, food, and athletics. He will live fifty years instead of thirty-five as at present.

There Will Be No Street Cars in Our Large Cities. All hurry traffic will be below or high above ground when brought within city limits. In most cities it will be confined to broad subways or tunnels, well lighted and well ventilated, or to high trestles with "moving-sidewalk" stairways leading to the top.

Trains will run two miles a minute, normally; express trains one hundred and fifty miles an hour. Cars will, like houses, be artificially cooled. Along the railroads there will be no smoke, no cinders, because coal will neither be carried nor burned. There will be no stops for water.

Automobiles will be cheaper than horses are today. Farmers will own automobile hay-wagons, automobile truck-wagons, plows, harrows, and hay-rakes. A one-pound motor in one of these vehicles will do the work of a pair of horses or more. Children will ride in automobile sleighs in winter.

There will be air-ships, but they will not successfully compete with surface cars and water vessels for passenger or freight traffic. They will be maintained as deadly war-vessels by all military nations. Some will transport men and goods. Others will be used by scientists making observations at great heights above the earth.

Photographs will be telegraphed from any distance. If there be a battle in China a hundred years hence snapshots of its most striking events will be published in the newspapers an hour later. Persons and things of all kinds will be brought within focus of cameras connected electrically with screens at opposite ends of circuits, thousands of miles at a span.

Wireless telephone and telegraph circuits will span the world. A husband in the middle of the Atlantic will be able to converse with his wife sitting in her boudoir in Chicago. Grand Opera will be telephoned to private homes, and will sound as harmonious as though enjoyed from a theater box.

Hot or cold air will be turned on from spigots to regulate the temperature of a house as we now turn on hot or cold water from spigots to regulate the temperature of the bath. Central plants will supply this cool air and heat to city houses in the same way as now our gas or electricity is furnished.

Ready-cooked meals will be bought from establishments similar to our bakeries of today.

Microscopes will lay bare the vital organs, through the living flesh, of men and animals. The living body will to all medical purposes be transparent. This work will be done with rays of invisible light.

Fast electric ships, crossing the ocean at more than a mile a minute, will go from New York to Liverpool in two days.

Moving Water - Have you ever noticed the water in your toilet moves on windy days? In many homes in the US, part of the plumbing system is a pipe that runs up and out to the roof. This outlet, called a "vent stack," allows sewage gases to vent outside instead of through the toilet, sink or tub, which would make the house reek. The stack also allows air to move through the pipes, which makes waste-water drain smoothly and keeps gurgling to a minimum.

When the wind blows over the vent stack outlet on the roof, the air pressure in the pipe is lowered. This is Bernoulli's principle in action, in your bathroom. The lowered pressure in the pipes creates a slight suction effect throughout the plumbing system, pulling on water in the toilet below. As the wind kicks up and dies down, the suction gets stronger and weaker, and the water in the bowl sloshes around accordingly.

Seven Unique Uses for Nail Polish - Dab a bit of clear nail polish on the screws on the side of your glasses to keep the screw from getting loose. Also good to put on cupboard door screws to tighten them up.

Dip the end of shoelaces in some to keep them from raveling.

Put on labels to smudgeproof them.

Put different colors on keys to distinguish. Also put a dot of the same color on door locks to match.

Cover costume jewelry to keep it from losing its luster.

Use it as a band aid for small cuts. It is almost like what hospitals use instead of stitches.

Freezing Candles - If you have candles in a glass, freezing them when done will make it easier to get the remaining wax out of the bottom.

Incidentally, freezing candles will not make them last longer.

Phosphenes - This is the name for the lights you see when you close your eyes and press your hands to them. It is like making your own personal Christmas lights.

Here are a few goodies from 2008 Bulwer-Lytton Fiction Writing Contest. *Sometimes I get so inspired.*

"As usual, Mr. Riddle came home from work, and, as usual, took the toy poodle, Fluffy, out for her walk, and, as usual, Fluffy "did her business" at the usual places, first at the bush, second, on the sidewalk, and third, in the grass, so that there, on the pavement, was evidence of Fluffy's evening sojourn: Mr. Riddle's little poodle's middle piddlle puddle." Dr. Ford Sutherland, Venice, Florida.

"The homicide detective was an aging woman with a crusty and somewhat ill-tempered personality, an individual who reminded me of the kind of woman my mother, a Sunday-school teacher, would have been if she had been a crusty and somewhat ill-tempered homicide detective." Bill Crumpler, McKinney, TX.

"Vito watched as Robert squirmed in his life vest while the Great White brushed against his chum-soaked and shackled body, but it wasn't until the terrible fish circled back, finally ending Robert's evening, that Vito, with the vision of the legless torso undulating up and down in the Farallon current had his epiphany, and uncovered one of life's truly great mysteries: when you shorten Robert you really do get bob." Paul Olson, San Jose, CA.

"Bryson the Plainsman seldom spoke a discouraging word, but he did when he filed for divorce after discovering his dear and an interloper played." Maree Lubran, Saratoga, CA.

Surfs Up - Just when you thought college was dull, they come up with a surfing course and it is not in California. English students will soon be able to spend two years learning to surf, in a new college course costing the British taxpayers £100,000. The surf school at the Bournemouth and Poole College in Dorset will be a full-time course teaching teenagers how to catch a wave.

Students will spend much of their "study" time on the beach and will go on residential trips to top surfing locations like Cornwall, Devon, and possibly abroad. In return, they will be awarded a BTEC National Certificate in Sport, equivalent to two A Levels, reports the Daly Telegraph.

The two year course, being subsidized by the taxpayer, will cost £4,012 pounds per place. Students will also take theory lessons in sports science and other aspects of the surf industry.

The Surf Academy will coincide with the completion of Europe's first artificial surf reef in Boscombe, Bournemouth.

Toilet Paper Facts - I am not so sure you have noticed, so I thought you should be informed that toilet paper is getting smaller. The standard size for years had been 4.5 by 4.5 inches, but now most manufacturers have gone to 4.5 by 4 or 4.5 by 4.3 inches.

The British pay twice as much as Germans or French, and nearly three times as much as the Americans for a standard four-pack roll.

Studies show that the average user of toilet paper uses about the same number of sheets whether it is three ply, two ply, or one ply. *So, when using the loo, one ply will do - and it's cheaper.*

New Use for Wasp Spray - A receptionist in a church in a high risk area was concerned about someone coming into the office on Monday to rob them when they were counting the collection. She asked the local police department about using pepper spray and they recommended to her that she get a can of wasp spray instead.

The wasp spray, they told her, can shoot up to twenty feet away and is a lot more accurate, while with the pepper spray, they have to get too close to you and could overpower you. The wasp spray temporarily blinds an attacker until they get to the hospital for an antidote. She keeps a can on her desk in the office and it doesn't attract attention from people like a can of pepper spray would. She also keeps one at home for home protection.

Bubble Wrap - Did you know bubble wrap is over 50 years old? Now you do. Of course we missed bubble wrap appreciation day, which was Jan 25 (started in 2001 in Bloomington, Indiana).

Here is a site that lets you pop the stuff online. A total waste of time, but you know you want to pop just a few.
http://www.snapbubbles.com/

Odd Book Prize Awarded - "Too Naked for the Nazis," the story of a music-hall act that outraged authorities in Hitler's Germany, has won an award for the year's oddest book title.

Organizers of the Diagram Prize said that Alan Stafford's cultural-history tome gained almost a quarter of votes cast, narrowly beating "Reading From Behind: A Cultural History Of The Anus."

The Diagram Prize was founded in 1978 and is run by trade magazine The Bookseller. The winner of the Diagram Prize for year's oddest book title, is decided by public vote.

Humorous self-help book "How to Poo on a Date: The Lovers' Guide to Toilet Etiquette" triumphed during 2014 as the quirky Diagram Prize. Organizers said the book, published by Prion Press, received 30 percent of votes in an online ballot.

Previous champions include "Bombproof Your Horse" and "Living With Crazy Buttocks." *Maybe I should have submitted my original book series, 'Terrible Tommy's Titillating Tidbits of Turpitude and Trivia.'*

Dallas Cowboys - The Cowboys, who began play in the NFL during 1960, were originally nicknamed the Steers.

The team's general manager, Texas E. Schramm, decided that having a castrated cow as a mascot might subject the team to ridicule, so he changed the name to Rangers. Then he feared that people would confuse the football team with the local minor league baseball team nicknamed the Rangers and finally changed the nickname to Cowboys shortly before the season began.

American Express - It was paying customers $300 to pay off their account and close it. After the company spent the better part of a decade trying to grow its customer base and actually grew it from 65 million in 2004 to 92 million, it was afraid of defaults from folks who were beginning to fall behind in their payments.

Spring Weed Killer - Get a head start as spring is beginning to blossom. Mix one ounce of vodka or vinegar, a few drops of dish soap, and two cups of water in a spray bottle. This works best on weeds that grow in direct sunlight. The vodka breaks down the waxy coating that protects the leaves, and helps the weeds dehydrate. Ants also do not like to cross a path of the mixture.

Pet Rocks - Gary Dahl got the idea for the Pet Rock, an ordinary rock, packaged in a pet carrier, requiring no food or care, at a California bar.

Pet Rocks made Mr. Dahl a millionaire practically overnight. He passed away March 28, 2015.

Shaft Tax - Most people think that all taxes are the shaft, but there really is a shaft tax. For calendar year 2015, the US tax imposed under § 4161(b)(2)(A) on the first sale by the manufacturer, producer, or importer of any shaft of a type used in the manufacture of certain arrows is $0.49 per shaft. The year before it was 48 cents.

Oregon Owns Water - According to Oregon water laws, all water is publicly owned. Therefore, anyone who wants to store any type of water on their property must first obtain a permit from state water managers.

A rural Oregon man was sentenced in 2012 to thirty days in jail and over $1,500 in fines because he had three reservoirs on his property to collect and use rainwater.

Oregon law that says all of the water in the state of Oregon is public water and if you want to use that water, either to divert it or to store it, you have to acquire a water right from the state of Oregon before doing that activity. The law states that the city of Medford, Oregon holds exclusive rights to "all core sources of water."

Car Tire Colors - Car tires were initially off white, due to the natural color of the rubber used. Pure vulcanized rubber is soft and wears out very quickly and tends to heat up and deform under load. Tire makers mixed zinc oxide in with the rubber that added temperature stability and hardness, and which made the tires bright white in color.

As the benefits of adding carbon black to the compound became known, that additive was used just on the tread portion, while the side of the tire remained the natural color, the original whitewall tires. Adding carbon black made the tires darker, and they lasted four to five times longer.

Binney & Smith began selling their carbon black chemicals to Goodrich Tire Company (now Michelin). *Binney & Smith would later switch to making school products, and, eventually, re-name their company after their most popular product, Crayola Crayons.*

There are a few tire manufacturers that make specialty color tires, mostly for car shows, and during 1961, Goodyear Tires introduced an experimental tire that was illuminated from the inside. Small incandescent bulbs were mounted inside the tire through holes inside the rim and the tire was made from a single piece of synthetic rubber. The synthetic rubber was created much thinner than a regular tire to allow for the light to penetrate the rubber. Due to the strict laws regarding the manufacturing of street-legal tires and the obvious hazard of having fragile glass inside them, Goodyear's illuminated tires never actually saw mass production.

Mourning Colors - Many colors are used around the world to signify mourning. Important information to know when traveling to avoid a potential faux pas.

In South Africa, red is the color of mourning.

In Iran, blue is the color of mourning.

In Egypt and Burma, yellow signifies mourning.

The ancient Egyptians and Romans used black for mourning, as do most Europeans and Americans.

Filipino people wear black or white for mourning.

Japanese wear black traditional Japanese clothing at funerals and Buddhist memorial services. Other colors, particularly reds and bright shades, are considered inappropriate for mourning dress.

In Thailand, black is the traditional mourning color. Purple is worn by widows mourning their husband's death.

In continental Europe and the UK, black is the mourning color. The color of deepest mourning among medieval European queens was white.

In Asia many people dress in different colors such as indigo, ruby-red and many more. In China, during the period of mourning family members of the deceased wear a piece of cloth on their arm for 100 days. A color of the cloth tells the relationship to the deceased. The children of the deceased will wear a black cloth, blue by the grandchildren, and green by the great grandchildren.

In the Middle East it is the norm that white symbolizes time of mourning and funerals.

In India the members of the mourning family and the people who come to participate in mourning all wear white clothes.

Violet and purple became the color of demi-mourning, worn after a widow or widower had worn black for a certain time, before she or he returned to wearing ordinary colors.

Aluminum Foil Facts - A friend of mine, Jeff Flanagan was wondering whether to cover pans with the shiny side or dull side of aluminum foil out.

Some background, the difference in appearance between dull and shiny is due to the foil manufacturing process. In the final rolling step, two layers of foil are passed through the rolling mill at the same time. The side coming in contact with the mill's highly polished steel rollers becomes shiny.

> It makes no difference which side, dull or shiny to use when wrapping, covering, draping, or using as a guard for drips.

However, when using non-stick aluminum foil place the non-stick (dull) side toward the food.

Aluminum foil has the lowest moisture-vapor transfer rate of all wrapping materials and is the most effective in preventing the loss of moisture and vapor from food, especially for long-term food storage or freezing.

Heavy duty aluminum foil is better for wrapping meats and poultry for the freezer, lining roasting pans for easy cleanup, lining the inside of a charcoal barbecue grill to keep it clean, tenting roasted turkey to prevent oven spatters and over-browning, also for making an oven packet for cooking chicken, fish, and vegetables.

Do not use aluminum foil to line the bottom of your oven. Place a sheet of heavy duty aluminum foil on the oven rack beneath a pie or casserole. The foil should be only a few inches larger than the baking pan to allow for proper heat circulation.

The argument of shiny side out to reflect heat is a myth as shiny reflects light, not heat. *Bottom line, according to Reynolds Aluminum no difference, except appearance. If you like shiny side up do it. If you like dull side up, do it.*

How to Disinfect Sponges - Quickly heating up your sponge in the microwave can kill bacteria including E. coli and refresh it for longer use. Make sure the sponge is damp and free of any cleaners before you pop it in the microwave. Heating up a sponge that has been soaked in soap or other industrial cleaners could cause it to emit unhealthy fumes.

Instead, soak your dirty kitchen sponges in water and a small amount of lemon juice or vinegar. Microwave them for up to two minutes on full power. The bonus is that the steam from the wet sponge will also clean your microwave.

Nine Plants to Clean Stale Air - We all know indoor plants are good to have for a variety of reasons. Some are better than others to help clean stale air.

Many of these plants remove toluene, which is a raw material used in the manufacture of polyurethane foam and TNT. Toluene is also a common solvent for paints, paint thinners, silicone sealants, many chemical reactants, rubber, printing ink, adhesives, lacquers, leather tanners, and disinfectants. Inhalation of toluene in low to moderate levels can cause tiredness, confusion, weakness, drunken-type actions, memory loss, nausea, loss of appetite, and hearing and color vision loss.

Areca Palm - Helps to remove toluene and xylene from the air and can help to increase overall air purification. Great for those who may have asthma or require effective air purification.

Money Plant - Helps to reduce the toxins benzene, formaldehyde, toluene, and xylene from the air. It can also help to increase overall air quality and purification.

Moth Orchids - Ideal for helping to increase purification of the air within homes. They are suitable for removing xylene and toluene and can increase air quality.

Dwarf Date Palm - Helps to reduce common toxins xylene, toluene, and formaldehyde from the air. This plant can also help to promote increased oxygen levels, and is able to improve air quality in highly exposed areas.

Spider Plant - Promotes high air purification. It is suitable for helping to decrease exposure to formaldehyde, toluene, and xylene.

Lilyturf - Helps to remove ammonia, toluene, xylene, and formaldehyde from the air. This plant is capable of increasing oxygen levels and can help to improve air quality. Great for people who are exposed to cleaning products, paint fumes, city or factory smog, or vehicle fumes. This plant can help clean the air for those with common lung conditions including emphysema and asthma.

Boston Fern - Helps to remove formaldehyde from the air and is said to act as a natural type of air humidifier. This plant can also remove xylene and toluene. It is said to be one of the best houseplants for air purification. Great for those living or working in areas where exposure to gasoline exists. They are ideal for homes exposed to city smog, and are suitable for those who may have asthma or breathing conditions.

Purple Waffle Plant - Helps to remove formaldehyde from the air. It can help to increase overall air purification, and is suitable for increasing the quality of the air within any home. Great for city homes that are exposed to smog and car fumes.

Bamboo Palm - Helps to remove formaldehyde and is suitable for acting as a natural humidifier for most indoor areas. It can also help to remove xylene and toluene. Great for those who live in high air pollution areas and areas where car fume exposure exists. Suitable for placing in homes or shops which may be exposed to gasoline.

Decanting Wine and Whiskey - According to the Scotch Whisky Association, whiskey, once bottled, is a finished product, "If you keep a 12 year old bottle for 100 years, it will always remain a 12 year old whisky."

The reasons whiskey remains basically the same while wine changes has to do with a couple factors: tannins and alcohol content. Wine has much more tannin content than whiskey. Whiskey has no innate tannins, and only gets a small amount from the barrel in which it ages. Tannins can cause change in a bottle of wine over time, for better or worse. Since whiskey has less tannins, it does not have much chance for major evolutions in flavor.

More important than tannins: alcohol content. Wines may have between 11% and 15%, or higher but almost all whiskeys are bottled at a minimum of 40% ABV. With such high alcohol content, the possibility for a dramatic chemical reaction from oxidation is much lower.

However, whiskey can change over time, especially if it has been exposed to sunlight or temperature fluctuations.

Wine decanters are specifically designed to encourage interaction between liquid and air, always without a cap. Whiskey decanters tend to be built for stability, have glass tops, and usually have a wide bottom. Air is not a factor in whiskey decanters, because it does make much difference.

So, wine is decanted for flavor and whiskey is decanted for looks.

Incidentally, do not use a lead crystal decanter, because over a long period of time it could leach into the whiskey.

Travel Tip - If you travel, those little hotel room packets of coffee are perfect to use in your bag with dirty laundry and at home for room odors. Unwrap the foil covering and toss unused coffee packet in with your dirty laundry. When you get home your bag will be less stinky. Leave the coffee packet in your bag while storing it for your next trip.

Pantone 2016 Colors - Pantone did something for the first time and named two colors for 2016's Color of the Year – Rose Quartz (pink) and Serenity (light blue). It also introduced politics into color choice.

It says, "joined together, Rose Quartz and Serenity demonstrate an inherent balance between a warmer embracing rose tone and the cooler tranquil blue, reflecting connection and wellness as well as a soothing sense of order and peace." *It continues with a Politically Correct BS description more of gender, and defies any common sense description of color, so I will end here.*

Star Wars and Guillotines - France was still executing people by guillotine when Star Wars first came out. Star Wars was first shown in theaters in May 1977. The last execution by guillotine was carried out on September 10th of the same year.

Star Wars Trivia - "I have a bad feeling about this" has been said in every Star Wars movie. The phrase even appears in other Lucas projects, such as the Kingdom of the Crystal Skull, Indiana Jones, and the Monkey Island.

In The Star Wars Universe, the sith, not the jedi, invented the first lightsaber. The Jedi used green and blue weapons with a single blade, the Sith's lightsaber was red.

In different movies Yoda has different number of toes. In The Phantom Menace he has 3 toes, in The Empire Strikes Back and Return of the Sith he has 4.

China Wealth - China has 190 billionaires, more than two million millionaires, and ranks a bit behind the US in number of high-net-worth individuals, according to research from Forbes magazine and Boston Consulting Group. *Not bad for a communist country.*

Thought for the Day - *"Murder is a crime. Describing murder is not. Sex is not a crime. Describing sex is."* — Gershon Legman

----

Read Old Newspapers and Magazines Online - Below are a few more ways to get your favorite reading online and for free.

Google News – Google News indexes thousands of newspaper websites from around the world and organizes news in clusters for easy reading. In addition to current news, Google News also offers access to stories published in old newspapers that you can search for free.

Google Books – If you are looking for an older issue of a magazine, Google Books might be the best place to find it. The magazines are scanned and searchable and can be read online using the standard Google Book interface. Decade's worth of material are available, and the magazines are laid out just as they were when they were originally printed, including the original articles, index, cover, and advertisements.

Trove – The National Library of Australia has a large selection of newspapers from across Australia archived online that anyone may read for free. All the newspapers are completely scanned and can be viewed online in any modern browser, or you may download them as a PDF for offline reading.

Library of Congress – The Library of Congress has a large repository of historic newspapers published in America between 1880 and 1922, available as PDFs. Though the library has made available newspapers from 14 states and Washington, DC., these states contain some of the largest newspapers and thus the archives are still a very valuable resource. Additionally, the site has a database with records of all newspapers printed in America from 1690 to the present.

The Olden Times – If you are looking for a popular article about a major historical event, the Olden Times may be a good place to look for it. Although it does not contain entire newspapers, it does have snippets including popular news articles, print advertisements, and personal information sections such as births and obituaries. All content is free, and the content ranges from 1788 to 1920.

OMA – Old Magazine Articles contains magazine pages covering from famous historical events. The articles can be downloaded as PDF files for free. They have been edited to remove advertisements from the original magazines.

BBC – The 'On This Day' section of BBC offers an online archive of some of the most significant stories broadcast by BBC News since 1950. You can select any date from the menu at the top of the page, and view the news from that date as well as today's historical news.

Power Balance Wristbands - You have seen the advertisements on TV. One of those companies was caught and the result is: "In our advertising we stated that Power Balance wristbands improved your strength, balance, and flexibility. We admit that there is no credible scientific evidence that supports our claims and therefore we engaged in misleading conduct in breach of s52 of the Trade Practices Act 1974. If you feel you have been misled by our promotions, we wish to unreservedly apologize and offer a full refund." *Nuff said.*

Do Not Call - If you ever receive a sales calls on your cell phone, you may wish to call 888-382-1222. It is the FTC National 'do not call' list and will block your number. You must call from the cell phone number you want to have blocked.

PS - Ignore those panic emails about numbers being sent to telemarketers. The only thing correct is that there is a 'do not call' list and you can use it. The rest is hooey.

FACTS ABOUT ART

Photography - Louis Jacques Daguerre was close to becoming the first person to develop a practical process for producing photographs in the early 1800s. He figured out how to expose an image onto highly polished plates covered with silver iodide, a substance known to be sensitive to light. The images he was producing on these polished plates were barely visible, but he did not know how to make them darker.

After producing another disappointing image one day, Daguerre tossed the silverized plate in his chemical cabinet, intending to clean it off later. When he went back a few days later, the image had darkened to the point where it was perfectly visible. Daguerre realized that one of the chemicals in the cabinet had somehow reacted with the silver iodide, but he had no way of know which one it was.

For weeks, Daguerre took one chemical out of the cabinet every day and put it in with a newly exposed plate. But every day, he found a less-than-satisfactory image. Finally, as he was testing the last chemical, he got the idea to put the plate in the now-empty cabinet, as he had done the first time. Sure enough, the image on the plate darkened. Daguerre carefully examined the shelves of the cabinet and found what he was looking for. Weeks earlier, a thermometer in the cabinet had broken and left a few drops of mercury on the shelf. it was the mercury vapor interacting with the silver iodide that produced the darker image. Daguerre incorporated mercury vapor into his process, and the Daguerreotype photograph was born.

Sears Tower no More - The world famous Sears Tower in Chicago had a name change to the Willis Tower after new tenants London-based Willis Group Holdings. The new name is part of the terms of a rental agreement between the owners of the Sears Tower and the Willis Group. Willis Group is not paying any extra money to make the name change.

Historic Photos - Historypin is a very interesting website that is a global project in partnership with Google. The site allows people to view and share historic places pictures online. It's an open community, which means everyone can upload an old photo, locate the place on a Google Map and Google Street View and pin it.

When uploading a photo you need to enter date and location. The site then pins the historic picture to a current picture in an overlay, to show past and present. There is a timeline across the top so you can look for pictures during various years. Great for history buffs, or those interested in genealogy. *It only has thousands of pictures so far, and this is the type of site that gets better as more folks add pictures.*

American Gothic - American Gothic is a famous painting that was created in 1930. Grant Wood entered the painting in a competition at the Art Institute of Chicago and won the bronze medal.

Since it came out at the onset of the Great Depression, it was viewed by many as a symbol of the steadfast American spirit. Many saw it as a struggling farmer and his wife who refuse to give up. The picture above shows the painting and its subjects. The woman was Wood's sister and the man was his dentist.

Google Tricycle - Google's tricycle-mounted cameras are shooting footage of the 17th century gardens of France's Chateau de Versailles destined for its Street View service. The tricycle carries nine cameras set to take automatic shots every six feet, providing footage of some of the most popular spots of the onetime home of Louis XIV, the main courtyard, Grand Canal, and Grand and Petit Trianon.

The palace and gardens on the western edge of Paris are visited by more than three million people a year. The pictures taken by the tricycle will complete those taken by car as it can get to places that are not accessible to historically interesting pedestrian areas.

Google began its photographic campaign of France and on to the northern city of Lille and the Mont Saint-Michel abbey in western France, also a popular tourist site.

Font Types and Buying - The type font used by marketers to convey a price promotion affects our perception of the product and purchase behavior.

It is widely accepted that non-serif fonts, such as Helvetica or Arial, are easy to process and should create a positive effect that consumers generally mis-attribute to the quality of the related product. As a result, many companies including Target, Mattel, Staples, and The North Face use Helvetica in their brand logos. Helvetica was also used in the posters for the television show Mad Men. From this, some could assume that when fonts are easier to read, they are more liked by consumers, who would increase purchases.

However, in a paper in the Journal of the Academy of Marketing Science, a team of researchers took a closer look at how consumers' buying decisions are influenced by fonts. They argue that when product and price information appears in difficult to read fonts, customers take more time to read and process the information, which should induce greater recall of that information and may lead to a perception that the product in question is a better value for their money. "Simply stated, we suggest that marketers might think that simplifying a consumer promotion might help increase sale. However we show that, in fact, a harder-to-read font makes them more likely to purchase a product, hence the paradox."

The researchers found that if a marketer wants consumers to notice the value communicated by a lower price, a difficult to read font might be beneficial and more effective. Even though consumers say they do not prefer difficult to read fonts or advertisements, the research shows they are actually more likely to purchase the related promoted offers.

Bottom line, when offers are monetarily similar, consumers prefer fluent fonts. However, even though consumers find prices in fluent fonts easier to grasp, prices promoted in harder-to-read fonts increase sales.

FAMOUS RECORDS

Record Firsts - Everyone likes to show the top ten lists from the past year, but for something different, here are top ten sports firsts from days gone by.

• The first to swim 100 meters in under a minute: Johnny Weissmuller (Tarzan), July 9, 1922

• The first sprinter to break 10 seconds in the 100m: Jim Hines, 9.9 seconds, at the 1968 AAU Championships

• The first high school student to break the four-minute mile: Jim Ryun, 3:58.3, in 1965, for Wichita East High School

• The first NBA player to reach 20,000 career points: Bob Pettit, 1964

• The first baseball player to reach 3,000 career hits: Cap Anson, 1897

• The first golfer to reach $1 million in career earnings: Jack Nicklaus, 1970, after taking second place in the Bing Crosby Pro-Am

• The first woman golfer to reach $1 million in career earnings: Kathy Whitworth, 1981, after taking third place in the U.S. Women's Open

• The first million-dollar gate for a fight: 1921, Georges Carpentier vs. Jack Dempsey

• The first Indianapolis 500 winner to average more than 100 miles per hour: Peter DePaolo, 101.27 mph in 1925, in a Duesenberg Special

• The first winning Super Bowl coach to wear headphones on the sidelines: Bill Walsh, San Francisco 49ers, Super Bowl XVI, 1982

INVENTIONS

It's in the Bag - Margaret Knight fought a sexist employee to claim her rightful title as the inventor of the flat-bottomed paper bag in 1858. She was working in paper bag factory when she noticed how difficult it was to pack things into the flimsy, shapeless sacks. So, she decided to invent a machine that folded and glued paper to make a flat-bottomed bag.

Knight spent many late nights drawing up plans before creating a wooden prototype. She couldn't, however, obtain a patent until she made one out of iron.

While it was being produced at machine shop, an employee named Charles Annan copied her idea and got a patent for it. Knight sued Annan for copyright infringement. Annan argued that, because she was a woman, she could not have been the true inventor. However, Knight's sketches and detailed plans helped her win the case. She ended up establishing her own paper bag company and received large royalties for her invention.

Dumpsters - The Dumpster was invented in Knoxville Tennessee by the Dempster brothers. The original name was the Dempster Dumpster. The Dempster-Dumpster system is a way of mechanically loading the contents of standardized containers onto garbage trucks. The Dempster Dumpmaster, was the first successful front-loading garbage truck, which really brought the word into everyday language.

A dumpster is a large steel waste receptacle designed to be emptied into garbage trucks. The word is a trademark of Dumpster, an American brand name for a type of mobile garbage bin.

Incidentally, dumpster diving involves people voluntarily climbing into a dumpster to find valuables, or useful items, including food and used clothing.

Pencils and Erasers - In 1858, there were lead pencils and there were erasers. That year, Hymen Lipman received his patent for putting the two together. A few years later, in 1862 Lipman sold his patent to Joseph Reckendorfer for $100,000. Quite a large amount at the time.

Reckendorfer sued the pencil company Faber for infringement. The Supreme Court of the United States ruled against Reckendorfer declaring the patent invalid, because his invention was actually a combination of two already known things with no new use. Faber is still in business making pencils and crayons.

The word "pencil" derives from the Latin word "pencillus", meaning tail or little brush. A typical pencil can draw a line 35 miles long, or write about 45,000 words. You cannot get lead poising from pencils, because they do not contain lead. More than half of all pencils are made in China. The typical six sided pencil uses less wood to make than round, is easier to sharpen, and has better grip to not roll off of a surface. There is no reason for the yellow color and many countries do not paint their pencils yellow.

Bathtub and Phone – It was invented in 1850 and the telephone in 1875. If you had been living in 1850, you could have sat in the tub for 25 years without the phone ringing once.

Slinky - Slinky was invented by Naval engineer Richard James, who knocked a spring off of a shelf when he was working to develop springs that could keep ship instruments stable in choppy waters.

The spring stepped down to a stack of books, then to the table, and then to the floor, where it righted itself into a cylinder. He tested it with neighborhood kids and the rest is history.

Hula Hoop - Many of you will remember the hula hoop craze from days gone by. They are still around and still fun. Do you know where they came from?

There was a famous radio and TV personality that was responsible for financing, manufacture, and promotion.

The person was very concerned that folks did not find out who was responsible and be swayed by his stardom. It was Art Linkletter, star of TV shows 'House Party', 'Kids say the Darndest Things', and more. *Many of my Terrible Tommy and Dirty Johnny jokes were inspired by his book.*

Winch Tourbillon Vertical - The WTV from Cabestan is built in a unique vertical manner in what is perhaps the most mechanical of mechanical wristwatches. The movement is wound with a large key that turns a set of visible cogs.

A set of wheels, pinions, and drums turn in synchronization to power the timepiece. There is no face to this watch either, but instead two rotating drums set atop a ball bearing. The vertical tourbillon, which is run by what looks like a small bicycle chain, is the first of its kind. The crystal consists of 6 hand blown pieces of Pyrex.

Water Water everywhere - This ingenious device (AM10 from AquaMaker in Texas) converts the humidity in the air into water. It can work practically anywhere in the world, even the desert (although with reduced efficiency). Water cooler sized models start at $1,799. The machines have been around since 2007 and produce about 36 liters of water within 48 hours.

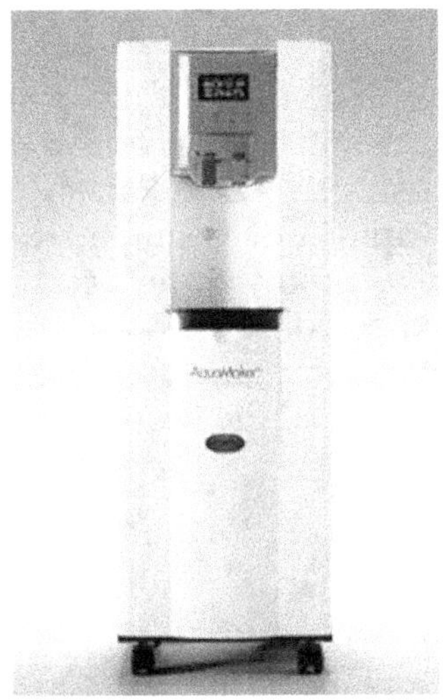

They use air filtering technology that prevents the growth of algae and bacteria on the condensing coils by removing between 85-99 percent of all air-borne particles, dust, mold spores, bacteria, and volatile organic chemicals.

Quiz - Two very popular and common objects have the same function, but one has thousands of moving parts, while the other has absolutely no moving parts. They do the same thing and both are non-exact. What are they?

Answer - Hourglass and Sundial

Elevator Close Buttons - Did you know most elevators built or installed since the early 1990s do not have close buttons that actually work, unless you use a fireman's or repair key? People push them, because the fact that the door eventually closes reinforces their belief that the button works. Doors are set on a delay timer to close. Older ones do work as advertised.

First Automatic Dishwasher - In 1850, Joel Houghton patented the first automatic dishwasher a wooden machine with a hand-turned wheel that splashed water on dishes. It was not much, but it was the first patent. In 1886, Josephine Cochran invented the first practical dishwasher. It was also hand operated. Dishwashers did not become household items until the 1950s.

Glowing Toilet Paper - The first packaged toilet paper was the 1857 invention of American, Joseph Gayetty and called Gayetty's Medicated Paper. In 1880, the British Perforated Paper Company created a paper product to be used for wiping after using the toilet, that came in boxes of small pre-cut squares. In 1879, the Scott Paper Company began selling the first toilet paper on a roll. However, toilet paper in roll form did not become common until 1907. In 1942, St. Andrew's Paper Mill in Great Britain introduced the first two-ply toilet paper.

Now you can buy the person who has everything a roll of glowing toilet paper. It is just the thing for hunting in the woods, when the power goes out, or when you don't want to turn on the lights. It costs about eight dollars a roll.

A Hundred (or so) Years Ago - During 1910 Thomas Edison demonstrated the first talking motion picture.

Georges Claude displayed the first neon lamp to the public on December 11, 1910, in Paris.

Fifty years ago, 1960 - The halogen lamp invented.

Wrapup the Leftovers - Saran wrap is really polyvinylidene chloride. In 1933, Ralph Wiley, a Dow Chemical lab worker, accidentally discovered polyvinylidene chloride.

Twenty Years of Inventions - During the years of 1870 to 1890, we had the invention of electric light, alternating current, the telephone, automobile, steam turbine, gas turbine, water heater, transformer, arc welding, phonograph, seismograph, development of vaccination and surgical techniques.

Also Boltzmann's development of thermodynamics and statistical mechanics; production of radio waves; the birth of the environmental conservation movement; and artworks by Rodin, Monet, Brahms, Dostoevsky, Tolstoy, Eliot, Chekhov and Twain. *All of this came a hundred years after the beginning of the industrial revolution.*

Water Heater Wrap - It is probably the most cost effective measure out of all the energy conservation measures and it has a one year or less payback. The cost is about $30 and savings varies from $30 to $50 per year, depending on the efficiency of your water heater.

Water heater wraps maintain the temperature of the water longer so the heating element or gas does not have to come on as often, and the less the elements come on, the longer the heater lasts.

The average household actually only uses hot water a little bit more than a hour a day, so for more than 22 hours a day, the water heater just maintains the temperature of the water. The vast majority of the cost to operate a water heater is maintaining the temperature of the water when nobody is using hot water. *Oh, and setting the limit down to 120 degrees will save at least another $30 annually.*

Vibrating Battery - No, not battery vibrator. Brother Industries Ltd developed small vibration-powered generators that can replace AA and AAA batteries.

Think of a flashlight that can be shaken to generate power to keep the light on. Reminds me of those wind up flashlights.

The new generator will semi-permanently eliminate the need to replace batteries and contribute to reducing the amount of wastes," Brother Industries said.

The generator can be used for a device that does not always consume electricity and has small power consumption, such as a TV remote, or LED flashlight.

Billboards Read You - In Tokyo, Japan, there are digital advertising billboards. They are fitted with cameras that read the gender and age group of people looking at them to tailor specific commercial messages.

A consortium of 11 railway companies launched a pilot project and has set up 27 of the high-tech advertising displays in subway commuter stations around Tokyo.

The camera can distinguish a person's sex and approximate age if the person walks in front of the display looks at the screen for a second. If data for different locations is analyzed, companies can provide interactive advertisements "which meet the interest of people who use the station at a certain time," the project said in a statement. *Scary when pictures you are looking at, look back at you.*

Origin of Frisbee - Walter Fred Morrison, like most other college kids in the 1930s, spent a great deal of time throwing around pie pans from the Frisbie Baking Company. It was after he joined the Air Force that he learned about aerodynamics and realized he was doing science during those pan-flinging sessions.

Fred took what he learned about basic aerodynamics from the Air Force and made a prototype of a better flying disc.

He used plastic to recreate it and named his creation the "Pluto Platter," which was ultimately renamed the Frisbee as homage to the original Frisbie baking plates.

MYTHS DEBUNKED

Baseball Myth - Abner Doubleday is routinely touted as the inventor of baseball, but there is little, if any historical evidence to back that claim. Much like Betsy Ross and the flag, Doubleday had a good story which circumvented the truth. When baseball started getting really popular, there was actually a committee called the Mills Commission organized with the purpose of tracking down the origins of the sport.

One of the men on that commission, Albert Spalding, did not like the fact that baseball was seen as a variation on the English game of Rounders. He wanted this new beloved pastime to be 100% American and Doubleday's story fit the bill perfectly. He had a decorated Civil War general who created the sport in his youth living in a small town in New York. And so the legend began. . .

Nine Shopping Myths Debunked - *Myth, You Should Always Buy in Bulk*
When confronted with a big package and a small package of the same item, cost-conscious shoppers often reach for the larger of the two, assuming a bulk discount. Unfortunately, this is not always the case. If you want to know whether you are getting a good value, calculate what you are paying per unit or per ounce. You may be surprised to find smaller packages can be just as or more economical than larger ones. I have noticed that Walmart regularly switches prices for which is higher on a given soda between two 24 can packages and one 48 can package.

Myth, You Don't Have to Pay Sales Tax for Online Shopping
While some retailers do sell goods online without charging state sales tax, this is not always the case. "These days, that myth boils down to a mix of misinformation and misunderstanding," says Ryan O'Donnell, director of marketing for a sales tax software company. "While it is true online shoppers can search and find options for tax-free purchases, in most cases, these amount to the seller failing to collect the sales tax." Even Amazon has been forced to charge sales tax for states in which it has facilities.

Myth, Sports Fans Buy New TVs Just for the Super Bowl
Another myth that is pushed by the wave of hype surrounding a big event is the idea that everyone rushes out to buy the biggest big screen they can afford before the Super Bowl. Polling shows the majority of

TV buyers said they bought their set in November or December, likely taking advantage of pre-Thanksgiving or Christmas sales to get TV deals. Generally every other month of the year, TV sales are fairly evenly distributed, until just before new models are introduced.

Myth, Black Friday Is the Best Day to Shop
This is not always true. Black Friday has some of the best deals of the year, but only on certain products. Do not get so caught up in the shopping holiday hype that you forget to consider whether you are getting a great buy or just an okay buy.

Myth, After Christmas Sales Can't Compare to Holiday Shopping
While it might not always qualify as the best time to shop, the week after Christmas generally offers very good deals. After holidays, retailers use steep discounts to bring shoppers into stores to clear out holiday inventory. Some of these post-Christmas sales actually start just before Christmas.

Myth, Retailers Always Clear Out Old Inventory in January
Though it is true that retailers are eager to get rid of old, outdated inventory when new products come out, not all products have straightforward release schedules. Consider cars, which have new models every year. The 2016 models were released in the fall of 2015, and by January those older models were likely long gone. However, in the automotive industry, as well as in many durable goods, year-end inventory reduction sales are significant because of inventory taxes which are calculated based in inventory on hand on December 31st.

Myth, If It is On Sale, Buy It
Not all sales are created equal. You have probably noticed that in certain stores things seem to be always on sale. When goods are always on sale, the sale price is really just the retail price under a different name. Be wary of these always-on-sale items. Think mattress, there seems to be a 'huge' mattress sale every day of the year.

Myth, Outlet Stores Have the Best Prices
Outlets suggest they are offering steep discounts on brand-name merchandise, with labeling that says you are paying $100 for something that sold for $300 at a flagship store. According to some estimates, more than half of merchandise at outlet stores was made specifically for those stores, using lower-cost materials and designs. Much of outlet stores also sell 'seconds' and discontinued items. Be aware that you are not getting as much value as the tag suggests. In addition, sales at the regular retailer sometimes beat outlet prices.

Myth, The Cheapest Retailer is Always Best
The best price is not always the best deal. A recent study from the University of Wisconsin-Madison's Wisconsin School of Business suggests that shoppers consider a retailer's reputation as well as its prices. Savvy shoppers will think twice before buying from a less reputable merchant. Will that seller not honor the price, not have the item in stock, add on extra shipping fees? However, many high-end and specialty stores offer the same products as their lower-priced competitors, but with no real increase in service value.

Microwave Myth Debunked - The myth is, people do not need to worry about getting food to proper temperatures throughout after a run through the microwave, because the radiation will kill bacteria.

This is an erroneous assumption and could lead to food poisoning. All microwaves do is make food hotter. The heat itself is the only thing killing germs. Microwaves are also notorious for cooking food unevenly. Experts recommend using food thermometers and checking various spots on the food when using a microwave, in order to ensure avoiding food poisoning issues.

Most microwave meals now contain similar instructions for their own legal protection and to avoid consumer complaints. The truth is that microwaves are perfectly safe in terms of radiation, but they are also not a magic box that will destroy all bacteria.

Whitening Toothpaste Myth - "Scientifically proven" labels on toothpaste containers are not entirely accurate. According to the American Dental Association, whitening toothpastes may be able to do something on the surface level. To get to the deep-down stains, you need more extreme treatments like bleaching. Several whitening toothpastes are available over the counter and have received the ADA Seal of Acceptance.

The ADA recommends that if you choose to use a bleaching product, you should only do so after consultation with a dentist. This is especially important for patients with many fillings, crowns, and extremely dark stains.

Since December 31, 2007, professionally (such as dentist) applied bleaching products are no longer eligible for the American Dental Association Seal of Acceptance.

SILLY STUDIES

WWF - It looks like the popular internet acronym and now may even bear some resemblance. In a recent report, the WWF (previously known as World Wildlife Fund) says, "The over-use and pollution of Earth's natural resources have become so extreme that, at current rates, a second planet will be needed by 2030 to meet the world's needs."

The report also added, "four and a half planets would be needed if everyone used as many resources as the average American." *I wonder what bar that study was conducted in and how it even got published by USA TODAY.*

Warming Thought - According to the ScienceDaily, the first eight months of 2010 tied the same period in 1998 for the warmest combined land and ocean surface temperature on record worldwide. Meanwhile, the June-August summer was the second warmest on record globally after 1998, and August was the third warmest August on record. Separately, another month's global average land surface temperature was the second warmest on record for August, while the global ocean surface temperature tied with 1997 as the sixth warmest for August. *What all that means is that global warming (now politically called climate change) has caused the world to be almost as warm as it was about twelve years previous.*

McGill University Study - Results from Canadian McGill University study, found that images of meat actually calmed men down and made them less aggressive.

The actual result of less aggression might reflect a genetic disposition to feel comfort at the sight of meat, with it being associated with gatherings of family and friends, the study's authors said.

Speaking of how ancient ancestors might have adapted their responses to the sight of meat ready for consumption, Kachanoff said "It wouldn't be advantageous to be aggressive anymore because you would've already used your aggression to acquire the meat, and furthermore, you would be surrounded by people who share . . . your DNA."

The research was conducted with 82 male subjects who were asked to inflict varying degrees of punishment on actors if they made errors while reading scripts. It was presented as a multi-tasking study to the subjects, who were sorting various pictures while the actors read.

The punishment was made by subjecting the script reader to various volumes of sound, with the highest levels believed by the subjects to be painful for the reader. The subjects were less likely to attempt to inflict pain on the reader if it was an image of meat they were looking at while the mistake was made.

Bruce Friedrich, vice-president of policy for People for the Ethical Treatment of Animals (PETA), called the study's results "interesting." "Clearly, eating meat does support horrible violence, but apparently somebody seeing meat that is not directly relatable to the animal does not cause people to become more aggressive." Kachanoff said his group had some vegetarians in the test group, and no major differences were found in their responses. *Studies like this prove that academics will go to great lengths to get their school to ante up for a barbecue.*

Another Stupid Study - US Navy culture leads to heavy drinking. The nature of the US Navy workplace leads to higher heavy drinking for sailors than for civilians, according to an article in the May, 2009 issue of the Journal of Mixed Methods Research published by SAGE.

Several issues specific to the Navy contribute to problem drinking, according to the study, including a culture that emphasizes drinking as a mechanism for bonding, recreation, and stress relief. These conclusions were reached using methods that included a statistical analysis of survey data as well as analyses of interviews and observations on bases, ships and submarines. *Isn't that interesting, only Navy people drink to bond, have recreation, and relieve stress. Hmmm.*

Vibrators - Church & Dwight, the company that produces OxiClean, Trojan products, Nair, Kaboom, and numerous products pitched by Billy Mays and others paid to have a vibrator study conducted.

The results - Two Indiana University studies conducted among nationally representative samples of adult American men and women show that vibrator use during sexual interactions is common, with use being reported by approximately 53 percent of women and 45 percent of men ages 18 to 60. Not only is vibrator use common, but the two studies also show that vibrator use is associated with more positive sexual function and being more proactive in caring for one's sexual health. *Conjures up visions of new late night commercials - H h h i i f f f f folks, G ggg ginsu vvv vibrators. . .*

Stupid Hammer Study - Scientists are studying hammering ability as a model for difficult motor tasks. The results presented at the Society for Experimental Biology meeting, indicate that there is a surprising difference in performance between the sexes, and that this difference is dependent on the hammering conditions.

When it comes to something as simple as hammering a nail, some people are naturals and get the job done after a few clean, sharp strokes of the hammer, whereas for the rest of us a similar challenge is likely to end up with the nail bent in the middle, a sore thumb, and a wounded pride.

The University of Massachusetts at Amherst measured hammering performance in men and women and found that men are more accurate than women when hammering under low light, and women are more accurate in brighter light, regardless of target size.

"We believe that our research indicates that humans have remarkable compensatory ability during difficult motor tasks such as hammering in the dark", said Dr Irschick, who in future studies is planning to focus on understanding how hammering ability evolves in humans from early development to adulthood. *I think he and his colleagues should go pound sand.*

Men and Memory - Another silly research study shows men who spend even a few minutes in the company of an attractive woman perform less well in tests designed to measure brain function than those who chat to someone they do not find attractive.

Researchers who carried out the study, published in the Journal of Experimental and Social Psychology, think the reason may be that men use up so much of their 'cognitive resources' trying to impress beautiful women, they have little left for other tasks.

Women, however, were not affected by chatting to a handsome man.

Shaving is Sexy - According to a Schick national research poll, men who shave regularly (5 times a week or more) have twice as much sex (15.5 vs. 7.8 times per month). They are also happier (89% vs. 82%), and more likely to report they are living their dreams (76% vs. 64%).

Eighty-two percent of women report a preference for cleanly shaven men and another 83% say it is sexy when a man has a smooth touchable face. Additionally:

    * 76% say they love it when their man shaves
    * 76% agree a "cleanly shaven man turns me on"
    * 64% say when their man shaves, they just can't keep their hands off of him
    * 78% would rather kiss a cleanly shaven man than a scruffy man
    * 64% would rather have sex with a cleanly shaven man than a scruffy one.

Also, according to the survey, women ranked body odor and dandruff the top two biggest turn-offs in a man. *I started shaving three times a day and I feel sexier already.*

Who Lies More - British men are more likely to tell lies than British women and feel less guilty about it, says the results of a poll of 3,000 people. Researchers found that the average British man tells three lies every day, that is equivalent to 1,095 a year. The average women lies about twice a day for 730 times a year.

Twenty-five per cent of men say they lied to their mother, but only twenty percent of women admit to having lied to their mum.

Seems like half the lies are used by both, as the bold ones below.

Men's most used lies -
1. **I didn't have that much to drink**
2. **Nothing's wrong, I'm fine**
3. I had no signal
4. **It wasn't that expensive**
5. **I'm on my way**
6. I'm stuck in traffic
7. No, your bum (butt) doesn't look big in that
8. Sorry, I missed your call
9. You've lost weight
10. **It's just what I have always wanted**

Women's most used lies -
1. **Nothing's wrong, I'm fine**
2. I don't know where it is, I haven't touched it
3. **It wasn't that expensive**
4. **I didn't have that much to drink**
5. I have a headache
6. It was in the sale
7. **I'm on my way**
8. Oh, I've had this ages
9. No, I didn't throw it away
10. **It's just what I have always wanted**

Deforestation - Fire occurrence rates in the Amazon have increased in 59% of areas with reduced deforestation and risks canceling part of the carbon savings achieved by UN measures to reduce greenhouse gas emissions.

Research from University of Exeter, published in June, 2010, in Science, analyzed deforestation and fire data from the Amazon. It found that carbon savings achieved by avoiding deforestation would be partially offset by increased emissions from fires.

Spiderman Useless Study - After extensive analysis, researchers at Cambridge University have concluded that the larger a person is, the more adhesives he would need to stick to a wall, making it virtually impossible for a normal sized human being to have the characteristics of Spiderman.

"If a human, for example, wanted to climb up a wall the way a gecko does, he would need impractically large sticky feet, and shoes in European size 145 or US size 114," said Walter Federle, senior author also from Cambridge's Department of Zoology.

Facebook Friends Study - A study done by an Oxford University professor of more than 3,300 Facebook users in the UK concluded that there were only 4.1 'dependable' friends out of a typical user's 150 Facebook friends. Friendships, the professor concluded. "Have a natural decay rate in the absence of contact, and social media may well function to slow down the rate of decay. However, that alone may not be sufficient to prevent friendships eventually dying naturally if they are not occasionally reinforced by face-to-face interaction."

TSA Pre-Check Study - According to a 2016 study from the Global Business Travel Association, it found that business travelers who are enrolled in the Transportation Security Administration's expedited screening program, TSA PreCheck, are much more satisfied with air travel than those who have not signed up."

TSA PreCheck is the program that allows pre-registered travelers to skip the long security lines and instead go through a much shorter, pre-screened queue. You do not have to take off any clothing or remove your computer from your bag. The data reveals that people prefer this. *If they had stood in a few lines, they would not have needed to do this silly study.*

Bacon and Nose Bleeds - According to a study conducted by the Detroit Medical Center, bacon can quickly and effectively treat a nosebleed by serving as a nasal tampon. For this bizarre method to work, one must plug the bleeding nostril with a piece of cured uncooked pork.

The team tested their bacon hypothesis on a girl who had Glanzmann thrombasthenia, a rare hereditary disease that causes prolonged bleeding. After sticking a piece of cured pork inside the girl's bloody nose, the bleeding stopped immediately.

The results of this bizarre scientific research were published in the Annals of Otology, Rhinology, and Laryngology. The researchers acknowledged that doctors had used cured pork to treat nosebleeds in the past. However, the practice was discontinued.

The researchers speculated that the high risk of acquiring parasitic and bacterial complications from stuffing one's nose with cured pork caused the unconventional treatment to be abandoned.

FACTS ABOUT GOVERNMENT AND LAWS

Top Ten Congressional Districts - Have you ever seen a map of Congressional Districts? As we approach this year and the resulting restructuring of Congressional Districts due to the new census results, you might enjoy some that have already been jiggered in interesting ways. Check the Illinois, Congressional District #4.

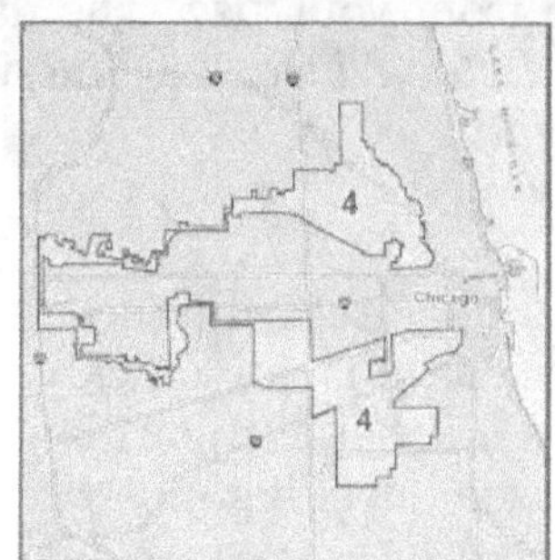

It looks like two distinct districts, but is really one connected by a median along the highway. Leave it to those folks in Illinois. *I wonder if it was done when Rod Blago was still in office?*

The Taxman Cometh - States have been feeling the pinch from unemployment causing them Medicaid outlay increases and tax income decreases, and the budgets are being squeezed. Rather than rein in spending as we are forced to do, states are looking for ways to increase current or make new taxes.

Cell Phone charges were up 2% in 2010 over 2009. The tax hikes, which could amount to as much as 75% in some localities. On average, 15% of a monthly cell phone service bill is already made up of taxes and fees, compared to 7% for most other goods and services.

E-book charges could start to be taxed not just by the state you live in, but also by the state where the server that you're downloading from is located. A buyer living in New Jersey who purchases a $10 e-book housed on a server in Texas might pay $1.52 in taxes (7% sales tax in N.J.; 8.25% in Texas). Taxes could add up to 21% of the total price, assuming multiple states apply taxes to the same transaction.

Cable Bills have already seen increases, such as Denton, Texas, where the city council voted to increase the public-access television fee (which pays for public, education and government channels) from 50 cents each month to 1% of the subscriber's bill. At an average cable bill of $75 per month, it goes to 75 cents from 50 cents.

Taxing Matters - Here are a few of the tax changes you might be affected by.

• Income taxes. Same as 2010, but the brackets are a bit higher Expires: end of 2012.

• 'Stealth' income taxes. Affluent taxpayers won't have deductions reduced. The old Pease limit cut 3% of itemized deductions and PEP cut the personal exemption, which is $3,700 for 2011. Expires: end of 2012.

• Investment taxes. For taxpayers in the 15% income tax bracket and below, the rate is zero. For those in the 25% bracket and above, the rate is 15% Expires: end of 2012.

• Estate and gift taxes. Top rate of 35% and one exemption of $5 million per individual for estate, gift and generation-skipping taxes. Expires: end of 2012. The annual exclusion for tax-free gifts remains $13,000 per donor. A giver may make an unlimited number of $13,000 gifts, as long as they are to different individuals. Gifts of tuition and payments for medical care also are exempt.

• Payroll taxes. A temporary two-percentage-point cut in the employee's share of Social Security taxes, saving a maximum of $2,136 per worker. No upper limit and each partner of a married couple can get the rebate. Expires: end of 2011. Will show up as an automatic adjustment to withholding. For the self-employed (whose tax rate falls to 10.4% from 12.4%), it will be built into a quarterly withholding worksheet the IRS hopes to release soon.

• Alternative Minimum Tax (AMT). The AMT limit is $47,450 for single filers and $74,450 for married couples Expires: end of 2011.

• Roth IRA conversion. The income limit for conversions has been permanently removed, so this year all taxpayers may still convert ordinary IRAs into Roth IRAs, but taxpayers who convert to Roth IRAs in 2011 no longer have the option of deferring conversion income into later years, as was true for 2010 conversions.

Those who converted in 2010 do have a year to decide whether to use this deferral.

• Foreign-account reporting. A new IRS reporting requirement on those with foreign financial assets above $50,000 in 2011. Details remain unclear, as the IRS has not yet issued regulations.

• Medical expenses. Workers with Flexible Spending Accounts (FSAs) may no longer use pretax funds to pay for many over-the-counter medicines—aside from insulin—without a prescription. But FSA funds may still be used for other, nonprescription medical items such as crutches, contact-lens solution or a wig after chemotherapy, if the individual plan allows it.

• Energy tax credits for homeowners. Extended the "25(C)" credit for energy-efficient improvements, but in a way that will be useful to few. The amount of the credit has shrunk to a maximum of $500 per taxpayer per lifetime, so those who took last year's $1,500 credit under this provision don't qualify. Expires at the end of 2011.

• Other changes. A deduction for state sales taxes in lieu of the state income tax deduction; and the tax-free donation of IRA proceeds to charity. They expire at the end of 2011. The American Opportunity Tax Credit of up to $2,500 for education expenses was renewed for 2011 and 2012. *How many of those were eliminated when they were supposed to be expired?*

What's a Whip - Both the Senate and House have majority and minority whips. A whip is a person, whose primary purpose is to ensure party discipline in a legislature, or whip it into shape. Whips typically offer inducements and threaten punishments for party members to ensure that they vote according to the official party policy.

A whip's role is also to ensure that the elected representatives of their party are in attendance when important votes are taken. The usage comes from the hunting term whipping in, such as preventing hounds from wandering away from the pack.

Sexy Over Sixty - Massachusetts House Bill 1668, (filed Jan 13, 2009) "An Act Relative to Posing or Exhibiting or Disseminating Material of an Elder or a Person with a Disability in a State of Nudity or Sexual Conduct" would make it a crime to "photograph with 'lascivious intent' a person over the age of 60 or a person with a disability who has been declared mentally incompetent."

If it is passed, a person violating the new provisions of the law "shall be punished by imprisonment in the state prison for a term of <u>not less than ten</u> nor more than twenty years, or by a fine of <u>not less than ten thousand</u> nor more than fifty thousand dollars, <u>or by both such fine and imprisonment</u>." This would include spouses photographing one another with "lascivious intent" and the person who poses.

State Democrat Representative Kathi-Anne Reinstein, (unmarried) says the bill she sponsored was intended to protect vulnerable (*elderly*) populations from sexual predators, but some disability advocates and law buffs have criticized the amendments as restricting the sexual freedom of seniors and people with disabilities.

Adding insult to injury, the proposal amends a bill designed to punish those who make child pornography. It treats fully functional adults who happen to be over 60 the same as children under 18; it explicitly takes away their right to consent to pose or be photographed nude.

I looked it up and she is from Revere, MA. with a population of 47,000, 84% Caucasian, and with 9,000 over 62 years old. She was born Jan 31, 1971.

Protection in the form of stealing people's rights isn't protection. This is the same argument that was used to deny women the right to vote 100 years ago: "Protecting" them from the upset of digesting political information and the pressures of citizenship."

Not only is this stupid and unnecessary, it is also unconstitutional. Do you think she might have seen her parents naked, and they were ugly?

Lincoln Revisited - The standing portrait of Lincoln was created soon after the American Civil War. Although it hung in many classrooms, Lincoln never posed for it. Instead, an unknown entrepreneur created it by cutting-and-pasting a head shot of Lincoln onto a portrait of the Southern leader John Calhoun.

This was done because there were hardly any heroic-style portraits of Lincoln made during his life.

In the Calhoun image, the papers on the table say "strict constitution," "free trade," and "the sovereignty of the states." In the Lincoln image, these words have been changed to read, "Constitution," "union," and "proclamation of freedom."

Opt Out - I was out checking one of my free credit reports the other day and found a tip at the bottom of the page. You can opt out of those annoying credit card and insurance offers for five years by calling 1 888 567-8688. I called and it took about three minutes. BTW, I get one credit report about every six months, because if you get all three together, you have to wait for a full year to get them again for free.

Don't Talk Back - The Obama administration planned to use the National Security Agency to screen Internet traffic between government agencies and the private sector, the Washington Post reported. *They said this was a continuation of the plan started by Bush, but I don't think this is what he had in mind.*

"We absolutely intend to use the technical resources, the substantial ones, that NSA has. But... they will be guided, led, and in a sense directed by the people we have at the Department of Homeland Security," Napolitano said.

Napolitano said the NSA would only be charged with looking at data going to or from the government system. *What other kind is there besides going to or coming from?*

"Each time a private citizen visits a 'dot.gov' website or sent an email to a civilian government employee, that action would be screened for potential harm to the network," the Post wrote. *How can anyone be comfortable viewing sites intended to inform us or complain to their elected officials, knowing the NSA will be. . .*

Four Constitution Day Facts for September 17

The U.S. Constitution has 4,543 words. It is the oldest and shortest written Constitution of any major government in the world. It contains 7,591 words including the 27 amendments.

Constitution Day is celebrated on September 17, the anniversary of the day the framers signed the document.

The oldest person to sign the Constitution was Benjamin Franklin (81). The youngest was Jonathan Dayton of New Jersey (26).

A proclamation by President George Washington and a congressional resolution established the first national Thanksgiving Day on November 26, 1789. The reason for the holiday was to give "thanks" for the new Constitution.

Stimulating Stimulus - *How the administration gets those 'saved or created' jobs numbers.* NEW YORK (CNNMoney.com) July - "The administration has said stimulus funds have already created or saved 150,000 jobs, and should create another 600,000 by summer's end.

The figures are based on estimates that each $92,000 in stimulus money spent creates one job for one year." *That's it folks. They are declared numbers and have no relation to jobs. The more they spend, the bigger the fib.*

Land Ownership - The United States government has direct ownership of almost 650 million acres of land, or nearly 30% of its total territory. These federal lands are used as military bases or testing grounds, nature parks, and reserves, and Indian reservations, or are leased to the private sector for commercial exploitation (e.g. forestry, mining, agriculture).

They are managed by different administrations, such as the Bureau of Land Management, the US Forest Service, the US Fish and Wildlife Service, the National Park Service, the Bureau of Indian Affairs, the US Department of Defense, the US Army Corps of Engineers, the US Bureau of Reclamation or the TVA.

Farming - 37.5% of the US population was involved in agriculture in 1900 and today less than half of one percent is in that business. We still have all the food we need, as well as supply other parts of the world.

There are 2.2 million farms and 50.4% of farms are less than 99 acres in size, with the average age of a farmer at 57.1 years old.

We export $115.5 billion of farm products a year. The top five farming counties in the US are in California. *All data from census.*

Census and ACS - The ACS is done annually, and is separate from the Census, but run by the Census Bureau. They changed the fine to $5,000 from $100 if you do not fill it out. This is the part where they ask you about income, etc. Each year approximately 3 million housing unit addresses in the United States and Puerto Rico are selected.

The American Community Survey (ACS) began full implementation of housing unit address in 2005. Since 2005, the ACS interviews samples of housing units in all counties in the United States (including the District of Columbia) and in all of the municipalities in Puerto Rico.

It is interesting to note that the census from 1870 asked for value of the house and value of the 'estate' of the main person in the house. It also asked about country of origin and native language. The census reports are available online for free after 75 years.

Big Spenders - Did you ever wonder who the big political spenders are? Here is a list of the largest spenders to influence votes. Notice that half are labor unions.

Rank	Organization	Total '89-'09	Dem%	Rep %
1	AT&T Inc	$45,656,394	44	55
2	Amer. Fedn of State, Cnty & Municipal Employees	$43,026,011	98	1
3	ActBlue	$42,628,917	99	0
4	National Assn of Realtors	$37,617,499	48	50
5	Goldman Sachs	$32,878,402	62	37
6	American Assn for Justice	$32,681,779	90	8
7	Intl Brotherhood of Electrical Workers	$32,680,295	97	2
8	National Education Assn	$31,113,780	93	6
9	Laborers Union	$29,816,800	92	7
10	Service Employees International Union	$28,889,132	95	3
11	Teamsters Union	$28,876,259	93	6
12	Carpenters & Joiners Union	$28,827,308	89	10
13	American Federation of Teachers	$28,194,891	98	0
14	Communications Workers of America	$27,958,106	98	0
15	Citigroup Inc	$27,583,712	50	49
16	American Medical Assn	$26,846,420	39	60
17	United Auto Workers	$26,509,902	98	0
18	Machinists & Aerospace Workers Union	$25,924,777	98	0
19	National Auto Dealers Assn	$25,613,758	32	67
20	United Parcel Service	$24,987,614	36	62

Wow, over 331 million dollars of union dues that did not go for the members welfare.

Seven Post Office Facts - Did you know that the amount of first class mail through the US Post Office has been less than junk mail since 2005.
The Post Office cannot lay off staff because union contracts prohibit layoffs.
It lost $20 billion since 2007.
Eighty percent of Post Offices lose money each year.
Federal law forbids closing post offices for solely economic reasons.
FedEx spends 43% of its budget on staff and the Post Office spends 80% on staff.
More than 47% of all mail does not go through the Post Office, but to competitors.

IRS - It happened in 1862. It started with the high cost of the US at war with itself. To help pay for the Civil War, Congress established the Bureau of Internal Revenue. President Abraham Lincoln signed the bill into law, for the feds to collect a three percent tax on incomes ranging from $600 to $10,000, and five percent on incomes over $10,000. <u>It was passed as a temporary law.</u>

The Bureau became the Internal Revenue Service in 1913 when the 16th amendment was added to the Constitution permitting the Government to collect a tax on income. *How ironic that a few days before we celebrate our independence, they took away our independence. . . from taxes.*

How to Change Time - The government began year-long experiments that may literally change time, at least the time on your microwave or coffee pot.

The time service department at the U.S. Naval Observatory, one of two official timekeeping agencies in the federal government, and the group that oversees the U.S. power grid is proposing an experiment which would allow more frequency variation in electricity than it does now. The purpose is to find ways to make the grid more cost effective.

Some clocks keep time based on the rate of the electrical current that powers them. If the current varies, clocks run fast or slow. Power companies monitor and correct the frequency to keep it constant.

Obviously, computers, TVs with cable, and other devices that are not plugged or get the time signal from another source in will not be affected.

The North American Electric Reliability Corp. which runs the nation's interlocking web of transmission lines and power plants says East Coast clocks may run as much as 20 minutes fast over a year, with other parts of the country having less of an effect. It is also possible that the effects will be negligible. *As Kermit says, "Time's fun when you are having flies."*

NASA - Interesting that the US space agency, the National Aeronautics and Space Administration (NASA), was authorized by Congress during 1958 and we now witness the end of a NASA space shuttle program. Many inventions and discoveries that touch us every day came as byproducts from that program. NASA holds 6,300 patents.

A few of the things from NASA that you may know, such as invisible braces, scratch-resistant lenses. memory foam (like tempurpedic beds), infrared ear thermometer, athletic shoe cool insoles, long distance communications via satellite, adjustable smoke detector, lightweight cordless tools (with Black & Decker), water filters, thermal gloves and boots, LED lights, heart pump, artificial limbs, aircraft anti-icing system, enriched baby food (in over 90%), freeze drying and thousands more.

NASA Satellite Data - Remote Sensing Journal reports that NASA satellite data from the years 2000 through 2011 show the Earth's atmosphere is allowing far more heat to be released into space than alarmist models have predicted. Dr Roy Spencer, who works on the space agency's temperature-monitoring satellites, claimed they showed 'a huge discrepancy' between the real levels of heating and forecasts by the United Nations and other groups. He used data from the satellite to dispute the notion of global warming. He says his data indicated that far less future global warming will occur than United Nations models predicted.

Related news - A federal wildlife biologist whose observation in 2004 of presumably drowned polar bears in the Arctic helped to galvanize the global warming movement has been placed on administrative leave and is being investigated for scientific misconduct, possibly over the veracity of that article.

A Taxing Matter - Why do gas prices end in 0.9 cents? Unfortunately, the origins of the increment are murky. Some sources attribute the practice to the 1920s and 1930s, when the gasoline tax was nine-tenths of a cent.

Stations would simply slap the extra 0.9 onto the advertised price of a gallon to give Uncle Sam his cut. Others theorize that slashing 0.1 cent off the price undercut competitors back in the days when gas was just a few cents per gallon.

Although most drivers simply ignore the extra 0.9 cents, oil companies certainly do not. In one year, Americans consumed 378 million gallons of gas per day, and that extra 0.9 cents per gallon was collectively worth nearly $3.5 million a day. On the flip side, you could also argue that customers collectively saved around $340,000 per day, thanks to stations' reluctance to round up to the next penny.

National Speed Limits - Sometimes the citizens win, but it takes a while. During the oil crisis of the 1970s, the US government was desperate to convince Americans to burn less gasoline. Realizing that cars are more fuel-efficient when driven at lower speeds, Congress decided to force people to drive slower. In 1974, it enacted a law that set the national speed limit at 55 mph, along with a threat: Any state that didn't comply with the rule would lose its federal highway funding.

Congress may have set the speed limit, but it was up to individual states to enforce it and many states did not appreciate being told what to do. In fact, some states made a mockery of the law. Nevada, for example, refused to write tickets to speeders unless they were caught traveling more than 70 mph; instead, offenders received $5 "energy wasting" fines.

So, did the lowered speed limit actually accomplish its goal? While the law did cut consumption by 167,000 barrels per day, the savings represented a drop in demand of about one percent. Highway fatalities also dropped with the lower speed limit, but some analysts have theorized that this reduction was the result of a general decrease in recreational driving rather than slower speeds.

Nonetheless, both state governments and average citizens whined about the law so much that Congress bumped up the speed limit to 65 mph in 1987, then did away with the law completely in 1995, putting speed limits back in the hands of the states, where it belongs.

Smithsonian - During 1846, the Smithsonian Institution in Washington, D.C. was established by the United States Congress as an institute of learning. An Englishman, James Smithson, made it possible to create the eponymous institute with his gift of $500,000. It was an enormous amount of money back then.

The Smithsonian Institution supports a wide variety of research projects and publications. It also houses the national museums of natural history, technology, art and history. One of the most popular is the National Air Museum which contains the Wright Brothers original biplane.

It is the world's largest museum and research complex and includes 19 museums and galleries as well as the National Zoological Park. Most Smithsonian museums and the National Zoo are free and open every day of the year except December 25.

The Smithsonian has something for everyone from every era. You can find Archie Bunker's chair and Fonzie's leather jacket among other treasures. It provides a much better experience than Disney World or any other amusement park, especially for school age children, from first grade through college.

If you are in the area, plan to spend a few days. If you are not in the area, there is much you can still learn from the comfort of your armchair and the Internet. You will be surprised at what you can learn. One of the few places around DC that is refreshingly free of politics.

Daylight Saving Time - It looks like we saved enough time this year. This weekend, at 2:00 AM on November 6th, Daylight Saving Time will end, and revert back to Daylight Standard Time (turn your clock back to 1:00 AM). Actually, the debate is still raging, whether clock shifting is a benefit or curse. It seems to me that all the debate, clock changing, and missed appointments more than offsets the benefit.

Am reminded of the Indian wise man who said that changing the clock was like cutting the bottom of a blanket off and sewing in on the top. *If you live in Arizona, Hawaii, or parts of Indiana, and other parts of the modern world, please disregard this message as you are smart enough not to believe in hobgoblins or time monsters.*

Statue of Liberty - The Statue of Liberty was presented to the American people by the French and unveiled in October 1886. The statue in New York Harbor is the work of French sculptor Frederic Auguste Bartholdi. He called it Liberty Enlightening the World. The 152-foot high statue, weighing 225 tons sits on Liberty Island.

Inscribed on a tablet inside the pedestal of 'Miss Liberty' is a poem by Emma Lazarus. It describes the statue of a woman holding a book and torch. The symbol of freedom, she waits for immigrants who must pass by her on their way to Ellis Island and admission to America.

"Not like the brazen giant of Greek fame, with conquering limbs astride from land to land; here at our sea-washed, sunset gates shall stand a mighty woman with a torch, whose flame is the imprisoned lightning, and her name Mother of Exiles. From her beacon-hand glows world-wide welcome; her mild eyes command the air-bridged harbor that twin cities frame. Keep ancient lands, your storied pomp cries she with silent lips. Give me your tired, your poor, your huddled masses yearning to breathe free, the wretched refuse of your teeming shore. Send these, the homeless, tempest-tost [sic] to me; I lift my lamp beside the golden door!"

On August 3, 1957, U.S. President Dwight Eisenhower changed the name from Bedloe's Island to Liberty Island.

Really Rich People - Half of the top 20 of the wealthiest people in the US are from the computer industry and 9 of the top 25 are family heirs.

Four Waltons (stores) $149B, Gates (Microsoft) $89B, two Kochs (energy) Bezos (Amazon) $85B, $96B, Zuckergerg (Facebook) $70B, three Mars (candy) $60B, Buffett (conglomerate) $75B, Ellison (Oracle) $58B.

These few distort the numbers so greatly because their wealth is so great. Over a quarter trillion dollars with just that handful of people. Add the next bunch and there is another quarter trillion dollars. The top 25 added together are worth well over half a trillion dollars.

The technology folks make up half of the top twenty and are all new wealth, made from working for a living. Their hard work and ideas created hundreds of thousands of jobs. Microsoft produced at least three billionaires and hundreds of millionaires. Apple also produced at least 300 millionaires.

Just 4 of the top 25 richest people in America made it from investing - Buffett companies and stocks, Soros and Paulson hedge funds, and Icann leveraged buyouts. Buffett and Soros are in their 80s, Kochs are 75, and Mars are in their 70s and 80s.

It is difficult to estimate how many millions of people are employed by these few and how many lives have been made better by them. Difficult to fault them for being wealthy when we buy their stock, which accounts for the vast majority of their wealth.

Earmarks and Pork Barrels - Earmarks are defined as, "Provisions associated with legislation that specify certain congressional spending priorities or in revenue bills that apply to a very limited number of individuals or entities."

Pork Barrel usually refers to, "Spending that is intended to benefit constituents of a politician in return for their political support, either in the form of campaign contributions or votes." It supposedly originated in a pre-Civil War practice of giving slaves a barrel of salt pork as a reward and requiring them to compete among themselves to get their share of the handout.

Both terms are derogatory and used interchangeably. Either are requested by only one chamber of Congress; not specifically authorized; not competitively awarded; and serve only a local or special interest. Below are a few examples.

$1,800,000 was earmarked for a climate model evaluation program. This is on top of the $2 Billion in stimulus money for the climate science program, and another half a billion in stimulus money that the White House directed to global warming. *I am getting hot just thinking about it.*

Fenelon Funicular - The Fenelon Place Elevator in Dubuque, Iowa is an incline railway running 296 feet from bottom to top. It first went into business in 1882, and has been owned by the same family since 1912. It was originally built so workers could get up the hill quickly to go home for lunch. Now visitors take the one dollar ride up the hill for the scenic views.

A while back, four inspectors from the US Transportation Security Administration arrived in black vehicles to secure the 'railroad' and conduct inspections and investigations to prevent attacks.

To give you an idea of how far 296 feet is, the farthest baseball throw was 445 feet 10 inches by Glen Gorbous of Canada August 1, 1957 while playing with the St. Louis Cardinals Triple A team.

A funicular is a railway up the side of a mountain pulled by a moving cable and having counterbalancing ascending and descending cars. *Yep, that's our government dollars at work. Oh, we are safe. They did not find any security threats or WMDs.*

Louisiana - The United States took possession of the Louisiana Territories from France in December 1803, just before Christmas. The treaty that France drew up, sold the territory to the United States for $15 million.

The Louisiana Purchase effectively doubled the size of the existing US. It was 827,987 square miles, at about $18 per square mile.

The area was later made into 15 states, created or *partially created from the Louisiana Purchase: Arkansas, *Colorado, Iowa, *Kansas, Louisiana, *Minnesota, Missouri, *Montana, Nebraska, *New Mexico, North Dakota, Oklahoma, South Dakota, *Texas and *Wyoming.

US government bailout in action - When Congress was done with it, the proposal for saving the US financial system ballooned to 451 pages and is loaded with pork barrel spending - including, a cut in taxes on toy arrows and an extended tax break on "wool products." Backers of the arrow tax exemption - section 503, say it reverses a 2004 law that sharply increased tax rates on cheap kids' arrows.

Also provisions for company credit for employee bicycle riders, cost recovery for motorsport racetrack facilities, tax incentives for investment in District of Columbia, Indian employment credit, income averaging for amounts received from Exxon Valdez incident, Paul Wellstone and Pete Domenici Mental Health Parity and Addiction Equity Act, special projects on Federal land, carbon tax code audit, etc. *I could go on.*

Leaving Paradise - For every home buyer coming into the state, there are three Californians selling and moving elsewhere. Prices have shot up 71% since 2011. Every year from 2000 through 2015, more people left California than moved in. According to census estimates, in the year ending July 1, 2008, the state lost 144,000 people, more than any other US state. The median house price averaging $473,000 in 2016, double the US average.

California has not seen such a prolonged period of departures outweighing newcomers since the downturn of the early 1990s. The jobs with the biggest net loss to other states from 2005 through 2015 were cashiers, cooks, truck drivers, material movers, retail sales reps and customer service reps.

According to those leaving:

> - soaring unemployment (third highest in the nation);
> the cost of living - taxes, food, gas, rents, home prices;
> - congestion;
> - overcrowding;
> - bad schools;
> - bad air;
> - a state government inching ever closer to bankruptcy;
> the omnipresent threat of more cuts to public services and tax increases.

WPA - The Works Progress Administration was in effect from 1935 to 1943, cost $11 Billion, and was designed to increase the purchasing power of persons on relief by employing them on useful projects. WPA's building program included the construction of 116,000 buildings, 78,000 bridges, and 651,000 miles of road, and the improvement of 800 airports. It also sponsored art projects and musical performances.

> Politicians have the unique ability to believe they are the one _in_ seven billion people, rather than just one _of_ seven billion people.

At its peak WPA had about 3.5 million persons on its payrolls. There was sharp criticism of the WPA by the Senate in 1939; the same year the WPA appropriation was cut, name changed to Work Projects Administration, several projects were abolished, and others were curtailed.

A strike of thousands of WPA workers to prevent a cut in wages on building projects was unsuccessful. Steadily increasing employment in the private sector caused further drastic cuts in WPA appropriations and payrolls.

Another NASA Failure - NASA launched an investigation into a carbon dioxide detecting satellite's failed launch, which disappointed and frustrated scientists studying global warming.

The Orbiting Carbon Observatory satellite failed to reach orbit after its 4:55 a.m. Eastern time liftoff, Feb 25, from Vandenberg Air Force Base in California, NASA reported. While the failure comes as a major disappointment to scientists hoping to use the satellite's data to study global warming, NASA is not giving up on this area of research, according to Michael Freilch, director of NASA's Earth Science division.

Money Supply - This book is like the money supply in Washington. If it is printed, it exists. They are both backed by nothing more than thoughts. This book is not free. We pay taxes on money we receive. You can decide you do not want to purchase a copy. You can decide that you no longer wish to earn money, but you cannot opt out of taxes.

Daylight Saving Time - Most countries in the world observe it, but in varying ways. Those closest to the equator do not need to, because the day and night are about equal at 12 hours. Those closest to the poles have the longest days in the summer. Polls show that some people enjoy it for the extra hours of sun at the end of the day.

The increase in electricity in the morning is less than the savings in the evening, with a net decrease of about one percent per day in the US. New Zealand saves about three percent a day. *When I was growing up, they said it was good for the farmers. I guess some farmer finally told them that cows and chickens can't tell time.*

California going Bookless – Then California Governor Arnold Schwarzenegger announced plans to phase out school textbooks in favor of digital learning aids. The measure allows California schoolchildren to ditch traditional math and science textbooks for digital versions.

"The textbooks are outdated, as far as I'm concerned, and there's no reason why our schools should have our students lug around these antiquated and heavy and expensive textbooks."

California is the first state in the United States to introduce such an initiative. The move comes as Schwarzenegger looked to slash spending across a range of sectors in a bid to narrow California's projected 24 billion dollar budget deficit.

Schwarzenegger said initial savings from the plan would be between 300-400 million dollars. If the scheme was widened to cover more subjects, hundreds of millions more would be trimmed from the annual budget, he said.

Shades of 1984 - For those who have not read George Orwell's book, "1984" it might be a good time to do so, or at least read an online summary of it.

> Government is the great fiction through which everybody endeavors to live at the expense of everybody else.

Tiburon, a town of 8,000 in Marin County, CA, officials want to photograph every car and use the license plate information to solve crimes in the town of 9,000.

Many see the plan as an intrusion into the rights of citizens, but officials say it is a sensible precaution that absolutely will not cross privacy lines. The town manager says, "The proposal has been misunderstood."

College Football -Unlike the original Founding Fathers, our current batch of politicians have more important stuff to discuss. While debating the wars, National Health Care, the waning economy, etc. Cars and banks are not enough, now they get into football.

A House subcommittee has approved legislation aimed at forcing college football to switch to a playoff system to determine a national champion.

The bill would ban the promotion of a post season NCAA Division 1 football game as a national championship unless that title contest is the result of a playoff. The measure passed by a voice vote by a House Energy and Commerce Committee subcommittee. *That should solve the economic crisis.*

Another View of the Economy - Household "wealth" fell by $5.1 trillion in the fourth quarter of 2008. To put that economic impact into perspective, let's look at it alongside the President's $787 billion stimulus package.

If you consider the magnitude of the loss on an individual basis, it is the equivalent of losing $5,100 at the racetrack one day, vowing to give up gambling forever, but finding $787 in your glove box and rushing back to get it all down on the next race.

Censor This - (*Forgive the rant, but more stupidity follows*) California Assemblyman Joel Anderson's proposed censorship of Google Map and Google Earth would blur images of hospitals, schools, places of worship, and government buildings in an effort to prevent terrorists from gathering information about the potential attack targets.

Military officials have indicated hospitals and schools are at risk for terrorist attacks if they can be easily identified.

Privacy groups and government bodies in the United States and United Kingdom have convinced Google to blur certain buildings and people's faces in Google's online image resources.

So now the terrorists will not be able to see a picture of the courthouse at 22 Main Street, because it is blurred - as if they need a picture. Of course this location information is not available elsewhere, like paper maps, online phone books, Yellow Pages, calling 411, etc.

Political Ages - Thomas Jefferson was 33 when he wrote the Declaration of Independence.

Theodore Roosevelt was 24 when he was elected to the New York State Legislature and became President at 42. John F. Kennedy was 43 when he was elected President. Ted Kennedy was 30 when he entered the Senate. Andrew Jackson joined the Senate at age 29, created the Democratic party and had a donkey as his personal totem. The party used the donkey symbol in honor of him.

CCRAP - In 2000, delegates of Canada's United Alternative convention needed a name for their newly formed political party. They came up with Canadian Conservative Reform Alliance Party, which in addition to taking roughly six minutes to pronounce was abbreviated CCRAP. Organizers quickly realized the blunder and changed the party's name to the Canadian Reform Conservative Alliance.

Land of The Free Land - Some communities need residents. Some need jobs. Some need development. In order to get those things, a few communities will give you free land.

For the most part, the places doing this are rural communities without much in the way of work opportunities, but doesn't the whole world work virtually now?

Several small cities in rural Kansas will give you a land lot if you agree to build housing of at least 1,000 square feet on it. If one lot is not large enough and you would like to garden, the city of Marquette, Kansas would be pleased give you a second lot adjacent to the first, also for free. These are developed lots with water, sewer, and electricity.

Muskegon, Michigan is giving away free land for companies that create new industrial jobs. You get five acres for 25 jobs; create 100 jobs and get 30 acres. The free sites have full utilities and easy access to highways, a deep-water port, railroads, and the Muskegon County Airport.

There are opportunities in Nebraska, Iowa, Maine, Michigan, Alaska, Kansas, Minnesota, North Dakota and Wisconsin.

Big Government - Small Government - Many discuss the size of big government, but most do not realize that the local governments are much larger than the federal government. State and local employment has been reduced, mostly through not filling vacancies, by 258,000, or 1.3%, to 19.2 million workers, reports the Bureau of Labor Statistics. Compensation for government workers accounts for half of the $2 trillion spent annually by governments. For workers who remain, compensation increased 2.5% compared with 0.8% for private-sector workers for the year ended June 30, 2010.

The federal workforce, meanwhile, grew 3.4% to 2.2 million during the past year and promises to keep growing. *The worst part of having this many federal and state workers, is that when they retire, we get to pay for them for the rest of their (and our) lives.*

Government Signs - The Federal Highway Administration decided that it takes way too much time for us to read road signs printed in ALL CAPITAL LETTERS. So, the newest FHA Manual of Uniform Traffic Control Devices says that all such signs must be replaced by those with an initial capital letter, followed by the remaining letters in lower case.

According to an article in the New York Post, New York City has already begun the process of changing its 250,900 signs. City officials estimate it at $110 each that amounts to $27.6 million, just for New York City. *Maybe this is a secret 'shovel ready' project to keep prisoners busy.*

One Dollar Bill Fact - Did you know one dollar bills are made in twelve different cities? They are made in Boston, New York City, Philadelphia, Cleveland, Richmond, Atlanta, Chicago, St. Louis, Minneapolis, Kansas City, Dallas, and San Francisco. Each has a letter associated with the city. They are, in order, A Boston, B New York, C Philadelphia, etc. Those letters are all associated with the numbers printed four times on the bill.

The black letter in the seal on the left side of the bill tells us which city it is printed in. The four black numbers toward each corner correspond to the letter. So, a bill printed in Philadelphia has a C in the seal and would have the number three printed, because C is the third letter of the alphabet. Incidentally, they print 16,600,000 bills a day. *I just checked my pocket and had bills printed in four different cities.*

Street Signs - The Federal Highway Administration is ordering all local governments, from the tiniest towns to the largest cities, to go out and buy new street signs that federal bureaucrats say are easier to read. The rules are part of a tangle of regulations included in the Manual of Uniform Traffic Control Devices.

The 800-plus page book tells local governments they:

-- Should increase the size of the letters on street signs from the current 4 inches to 6 inches on all roads with speed limits over 25 miles per hour.

> The CIA task force assessing damage from leaked US diplomatic documents named the 'WikiLeaks Task Force', has the same abbreviation as a popular online acronym, WTF.
>
> *How appropriate.*

-- Install signs with new reflective letters more visible at night by January 2018.

-- Whenever street name signs are changed for any reason, they can no longer be in ALL CAPS.

In Milwaukee this will cost the city nearly $2 million, or double the city's entire annual budget for traffic control.

"If you can't read it, you can't see it, or you can't comprehend it, it could be a distraction to you," said the Federal Highway Administrator. "You could be in an accident, negative consequences could occur." *Hmmm, now about those illegal aliens that can't read English. . .*

Cleveland Recycles - The city plans to sort through curbside trash to make sure residents are recycling and fine them $100 if they do not. The move is part of a high-tech collection system the city with new trash and recycling carts embedded with radio frequency identification chips and bar codes.

The chips will allow city workers to monitor how often residents roll carts to the curb for collection. If a chip shows a recyclable cart has not been brought to the curb in weeks, a trash supervisor will sort through the trash for recyclables.

Trash carts containing more than 10 percent recyclable material could lead to a $100 fine. It plans to roll out to nearly all of the city's residences.

The city stepped up enforcement of ordinances governing trash collection by issuing 2,900 tickets, nearly five times more tickets than in the previous year. Those infractions include citations for people who put out their trash too early or fail to bring in their garbage cans from the curb in a timely manner. The Division of Waste Collection is on track to meet its goal of issuing 4,000 citations a year. Fines for excessive trash will range from $250 to $500 depending on the amount.

The Washington, D.C. suburb of Alexandria, Va., announced it would also issue carts to check whether people are recycling.

Bees - Keeping bees in New York City is illegal, so for years beekeepers have kept their hives on roof tops or in community gardens. If a neighbor makes a complaint, the owners must disassemble their hives or face steep fines and exterminator fees.

Recently a city council bill was introduced to legalize beekeeping. *That will certainly help with the billion dollar budget shortfall the city faces.*

Library of Congress - The U.S. Library of Congress has begun uploading its audio archives to iTunes, and it will soon begin to post videos on YouTube, in an effort to make its materials easier for the public to access.

The decision to post audio and video on iTunes and YouTube follows a successful launch of a library photo archive on Flickr. Since January 2008, the library's photos on Flickr have been viewed about 15.7 million times, and more than 20,000 Flickr users have added the Library of Congress as a contact.

> *Ideas in politics are much like poetry;*
>
> *they need no inner logical structure.*

Some items - 100-year-old films from Thomas Edison's studio, book talks with contemporary authors, early industrial films from Westinghouse factories, first-person audio accounts, a rough draft of the Declaration of Independence and the contents of President Abraham Lincoln's pockets on the night of his assassination.

Salt Lake Liquor - Utah is easing its liquor laws again to encourage tourism, but the state's most-visited city is stuck. A review of state records shows Utah is quickly running out of liquor licenses for bars and restaurants.

State lawmakers, most of whom are Mormon and do not drink, limit the number of bars and restaurants that can serve liquor based on the state's population and no more than 361 bars can open in Utah and no more than 546 restaurants can serve beer, wine, and liquor.

The dwindling supply of licenses is a direct threat to Salt Lake's downtown nightlife district. Finding and getting to bars can be a nightmare for tourists thanks to a decades-old city ordinance that limits the number of bars that can operate to two per block face.

The mayor is seeking to lift the two-bar limit so existing pockets of nightlife can continue to grow on the heels of a major change in state law, that customers will no longer have to fill out an application and pay a fee to enter a bar.

New licenses would only become available as existing licenses are forfeited or the population grows. *Who says religion and politics don't mix.*

\---------------------

> "Those who hammer their guns into plows will plow for those who do not."
> ~Thomas Jefferson

Guns for Sale - Smith & Wesson shares have increased 338% since hitting a low of $1.53 in October 2008. The government run National Instant Criminal Background Check System reports that it received 1.3 million applications in March 2009. This is a 30% jump from the previous year and an 80% jump from 1999. California, Kentucky, and Texas are the leaders requesting new applications.

The government's plan to curb gun buying seems to be working just like other government curbing programs, such as curbing spending.

\-----------------------

Fun with Words - According to the government, Webster needs to be updated.

Let's spend a trillion dollars on healthcare and call it a *savings.*

Let's change the definition of illegal (not conforming to the law) to *get free stuff.*

Let's add 26 million people to the healthcare system and call it *reducing costs.*

Let's call the new healthcare system universal by including illegal aliens, but *leave out nine million Americans and exempt the politicians from participation.*

Let's spend a 1 or 2 trillion dollars for fiscal stimulus to get us out of a 2009 recession, but *not actually plan to spend most of it until 2011.*

Let's take over the auto companies, but say *we do not want to be in the car business.*

Let's lower the pay of CEOs to save money, but *raise the pay of politicians.*

Let's berate auto CEOs for flying to Washington and wasting our money, but *give Pelosi and others a free plane ride back and forth to California.*

Let's call people rich, if they make over $250,000 a year, but *tax them as rich starting at $200,000.*

Let's say we are getting rid of lobbyists, *and make them paid consultants.*

Let's say we are the government of the people, by the people, and for the people - *Oops, sorry, no one has said that for a long time.*

Czar - Our government has appointed <u>czars</u> for autos, healthcare, insurance, and finance, so I decided to look up the definition. It is taken from the word Caesar, which means emperor, a male monarch or emperor, title of the ruler of Russia, a person having great power. *Scary, isn't it? The US could have more czars than Russia. Maybe that's why Obama really went to Russia, to find out the optimum number of czars the US should have.*

The New York City Police Department has a $4.8 billion annual budget, larger than all but 19 of the world's armies.

Dollar Coins - Did you ever wonder who the heck Sacagawea (sacka ja wee a) was and what her baby's name was. The Shoshone woman, Sacagawea, a member of the Lewis and Clark Expedition, is shown on the coin carrying her son Jean Baptiste Charbonneau, who was later nicknamed Pomp. She was a slave girl, given to Toussaint Charbonneau, a French trader born in Montreal. She was six months pregnant when she joined the expedition.

The 2009 Sacagawea dollar, along with the Presidential Dollar series, is one of the two current United States dollar coins.

The coins are made from pure copper with a manganese brass outer clad. Unlike most other coins in circulation, the outer alloy has a tendency to tarnish quite severely in circulation, resulting in a loss of the golden patina. The Mint suggests the uneven tarnishing effect gives the coins an antique finish that accentuates the profile and adds depth to the depiction of Sacagawea and her child.

The first Native American series coin was released in January 2009 and has a reverse that depicts a Native American woman sowing seeds of the Three Sisters, symbolizing the Indian tribes' contributions to agriculture. Like the Presidential Dollar, the year of issue, mint mark, and motto E Pluribus Unum have been moved to the edge of the coin to allow more room for the design.

Unlike the Presidential $1 coins from before 2009, "In God We Trust" will remain on the front and the vacant space on the edge lettering will be taken up by thirteen stars, symbolizing the Thirteen Colonies.

The chief stumbling-block to the success of the golden dollar is the continued presence of the $1 bill. The lesson demonstrated by the Susan B. Anthony, experience, and learned by all countries that have introduced a high-denomination coin since 1979, is that the equivalent paper note must be removed from circulation. The only country not to learn that lesson is the United States.

Although the Sacagawea dollar is not widespread in the United States, it is very popular in Ecuador and other foreign countries that have made the US dollar their currency. An estimated 500 million coins, approximately half of those minted, are used in Ecuador, El Salvador, and other Latin American countries.

How Lobbyists Get Their Name - A lobbyist is a person who tries to influence legislation on behalf of a special interest. One story states that the term originated at the Willard Hotel in Washington, DC, where it was used by Ulysses S. Grant to describe the political wheelers and dealers frequenting the hotel's lobby in order to access him as he was often found there, enjoying a cigar and brandy.

There is an online lobby data base to find out what is being spent by lobbyists on Washington politicians. You can check by various criteria or country. *We do not condone bribes in the US, but lobbyists; well that's a different story.*

Stimulated Pork - The term, pork is sometimes used to describe legislative appropriations meant to favor specific projects, to gain favor, or repay political debts for legislators. Now we have something new - stimulated pork.

The USDA's Agricultural Marketing Service spent $24.3 million of stimulus funds for pork. It bought $16.9 million of canned pork, $2.6 million of ham, and $4.8 million of sliced ham. The Agriculture Department is sending the meat to food banks as part of a $150 million effort to feed hungry Americans.

Stimulating Stimulus Study - As part of the past stimulus, Kaiser Permanente received 25 million dollars and embarked on a two year genetic analysis of 100,000 older Californians. Genetic data from a diverse group of California patients will be gleaned from samples of saliva.

Does not look like any new jobs were created, but researchers will be able to study the data and seek insights into the interplay between genes, the environment, and disease, along with access to detailed electronic health records, patient surveys, and records of environmental conditions where the patients live and work.

The object is to produce a very large amount of genetic and phenotypic (what organisms look like) data that investigators and scientists can begin asking questions of. Researchers will look for genetic influences that determine why some people suffering from cardiovascular disease and type 2 diabetes deteriorate more rapidly than others, and find which genetic factors reduce the effectiveness of various drugs or make them hazardous. *I thought the stimulus money was to be spent to stimulate jobs?*

Economic Recovery - There is an interesting web site that shows where the recovery money is being spent. It shows many of the projects funded by the ARRA. It is a fun read if you want to scare yourself with details or where your tax dollars were being spent, like waterless latrines in Arkansas and a picnic shelter at Turkey Point Park in Kansas.

A good deal were for construction projects as they were supposed to be, but pork always finds its way in. A few more goodies, $5 million and another $1.75 million, the Jennie-o Turkey Store, MN, (the only description for both is "small turkey deli breasts"). $3 million to Accenture to help construct a data warehouse for the Farm Service Agency. $707,000 to increase demand for the National Health Service. $90 million to Leland Stanford University to develop three x-ray instruments. $27.9 million for "The purpose of this procurement is to obtain the services of a broadband industry consultant to implement the statutory requirements of the American Recovery Act and Reinvestment Act of 2009."

Especially interesting were the amounts to outlying areas, such as the $2 Billion to Puerto Rico, $93 million to the Virgin Islands, $78,000 to the American Samoa Coalition against domestic and sexual violence (*that is a real jobs booster*). Guam received money for Catholic Social

Services, Salvation Army, Guam coalition against social assault, Soroptimist Club of Guam, an organization of business women, and more. *Seems some folks like pork more than I do.*

Big Brother Tracks Trash - *It could happen here.* In England, More than 2.5 million homes now have wheelie bins fitted with microchips to weigh their contents. This was an increase of nearly two-thirds in just a year. The bins, which can be electronically identified and weighed, are designed for 'pay-as-you-throw' rubbish tax schemes. Families that put out more waste will pay higher taxes to their local council.

The spread of chipped bins marks the revival of a tax idea that the Government appeared to have abandoned, but the latest check showed 20% of all those that collect household rubbish. According to the responses from town halls, 2,629,052 homes have now been given bins with chips.

A spokesman for the Department of Environment, Food and Rural Affairs said: 'There are no Government plans to introduce microchips in bins. Any use of microchips is a local authority decision - some councils use them to monitor levels of waste. This is not about spying on people or fining them.'

However, back in 2008 nearly 100 councils ran investigations into the contents of their residents' bins, in some cases to check on what rubbish they dump and in others to try to obtain information on their incomes and lifestyles. *Sounds like taxing is coming to both ends of the consumption cycle.*

Census Jobs - I recently read about a friend of a friend who just started her job with the Census Bureau. She will have two days of training for her job, which will consist of opening envelopes, removing the documents, and straightening the papers as needed to be scanned by someone else. Another person will check the envelopes to make sure they are empty. They are paid $17 an hour, but no benefits. *Hmm, sounds like easy money.*

Unreliable - TRUE - From the UK Telegraph paper, Nicole Mamo, 48, wanted to post an advert for a £5.80-an-hour domestic cleaner on her local Jobcentre Plus website.

The text of the advert ended by stating that any applicants for the post "must be very reliable and hard-working".

But when Ms Mamo called the Jobcentre Plus in Thetford, Norfolk, the following day she was told that her advert would not be displayed instore.

A Jobcentre Plus worker claimed that the word "reliable" meant they could be sued for discriminating against unreliable workers. *Makes me want to go ARRRGH! What hath politics wrought?*

Tall Presidents - Did you know that in the past 27 US presidential elections, the shorter candidate has won only six times? Handlers for Jimmy Carter (5' 9") went to great lengths to prevent him from having to stand next to the taller Gerald Ford (6 foot+). It worked, Carter won.

Eighteen presidents have been 6 foot or taller. James Madison was the shortest at 5 foot 4.

Mitt Romney is 6'2", Barack Obama is 6'1", Donald Trump is 6'2".

> Michigan is the only state that has a statute prohibiting height discrimination

Did you also know that Napoleon was 5 foot 6 or so, depending on what you read), Paul Simon and Dudley Moore 5 foot 2.

Queen Elizabeth and Stamps - The world's first adhesive postage stamps were issued by Great Britain in 1840, as the "Penny Black" depicting Queen Victoria. It began designating British stamps by the depiction of the country's sovereign. Great Britain is the only country allowed by international postal regulations to omit a text name of the issuing country.

In 1966 Arnold Machin sculpted a bust of Queen Elizabeth for the Royal Mail. It has been in continuous use since then, and has been reproduced more than 320 billion times. Three copies of the original bust were known to exist, but recently a fourth one was discovered at the Machin family home.

Lost in Translation - When officials asked for the Welsh translation of a road sign, they thought the reply was the answer they needed.

All official road signs in Wales are bilingual, so the local authority e-mailed its in-house translation service for the Welsh version of, "No entry for heavy goods vehicles. Residential site only."

Unfortunately, the e-mail response to the Swansea council said in Welsh, "I am not in the office at the moment. Send any work to be translated."

Red Light Photos - California's three-judge appellate panel unanimously found a total lack of evidence from Santa Ana, California red light camera program and become increasingly upset at the conduct of cities and photo enforcement vendors.

The decision calls into question the legitimacy of the way red light camera trials are conducted and setting a precedent that applies to the county's three million residents and others around the country.

The attorney objected to the admission of the red light camera photographs, because the city had failed to lay a proper foundation for the evidence and the photos contained hearsay evidence. The court said the photographic records were created by a for-profit company, not a state or local government agency and the document that they created cannot be and is not an 'official record' under Evidence Code section 1280."

Bottom line - All charges were dismissed. *This may go a long way to eliminating those pesky cameras atop the lights around the country. More proof that if you get a ticket, go fight it in person, the odds are in your favor.*

In God We Trust - Although many people thought E pluribus unum was the motto, there was no official US national motto before 1956.

"In God We Trust" had been on coins since the 1800s, but it was not officially the motto of the United States of America until the congressional act designating it so in 1956. *Coincidentally, it is also the official motto of Nicaragua.*

A Brief History of the Dollar - The term 'dollar' has been around for thousands of years. Common history says it comes from the Czech name Joachimsthaler.

Thaler is a shortened form of the term. It was pronounced like 'taller'. Talers were around as recently as the 1960s in Hungary, Bohemia, and other German States.

Dalers were used in the Scandinavian countries from the 1500s until the 1920s.

The English pronunciation 'dollar' was also used for Spanish Pesos and Portuguese pieces of eight and a few other European currencies.

The US minted its first dollar in 1792. Currently, an average paper US dollar lasts about 21 months before it wears out.

Canada officially changed to the (Canadian) dollar in 1853, but they were minted in Britain until 1908. Australia and New Zealand changed to the (Australian and New Zealand) dollars, from the Pound, in the 1960s. Many other countries use a dollar as the official currency, but not all dollars are US dollars and not all are tied to the US dollar for their value.

In January 2010, Zimbabwe issued a $100 trillion note, making the note the highest denomination in the world.

Britain officially changed to the decimal system and divided the pound into 100 pennies in 1971. *Now you know why dollars make sense. . . or cents. Speaking of cents, the Lincoln penny has been around for over a hundred years.*

Yield - The sign on the highway that tells you to yield to oncoming traffic is not as old as you might think. Oklahoma police officer Clinton Riggs came up with the "yield" sign in 1950, which spread from its birthplace in Tulsa to all corners of the US.

He spent more than a decade experimenting with the sign, according to the Tulsa Police Department's history book. His goal was a sign that would not only control traffic at an intersection, but would also attach liability in a collision if one driver failed to yield.

Unions - Seems unions are suffering based on labor figures by the US Bureau of Labor Statistics. The overall unionization rate in the US was 12.1 percent, down from 12.4 percent the previous year.

The number of union workers employed in the private sector fell from approximately 7.91 million in 2008 to 7.4 million in 2016, while the number of public-sector union workers dropped from 7.86 million to 7.1 million during 2016.

In California, the highest unionized state, unionization rates were down across a range of groupings, with the most significant losses in:

  * Transportation and utilities fell from 41.7 percent to 36.4 percent
  * Public administration fell from 58.1 percent to 52.1 percent.

US Employment Numbers - Much talk about jobs saved, jobs created, company hiring, etc., but there is one number that is without politics. How many people actually have jobs is answered below. Does <u>not</u> show how many have entered the workforce since 2004, but are currently unemployed.

Employed Americans per US Bureau of Labor Statistics (not seasonally adjusted) -
July 2004 - 139.7 - Population 292.81 million
July 2010 - 138.9 - Population 309.35 million
June 2017 - 127.3 -   Population 325.34 million

Easy to notice the population increases versus the workforce decreases.

Going Metric - Back when I was in grade school, they were going to change the country to the metric system and began to teach us meters, kilometers, etc., but somewhere along the way gave up. Actually, the metric system is easier to use, once you have learned it.

History shows that the US mint created the first decimal currency in the world in 1792. Congress first authorized the use of metrics in 1866 and in 1875 became one of the original seventeen signatory nations to the Treaty of the Meter.

Congress passed the Metric Conversion Act of 1975 "to coordinate and plan the increasing use of the metric system in the United States." It also established the US Metric Board, which was dissolved in 1982. The Omnibus Trade and Competitiveness Act of 1988 amended the Metric Conversion Act of 1975 and designated the metric system as the "preferred system of weights and measures for United States trade and commerce."

It is back. The National Institute of Standards and Technology has issued two publications calling for the amendment of labeling laws to allow the <u>voluntary use of only metric units</u> on some consumer products. It says that adoption of metric labeling will simplify domestic and international commerce.

So, the current Fair Packaging and Labeling Act (FPLA), which has both, is recommended to be the Uniform Packaging and Labeling Regulation (UPLR), which has only one - metric. *This time they forgot the 'first teach 'em in school' part.*

Only 91.44 meters for a touchdown, hmmm. Hey, don't judge me until you have walked almost two kilometers in my shoes. It's 29 today, damn it's hot!

Comparisons:

* 1 gram is about the weight of a paperclip.

* 1 kilogram is a little more than 2 pounds.

* 1 liter is a little more than a quart.

* 1 kilometer is a little more than half a mile.

* 1 meter is a little more than a yard.

* 1 centimeter is a little less than half an inch.

* 1 millimeter is about the width of a pencil point.

Since we have decided to go with one unit of measurement, maybe we should consider going back to one language (English) on our packages. . .

Oil Wells in the Gulf of Mexico - API says, "There are 3,559 platforms in the Gulf that have been operating safely for 30 years. An excellent safety record. From 1947 until now, spills in the Gulf represented 1/1000th of 1% of all the oil produced. That's multiple times better than natural seepage. Much better than nature."

These are some of the US agencies that cover oil and gas drilling and production:
Bureau of Land Management,
Department of Energy,
Department of Interior,
Department of Transportation, Office of Pipeline Safety,
Energy Information Administration,

Environmental Protection Agency,
Environmental Protection Agency - Oil Program,
Environmental Protection Agency - Region 8 (Utah, etc.),
EPA Spill Prevention Control and Countermeasure (SPCC) Site,
Federal Energy Regulatory Commission,
Fossil Energy.Gov (DOE),
Minerals Management Service,
National Energy Policy Development Group (The White House),
National Petroleum Technology Office (DOE),
National Response Center,
Utah School and Institutional Trust Lands Administration.

Checks Going Away in UK - Paper checks, or Cheques (as they spell it) are scheduled to be phased out by October 2018, according to the BBC. The board of the UK Payments Council has set the date in a bid to encourage the advance of other forms of payment.

The first cheque was written 350 years ago and the decision will be greeted with disappointment by some small businesses and consumers.

The target date for the closure of the system that processes cheques has been set for 31 October 2018, after the board described the payment method as in "terminal decline".

> "Politics is not the art of the possible.
> It consists in choosing between the disastrous and the unpalatable."
> ~ J. K. Galbraith

However, there will be annual checks on the progress of other payments systems and a final review of the decision will be held before that date. "The goal is to ensure that by 2018 there is no scenario where customers, individuals or businesses, still need to use a cheque," the Payments Council said in a statement.

Personal cheque payment volumes reached a peak of 2.4 billion in 1990, and have since fallen steadily to 663 million in 2008 and down to 344.6 million during 2016.

Tax Cuts - In the unkindest cut of all, New York State is now imposing a tax on cuts. A recent audit by the state Department of Taxation and Finance slammed 33 Bruegger's Bagels franchises for failing to charge sales tax on sliced bagels. Unsliced bagels are exempt.

The audit also found that Bruegger's failed to charge tax on meals consumed on the premises.

The state slapped the owner with a hefty bill for back taxes and demanded that he begin collecting. *That is not a tax cut, it is a tax on cuts. Maybe Bruegger's should pass out knives for patrons to cut their own taxes by cutting their own bagels.*

Lights Out - The last major GE factory making incandescent light bulbs in the United States turned out the lights, literally, marking an exit for a product that began during the 1870s.

It is the result of a 2007 energy conservation measure passed by Congress that set standards essentially banning ordinary incandescent bulbs beginning in 2012. Other countries are doing the same. Some stores have announced phasing out incandescents as early as the end of 2010.

Much controversy remains as to whether the high cost of replacement bulbs is really offset by the savings in electricity. Of course, the US does not produce the replacement bulbs, they all come from overseas, so US jobs are leaving with the bulbs. LEDs appear to be the winner over all the others.

Senate Friday Votes - The US Senate had four votes on Friday during 2013, no Friday votes during 2014, fifteen Friday sessions (can't find votes) 2015.

MARRIAGE TRIVIA

Strange Marriage Customs - For the 3 days and 3 nights following weddings of Tidong people from northern Borneo, both the bride and groom are prohibited from urinating, defecating, or bathing. They believe that custom will lead to a long, happy, and fertile marriage. In order to achieve this, the newlyweds are allowed to eat and drink only very small amounts and are watched very closely for compliance by family members.

Bullet proof vests, fire escapes, windshield wipers, and laser printers were all invented by women.

Friends of Scottish brides-to-be take her by surprise and cover her with eggs, spoiled milk, feathers, and other disgusting slop and parade her around town. The purpose is to prepare the bride for marriage, because it will make marital problems seem easier by comparison.

Polterabend is a German pre-wedding tradition where friends and family come together for an informal party and break dishes, flowerpots, tiles, toilets, etc., except glasses or mirrors. The bride and groom must clean everything up to symbolize working together through future difficulties.

Men vs. Women -

- 3.9% of all women surveyed say they never wear underwear.
- 80% of American men say they would marry the same woman if they had it to do all over again.
- 50% of American women say they would marry the same man.
- 58% of men say they are happier after their divorce or separation.
- 85% of women say they are happier after divorce or separation. (*I think this varies with age.*)
- <3% of mammal species are monogamous, including Dwarf Mongooses, Beavers, otters, foxes, and Prairie Voles.

Wife Carrying - This is a sport in which male competitors race while each carrying a female teammate. The objective is for the male to carry the female through a special obstacle track in the fastest time. The sport was first introduced at Sonkajärvi, Finland.

Several types of carry may be practiced: piggyback, fireman's carry (over the shoulder), or Estonian-style (the wife hangs upside-down with her legs around the husband's shoulders, holding on his waist).

Major wife-carrying competitions are held in Sonkajärvi, Finland (where the prize depends on the wife's weight in beer), Monona and Minocqua, Wisconsin, Marquette, Michigan, and Ranchester, Wyoming, among others.

The North American Wife Carrying Championships take place every year on Columbus Day Weekend at Sunday River Ski Resort in Newry, Maine. The 18th Annual event will take place 2018. Many North American Champions go on to compete in the Finnish World Championship. *I am sure they hold it on Columbus Day so it does not interfere with the Super Bowl.*

> Married men, on average, change their underwear twice as often as single men.

Ring Finger - The Chinese have a good explanation for what the fingers represent.

The Thumb represents your Parents
The Second (Index) finger represents your Siblings
The Middle finger represents your Self
The Fourth (Ring) finger represents your Life Partner, and
The Last (Little) finger represents your Children

First, open your palms (face to face), bend the middle fingers down and hold them together - back to back. Second, open and hold the remaining three fingers and the thumb - tip to tip.

Now, try to separate your thumbs (representing the parents). They will open, because your parents are not destined to live with you (or you with them) forever.

Join your thumbs as before and separate your Index fingers (representing siblings). They will also open, because your brothers and sisters will have their own families and will lead their own separate lives.

Now join the Index fingers and separate your little fingers (representing your children). They will open too, because the children also will get married and leave.

Finally, join your Little fingers, and try to separate your Ring fingers (representing your spouse).

You cannot do it, because husband and wife should remain together all their lives.

Divorce Rate - Just read that 67% of second marriages and 73% of third marriages end in divorce. The average divorce rate for first marriages is about 41% in the United States, and the divorce rate figures have been declining.

Greatest Love Letter - A heartfelt birthday message from Johnny Cash to his wife June has been voted the greatest love letter of all time. It was hand written and the text is below.

We get old and get used to each other. We think alike. We read each other's minds. We know what the other wants without asking. Sometimes we irritate each other a little bit. Maybe sometimes take each other for granted.

But once in awhile, like today, I meditate on it and realize how lucky I am to share my life with the greatest woman I ever met. You still fascinate and inspire me. You influence me for the better. You're the object of my desire, the #1 Earthly reason for my existence. I love you very much.

Happy Birthday Princess.

John

> **If you are wrong and you shut up, you are wise.**
>
> **If you are right and you shut up, you are married.**

Food Facts

FUN FOOD FACTS

Bacon Potato Pie - Now McDonald's Japan is serving bacon potato pie, made with mashed potatoes mixed with bacon and cheese and deep fried. *Why not serve that everywhere?*

Pork Powered Protein - The protein found in bacon is extremely valuable to maintaining our energy levels and a fully functioning, healthy body, with a minimum of those nasty, waist, thigh, and butt expanding, fat building carbohydrates.

Burger Franchise - It is not what you think. Packaging up urgent care services like a Burger King and selling franchises across the country is the new American dream.

Maryland physician, Dr. Scott Burger and his partners have run an urgent-care center, named Doctors Express, for the past few years. Now, Burger wants to blanket the US with Doctors Express franchises. He and his partners hope to open 3,000 such centers around the country during the coming years.

His first franchisees opened their doors in Temple, TX, (*of course Texas*) with about two dozen more locations set for future launches in Georgia, New Jersey, South Carolina, North Carolina, Colorado and Virginia.

The model will have a physician on duty during all of its hours of operation. Doctors Express locations will also have digital X-ray equipment, a lab, and a pharmacy on location. In addition to providing urgent treatment, the centers will also conduct drug screenings, do pre-employment physicals, and provide vaccinations.

It has since been bought out by American Family Care, which is the nation's leading provider of urgent care, accessible primary care, and occupational medicine, with more than 180 clinics and 600 in-network physicians caring for nearly 3 million patients a year.

McDonald's Choices Around the World - McDonald's also serves spaghetti in the Philippines, hot dogs in Japan, pork burgers in Thailand, seaweed seasonings all over Asia, lobster salad on a bun and Poutine in Canada, ham and cheese on flat bread in France, pizza pockets in Morocco, fried salmon on a bun in Norway, fried beef stew on a bun in Poland, bacon and ketchup on a bun in England, bratwurst in Germany (of course), and beer in many countries, but not, alas, the US. . . yet.

Pink Pearls - The Pink Pearl apple is an inner pink-flesh apple cultivar with cream colored skin developed in 1944 by Albert Etter, a northern California breeder. US plant patent 723 for the Pink Pearl was obtained later that year. It is the offspring of the Surprise apple, an old English variety and was cultivated from an older rosy-fleshed apple introduced by German settlers in the mid 1800s. It is different from the Pink Lady apple, which has pink skin and is not a novelty.

Pink Pearl apples are low in calories, high in water content and contain vitamins A, C and B. They also contain a dietary fiber known as pectin, which has been shown to lower cholesterol levels, and trace amounts of boron, which has been touted for its ability to help build strong bones. Great for pink applesauce or as a color burst in salads.

Pink Pearl apples are generally medium sized, with a conical shape. They are named for the color of their flesh, which is a bright rosy pink, sometimes streaked or mottled with white. They have a translucent, yellow-green skin, and a crisp, juicy flesh with tart to sweet-tart taste. Pink Pearls are grown in various countries, but generally available in the US from California, Michigan, Ohio, Oregon, as well as Canada, England, and Australia.

Burger King Cologne - Now you can smell like a burger. I am still hoping this perfume is a joke. It's called Flame, and for a mere $3.99, you can smell like "the scent of seduction, with a hint of flame broiled meat."

BPA Update - More good news. The FDA has reached a conclusion about BPA, the chemical that first made consumers worried about plastics that could act like hormones. Late in 2014, the agency issued a statement reiterating its position that products made with BPA are safe.

Bangers and Mash - The British meal of sausage and mashed potatoes goes back a long way. Sausages can be traced back to ancient times. Victorians were skeptical of what was in a sausage, suspected horse meat, and nicknamed them 'Little Bags of Mystery'. After the outbreak of the World War, food shortages led to a dramatic reduction of meat in sausages, so producers packed them out with scraps, cereal, and water, which caused them to pop when cooked over hot fires. That is how the name bangers came to be. The mash comes from the way potatoes are cooked - mashed.

Sriracha Sauce - Rooster sauce, as it is also known has around since the 1980s. During the early 1980's, David Tran immigrated to the United States from Vietnam and settled in Los Angeles. He was unable to find a hot sauce that he liked and began making his own. His recipe was modeled and named after the local hot sauces in Sri Racha, Thailand.

He began selling the sauce out of the back of his van and as the popularity of the sauce grew. Huy Fong Foods grew swiftly and today over ten million bottles of Huy Fong Foods Sriracha Sauce are sold every year.

The bright red, multi-purpose hot sauce is made from red chili peppers, garlic, vinegar, salt, and sugar. The sauce is hot and tangy with just a hint of sweetness. The flavor is unique, addictive, and very versatile.

Sriracha sauce is often served as a condiment in Thai, Vietnamese, and Chinese restaurants throughout the United States. The most popular brand is manufactured in the US by Huy Fong Foods, which is owned by Tran.

Five Frozen Food Facts - Frozen foods do not require any added preservatives to keep them safe and consumable, because microbes cannot grow on food that is at a temperature less than 0°F. The microbes do not die at that temperature, but they stop multiplying and can come back as food is unfrozen.

Despite some freezer burn is just the result of air hitting frozen food and allowing the ice to sublimate; other color changes can be blamed on long freezing times or poor packaging. It might look gross, but if your frozen food has maintained a proper temperature, it is fine to eat.

Freezing food typically keeps items edible indefinitely, although taste and quality may diminish over time. Some items that stay tasty even after long freezes include uncooked game, poultry, and meat, which are still good after up to a year in the freezer.

Even though freezing food was used as a storage technique in cold weather climates for many years, it is believed it was first applied to industrial food sales sometime in the 1800s, when a Russian company froze a small quantity of duck and geese and shipped them to London. By 1899, the Baerselman Bros. company adapted frozen storage for their own Russia-to-England food shipping business, though they initially only operated during cold weather months.

> *old wives' tale debunked -* Freezing food does not remove any nutrients.

Potatoes Business - The potato is the world's fourth largest food crop, following rice, wheat, and corn/maize. The Inca Indians in Peru were the first to cultivate potatoes around 8,000 BC to 5,000 BC. They first came to the US in 1621.

Did you know there is a National Potato Council, Potato Association of America, World Potato Congress, US Potato Board, US Potato Promotion Board, among others. In addition, Michigan has Mich. Potato Industry Commission, Mich. Seed Potato Assoc., and Potato Growers of Mich. There are more than 100 varieties of potatoes in the US. There are many more types of potato chips from around the world.

Michigan supplies over a third of all potato chips in the US. Its annual Winter Potato Conference is one of the biggest in the country. It is overshadowed by the Potato Expo, the largest conference and trade show for the potato industry held in North America.

Potatoes contain many of the essential nutrients that the dietary guidelines recommend Americans increase in their diet. Potatoes eaten with the skin provide nearly half of the Daily Value for vitamin C and are one of the best sources of potassium (more than a banana), iodine, iron, other trace minerals, and fiber. One medium-sized potato has 100 calories and provides complex carbohydrates needed to fuel our brains. Potatoes contain no fat.

Researchers at Queen Mary, University of London noted that a small "bag of ready-salted crisps" contains less salt than a serving of "Special K, All-Bran, Golden Grahams, Cheerios, Shreddies, and every brand of cornflakes on sale in the UK."

Veal, Beef, and Offal - Veal comes from calves. It can be produced from a calf of either sex and any breed, but most veal comes from male calves of dairy cattle breeds. Limited numbers of male dairy calves are needed for breeding and the rest are sold to the veal industry. *Incidentally, rennet (necessary for cheese making) is extracted from part of the fourth stomach chamber of harvested young, unweaned calves used for veal production.*

Beef comes from older cattle and can be harvested from bulls, cows, heifers, or steers. When a cow is slaughtered, its beef is so fresh it is considered 'green'. Green beef is tough, bland, and has no sustained juiciness. Aging causes natural enzymes to break down the muscle fibers, making it more tender. Most aging takes place within one to two weeks. *Incidentally, Kobe beef, prized for its intense marbling, refers to beef from the Tajima strain of wagyu cattle, raised in Japan's Hyogo Prefecture according to rules from the Kobe Beef Marketing and Distribution Promotion Association. There are only about 3,000 head of cattle that may qualify as Kobe. No beef from Japan was allowed to be imported into the US by the USDA, starting during 2009. US 'Kobe-style' beef comes from domestically raised wagyu crossbred with Angus cattle. Black Angus is the most common beef breed (sixty percent and greater than the next seven breeds combined) of cattle in the US and its meat is used by McDonald's and Hardees.*

Offal is also called variety meats or organ meats and refers to the internal organs and entrails of a butchered animal, such as calves, pigs, sheep, and lambs. It includes most internal organs, but not muscle and bone. Certain offal dishes, including foie gras, pâté, and sweetbread are considered gourmet food in international cuisine. Others remain part of traditional regional cuisine including Scottish haggis, Jewish chopped liver, Southern US chitlins, Mexican menudo as well as many other dishes. Intestines are traditionally used as casing for sausages.

Bacon Mashed Potato Waffles - Add crumbled bacon, butter, and garlic powder to mashed potatoes and cook it in a waffle iron. Add more bacon and cheese on top, then broil until cheese melts.

Ten Salt Types - Salt is the most important ingredient in cooking. Without it, most meals would taste bland and unexciting. Salt is a crystalline mineral made of two elements, sodium (Na) and chlorine

(Cl). Sodium and chlorine are absolutely essential for life in animals, including humans. They serve important functions like helping the brain and nerves send electrical impulses. The main difference between the salts is the taste, flavor, color, texture, and convenience.

Refined Salt (table salt) is the most common. It is usually highly refined. It is heavily ground and most of the impurities and trace minerals are removed. The problem with heavily ground salt is that it can clump together. For this reason, various substances called anti-caking agents are added so that it flows freely. Food-grade table salt is almost pure sodium chloride, at 97% or higher. Iodine is often added to table salt.

Kosher Salt is used for all cooking. It dissolves fast, and its flavor disperses quickly, so chefs recommend tossing it on everything from pork roast to popcorn. Kosher salt got its name because its craggy crystals make it perfect for curing meat, a step in the koshering process. Cooks prize crystals like these, because their roughness makes it easy to pinch a perfect amount.

Himalayan Pink Salt is harvested in Pakistan. It is mined from the Khewra Salt Mine, the second largest salt mine in the world. Himalayan salt often contains trace amounts of iron oxide (rust), which gives it a pink color. It also contains small amounts of calcium, iron, potassium, and magnesium, and slightly lower amounts of sodium than table salt.

Black Salt, also known as Kala Namak, is actually a pinkish-grey color. It is mined in India and has a strong sulphuric smell. It is commonly used to spice food in Southeast Asia and has recently become more popular in the US among vegan chefs who use it for the flavor.

> *The main purpose for salt is to add flavor, not nutrition.*

Flaked Sea Salt adds a complex flavor to steamed vegetables or shellfish. This salt adds a hint of briny flavor. It comes from England's Essex coast. Its texture is soft, with sheer, pyramid-like flakes. This is the fastest-dissolving of all of the salt grains.

Celtic Salt is a type of salt that originally became popular in France. It has a greyish color and also comes from and contains a bit of water, which makes it quite moist. Celtic salt contains trace amounts of minerals and is a bit lower in sodium than table salt.

Rock Salt is used for making ice cream and de-icing. Rock salt is paired with ice in old-fashioned hand-cranked ice cream makers to regulate the temperature. It is also used to de-ice sidewalks and driveways during the winter. It is not sold for use directly on food. It is usually packaged in an organic, unprocessed form. It has large, chunky, non-uniform crystals. Minerals and other harmless impurities can give it a grayish color.

Crystalline Sea Salt is used for adding a pungent burst of flavor to just-cooked foods. These crystals can complement anything from a fresh salad to a salmon fillet. It comes from coasts from Portugal to Maine, California to the Pacific Rim. It can be either fine or coarse. The size of the irregular crystals affects how fast it dissolves. It varies in color, depending on the minerals it contains. These natural impurities can add subtle briny, sweet, or bitter flavors to the salts.

Fleur de Sel is a special-occasion table salt. It is delicately flavored and adds a perfect hint of saltiness to freshly sliced tomato or melon. It comes from coastal salt ponds in France. Some call it the caviar of sea salt and it is hand harvested. It is crystalline and melts slowly in the mouth.

Pickling Salt is used for brining pickles and sauerkraut. It is also used to brine a turkey, and is more concentrated than kosher salt. Pickling salt may come from the earth or the sea. It is almost one hundred percent sodium chloride and is the purest of salts.

Bad Fats - Not all trans fats are bad fats. Generally, bad fats are manufactured trans fats. They are also known as hydrogenated or partially hydrogenated vegetable oil. Manufactured trans fat is a heavily processed vegetable oil. Partially hydrogenated vegetable oil is one of the top ingredients in most packaged foods: cookies, snack chips, pretzels, most peanut butter, and shortening. Many fast food chains fry their foods in partially hydrogenated oils.

All hydrogenated and partially hydrogenated oils are trans fats.

Natural trans fats are found in dairy products and certain other foods. They have not shown to be harmful.

Vegetable shortening and most margarines contain trans fats. Trans fats begin as natural, polyunsaturated fats that are then exposed to chemical processes that change the molecular structure by artificially saturating the fat with hydrogen in the manufacturing process. Manufactured trans fats are synthetic saturated fats.

Manufactured trans fat raises LDL (bad) cholesterol levels and lowers HDL (good) cholesterol levels. It raises levels of triglycerides, another form of lipid, which can increase the risk of heart disease.

Commercial baked goods such as crackers, cookies, cakes, and many fried foods like doughnuts and French fries may contain trans fats. Shortening and margarine may also be high in trans fats. In the United States, if a food has less than .5 grams of trans fat per serving, the food label can read 0 grams trans fat.

According to the Mayo Clinic, in a healthy diet, 25 to 35 percent of your total daily calories can come from fat, but saturated fat should account for less than 10 percent of your total daily calories.

Monounsaturated fat, found in olive, peanut, and canola oils is a healthier option than saturated fat. Nuts, fish, and other foods containing unsaturated omega-3 fatty acids are also good choices of foods with monounsaturated fats. *Consumption of bad trans fats has gone down in recent years and decades.*

Smell the Coffee - Mocha Java Coffee has no chocolate in the Mocha or Java bean. Mocha is the name of the port in Yemen, where all African coffee beans are traded and transported. Java is the name of an island in Indonesia where the Java bean originates. Both coffees are dark bean and provide a bold coffee, when you mix the two beans together you get Mocha Java coffee.

Spoiling the Bunch - One bad apple can really spoil the bunch and the same may be said for bananas, cantaloupes, and a number of other fruits and vegetables. It is all due to a plant hormone called ethylene.

Ethylene is a natural plant hormone released in the form of a gas. It triggers cells to degrade, fruit to turn softer and sweeter, leaves to droop, and seeds or buds to sprout. While some fruits and vegetables are high ethylene producers, others are more sensitive to it.

You can use this knowledge to extend the life of your produce by keeping certain items separate in the fruit bowl or refrigerator drawer. Ethylene is the reason you should not store onions and potatoes together.

Ethylene may also be used when you want to accelerate ripening. This is the principle behind placing unripe fruit inside a paper bag or other closed container, which concentrates the ethylene. Adding another high ethylene fruit, such as a ripe apple or banana, may also speed up the process.

Ethylene producing foods include: apples, apricots, avocados, bananas, blueberries, cantaloupe, cranberries, figs, green onions, guavas, grapes, honeydew, kiwifruit, mangoes, nectarines, papayas, passion fruit, peaches, pears, persimmons, plums, potatoes, prunes, quince, and tomatoes.

> Separate your fruits and veggies to let them ripen naturally, unless you are in a hurry, then pair them up to speed the process.

Ethylene sensitive foods include: Asparagus, blackberries, broccoli, Brussels sprouts, cabbage, carrots, cauliflower, chard, cucumbers, eggplant, endive, garlic, green beans, kale, leeks, lettuce, okra, onions, parsley, peas, peppers, raspberries, spinach, squash, strawberries, sweet potatoes, watercress, and watermelon.

Frying, Sautéing, Searing, Simmering, and Stir Frying - Most people know there is a difference between sautéing and frying, but not exactly what the specific difference is. The same is true for "searing" and simmering, or stir frying and pan frying. Frying is the generic term for cooking any type of food in oil or fat. It is all-encompassing.

Sautéing involves cooking food in a shallow pan with a little oil or fat, over high heat. Usually you only sauté with thinly cut or sliced food, little to no liquid, and for relatively short periods of time.

Searing is similar, but only refers to the process of browning the surface of food. This means you can get the job done with any cooking instrument and any cooking method, whether it is sautéing, grilling, roasting, or something else. When you put a steak in a screaming hot pan and try to get that tasty crust on the outside, you are searing it.

Simmering refers to the process of cooking liquid-heavy dishes on the heat just below the boiling point. To do this, you specifically bring the liquid to a boil, and then reduce the heat until it almost stops bubbling, and maintain that heat.

Stir frying traditionally involves a wok or a high-walled pan, and involves cooking food in very hot oil while constantly moving the food around to ensure even cooking. Stir frying is similar to sautéing, but traditionally refers to cooking more food and constantly moving it to make sure it cooks through, but does not brown or burn.

Shallow and deep frying are generic terms and refer mostly to the amount of oil used to cook the food. For example, you can interchange sauté and shallow fry, but since sautéing refers to cooking with a small amount of fat or oil, deep frying is different because it involves submerging your food in hot fat or oil.

Pan frying is characterized by the use of just enough oil to lubricate the pan during the cooking process. With greasy foods that produce their own oil or fat, like bacon, you do not need oil. It also usually refers to the use of shallow, low-walled cooking pans, unlike deep frying or stir frying.

Fried Chicken Tips - Vodka is much more volatile than water, which is the main component of buttermilk, pickle juice, or pretty much any other fried chicken marinade. As such, it evaporates much more rapidly and violently. This helps drive moisture off the crust of the chicken faster, while also creating bigger vapor bubbles, adding surface area to the crust. Both of these mean crisper, lighter fried chicken. Only about two tablespoons of vodka is needed.

Brine helps chicken retain moisture. As chicken sits in a brine, the salt dissolves proteins in the meat's muscle structure, loosening it and allowing it to retain more moisture as it cooks. Brined chickens lose 30 to 40% less moisture than un-brined chickens. Add half an ounce of salt for every cup of marinade.

For each cup of dredging flour called for in the recipe, drizzle about two tablespoons of marinade/liquid into it. After drizzling, work it into the flour with fingers or a whisk then add the chicken pieces to coat. This process makes little chunks, which make chicken crispier.

Sliced Bread - Bread is an ancient food that has been eaten for tens of thousands of years. However, pre-sliced bread, which makes a bacon butty a convenient task, did not happen until the early 1900s, when a man named Otto Frederick Rohwedder of Davenport, Iowa invented a device to automate this process. He solved part of the staleness problem by wrapping the thinly sliced loaves in wax paper immediately after slicing was complete.

Pre-sliced bread was a hit and within a decade people who had access to it were eating more bread per person than before. Then they began experimenting with various new ingredients and spreads to put on the thin bread slices.

How to Clean a Cheese Grater - Remove Cheesy Residue from a Grater with bread. If you have residue on your box grater after grating soft cheese, grate a piece of stale bread to get rid of it and make clean up easier. (via Paula's Weekly Kitchen Tip on Facebook -The trial: "I grated 4 ounces of Monterey Jack cheese, leaving the expected cheesy mess on my metal box grater. I then took the stale heel of a loaf of sourdough and raked it over the same side of the box grater, making sure to cover the entire surface. It worked.")

More Sandwich Origins - It is difficult to think of sliced bread and not think of sandwiches.

Monte Cristo - The precise origin of the Monte Cristo is unknown, although most experts believe that it was an Americanized version of the Croque Monsieur. Versions of it appeared under other names in the mid-20th century, and by 1966, it was found on menus in Disneyland with its romantic-sounding name. Although there are variants today, typically a Monte Cristo will have either turkey, ham or chicken and sliced cheese between two pieces of white bread, dipped in egg and pan fried until golden. It is said that, to be traditional, it should be served with jelly on the side.

Patty Melt - The Patty Melt is said to have originated in Southern California in the restaurant chain of William "Tiny" Naylor in the 1940s or 1950s. The traditional recipe has a ground beef patty topped with either American, Swiss, or cheddar cheese and grilled onions on rye bread, pan fried in butter.

Po' Boy - Originating in New Orleans, Louisiana, the Po' Boy Sandwich can be made a number of ways. The Roast Beef Po' Boy has mayonnaise and shredded lettuce, roast beef, and debris gravy on top of a long white roll or baguette. Other versions, such as the Oyster and Shrimp Po' Boys, have the seafood battered and deep fried, then served atop baguette with a selection of mayonnaise, hot sauce, tomato, lettuce and dill pickle. One story of its name comes from the labor movement lore. In 1929, NOLA streetcar workers went on strike; to help support them, the Martin Brothers offered to feed the strikers. So many took them up on their offer that, as strikers entered their shop, supposedly one brother would say, "Here comes another poor boy."

Reuben - Although many attribute the origin of the name of the Reuben Sandwich to Reuben's Restaurant in New York, experts were persuaded by the claim of Reuben Kulakofsky of Omaha Nebraska. Using old copies of menus and a sprinkling of folklore, they determined that Kulakofsky, a grocer, invented the sandwich in the first half of the 20th century. Traditionally, a Reuben has a thick pile of corned beef, a slice of Swiss cheese, and a pile of sauerkraut on grilled rye bread.

Sloppy Joe - It is made by mixing and cooking tomato sauce, ground beef, onion, salt, pepper, and spices then heaping on a soft white bun. Like so many others, the exact origin of this sandwich is contested, probably because it evolved over time. There are claims that it originated at Sloppy Joe's Bar in Old Havana, Cuba during the 1920s. Others claim it was from a different Sloppy Joe's restaurant in Key West, Florida, known to have been frequented by Ernest Hemingway. By the 1950s, the Sloppy Joe sandwich became popular, particularly in the Midwest.

S'more - It is technically a sandwich, made with two graham crackers sandwiching a thick piece of chocolate and a melted marshmallow. The S'more was named from people asking for 'some more', which appears to be the original name. The origin is typically credited to the Girl Scouts who included the recipe for 'Some Mores' in their 1927 publication Tramping and Trailing with the Girl Scouts.

Bottled Water True Cost - The Pacific Institute finds that it took approximately 17 million barrels of oil equivalent to produce plastic for bottled water consumed by Americans in 2006, enough energy to fuel more than 1 million American cars and light trucks for a year.

There are 50 billion water bottles consumed every year, about 30 billion of them in the US. The manufacture of every ton of PET (polyethylene terephthalate bottles) produces around 3 tons of carbon dioxide (CO_2). Bottling water thus created more than 2.5 million tons of CO_2 in 2006. In addition to the water sold in plastic bottles, the Pacific Institute estimates that twice as much water is used in the production process. Thus, every liter sold represents three liters of water.

Club Soda, Mineral Water, Seltzer, and Tonic - *Club Soda* is often mistaken for and swapped out for seltzer water. The two are similar, but different. Club soda contains sodium salts and/or potassium salts. Like seltzer, it makes a good addition to batters, and makes matzo balls extra fluffy.

Mineral Water or sparkling water also contains minerals. Sparkling mineral water gets both its effervescence and minerals from the natural spring it is drawn from. The US FDA states mineral water must contain "no less than 250 ppm total dissolved solids that originates from a geologically and physically protected underground water source." Mineral water, because of its salt content, tends to be more acidic and while the carbonation is often added to mineral water during its plant treatments, the carbonation is often collected from natural sources. Mineral water is generally not used as a mixer and is best complemented by just a squeeze of citrus. Mineral water contains higher amounts of magnesium and calcium.

Seltzer Water is artificially carbonated water with no added ingredients. The beverage got its start (and name) in the German town of Selters, which was known for its sparkling springs that supposedly had remarkable healing powers. Seltzer is a cheap alternative to designer mineral waters.

Tonic Water is carbonated water to which quinine has been added to give it a characteristically bitter taste. Quinine was originally created from the bark of the cinchona tree that is native to South America and has been used to treat malaria since the 17th century. Its taste was so bitter and unpalatable that the medicine, while effective, was unpopular. British officials in the 19th century decided to add soda water in an attempt to make quinine easier to take. British soldiers found that gin was also great to mask the taste, making the gin and tonic a popular drink. Quinine glows in UV light, so you can use a black light to show off glowing drinks using tonic water.

White Bread vs. Wheat Bread - Not all wheat breads are created equal. Most white bread is made with refined grains that skip much fiber and nutrients. However, there are whole-wheat white breads that are just as healthy as whole-wheat breads. Regardless of color preference, it is important that the bread contains bran, germ, and endosperm.

New Way to Slice Pizza - For those who have friends or family who love crust and some who do not, here is a novel way to satisfy both.

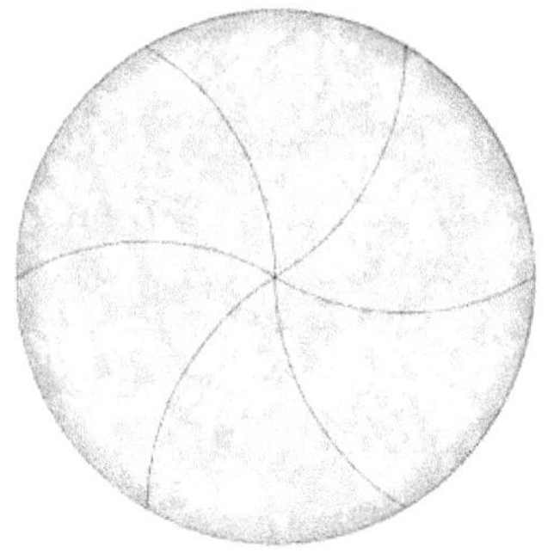

Make a few gently curved lines and join corners to middles. Six slices each, with crust and no crust.

Bacon Facts

Bacon Increases Intelligence - Bacon is full of a very important nutrient called choline, which helps increase our intelligence and memory and has been shown in University studies to help fight off the debilitating effects of Alzheimer's Disease and other chronic mental impairments.

Bacon Vitamins and Minerals - Bacon provides substantial amounts of important, necessary vitamins and minerals our bodies need to function healthfully. From bacon, we receive: 65% of our Recommended Daily Intake of Thiamin (Vitamin B1) as well as 47% of Niacin (Vitamin B3), 38% of Vitamin B12, 36% of Zinc, 24% of Vitamin B6, 22% of Riboflavin (Vitamin B2), 22% of Phosphorus, 10% of Pantothenate, 10% of Magnesium, 9% of Iron. The Protein to fat balance in bacon is actually 4 to 1, which is one of the highest protein to fat balances found in any meat, fish, or fowl.

Nitrates and Nitrites – While it is true that nitrates and nitrites are unhealthy for your body, what most pro-veggie, chicken, and fish nutritionists fail to tell us is that we can easily avoid nitrates and nitrites by simply not burning, charring, and over cooking bacon. It can also be avoided by baking bacon in the oven.

If you include some dairy and citrus with your bacon meal, vitamins A, D and E work to effectively prevent conversion of nitrates and nitrites into toxic nitrosamines in the stomach, rendering them harmless to the body.

Fat and Flavor - People have heard stories for years that bacon is full of harmful fat, but facts show the opposite, as bacon helps to fully satiate appetite with high protein, low carb energy, helping the body lose weight, raise metabolism, and build leaner, stronger muscles. Bacon actually has less total fat, saturated fat, and cholesterol than many cuts of beef and chicken. Some fish have less fat and cholesterol than bacon, but bacon has more protein and does not contain mercury toxin. One strip of bacon has 43 calories and .1g carbohydrates.

Bacon, Pancetta, and Prosciutto - Bacon and pancetta have the most in common. They are both typically made from pork belly and both are cured for a certain length of time. Both are also considered raw and need to be cooked before eating.

The process for making the two is slightly different. Pancetta is simply cured with salt, but spices and other aromatics are often added to infuse the pancetta with other flavors. Pancetta is sometimes sold sliced paper thin, or cubed. The thin slices can be wrapped around vegetables or meat before cooking. The pancetta cubes are often used like bacon, sautéed with onions or garlic to form the base of a soup, pasta, or risotto.

Bacon is also cured, like pancetta, but the meat is smoked after it has been cured. This is usually a cold-smoking process, meaning that the bacon isn't actually heated or cooked during smoking and remains raw. Smoking can be done with a wide range of woods, from apple to maple, which each give their own distinctive flavors to the meat.

So pancetta is cured and unsmoked, while bacon is cured and smoked, but both need to be cooked before being eaten. They can be used interchangeably in dishes.

Prosciutto is very different from either bacon or pancetta. Prosciutto is made from the hind leg of a pig (ie, the ham), and outside Italy, calling it prosciutto indicates a ham that has been cured.

The quality of prosciutto depends on the curing process. The outside of the ham is usually rubbed with just salt and sometimes a mix of spices. This draws out moisture and concentrates the flavor while the ham slowly air-dries. This process can take from a few months to a several years depending on the desired result. Once cured, prosciutto is usually thinly sliced and eaten as is, uncooked. Sometimes prosciutto gets lightly cooked as a finishing touch to a pasta sauce or other dish, but this is more to bring out the aroma and merge flavors.

Bacon Happy - Bacon makes us feel happy, satisfied, and blissful, which greatly reduces stress in our lives and effectively relieves the negative effects of frustration, self deprivation, and sense of lack in our existence.

Bacon Up - Holy Disaster - US bacon reserves hit 50-year low. Prices continue to go up in a sizzle. The average price of bacon across America has risen 14 percent since June of last year, according to the Bureau of Labor Statistics.

Analysts are reporting an 18% increase in the wholesale price of pork, with the surge expected to have a continued rise on the price of bacon and sausages.

Pig farmers can't keep up with the world's sizzling appetite for those fatty, juicy, smoky strips of sheer eating pleasure. US Department of Agriculture, "Today's pig farmers are setting historic records by producing more pigs than ever," said Rich Deaton, president of the organization. "Yet our reserves are still depleting."

Hog farmers export approximately 26 percent of total production, the Bacon Council said. China still produces almost four times the amount of pork as the US, so the US may need to reduce exporting in order to satisfy local demand or risk rising imports. *Bottom line, eat more bacon now before the next increase.*

Coffee and Cirrhosis

According to new research published online Jan. 25, 2016 in the journal Alimentary Pharmacology and Therapeutics, drinking more coffee could lower the risk of alcohol-related cirrhosis.

While there are observational studies that have already been reported regarding the link between coffee and cirrhosis, the researchers wanted to conduct a systematic review and meta-analysis to establish the inverse relationship between the two.

They found that by adding two or more cups of coffee a day, a person can reduce the risk of developing liver cirrhosis by 44 percent. The inverse association continues as the number of cups increases. For every additional three cups, the risk was reduced 57 percent; and for every four cups added, the risk was further reduced to 65 percent.

"Cirrhosis is potentially fatal and there is no cure as such," said lead study author Dr. Oliver Kennedy of Southampton University in the U.K. "Therefore, it is significant that the risk of developing cirrhosis may be reduced by consumption of coffee, a cheap, ubiquitous, and well-tolerated beverage."

According to the National Institution of Diabetes and Digestive and Kidney Diseases, cirrhosis is a condition in which the liver, the body's largest internal organ, gradually gets worse and is unable to perform its normal functions, because of chronic damage.

There are some limitations to the study as it was not able to account for other risk factors of liver disease, such as obesity and diabetes. The study also did not mention whether the type of beans or brewing method is significant to the results.

According to one expert, while the findings of the study showed positive effects of drinking coffee on the risk of cirrhosis, it should not give people the false hope that coffee can lessen the seriousness or extent of the liver damage.

"Unfortunately, although coffee contains compounds that have antioxidant effects and anti-inflammatory properties, drinking a few cups of coffee a day cannot undo the systematic damage that is the result of being overweight or obese, sedentary, excessive alcohol consumption or drastically mitigate an unhealthy diet," said Samantha Heller, a senior clinical nutritionist at New York University Langone Medical Center in New York.

Nine Big Banana Facts

Eating two bananas can give you enough energy for a 90-minute workout.

Bananas fight against depression. This is because bananas contain a protein called tryptophan, which converts to serotonin. Serotonin helps you relax and can make you feel better.

Bananas contain Vitamin B6, which regulate blood glucose levels and can put you in a better mood.

The Vitamin B6 will also help fight nerves and stress.

Bananas are high in potassium and low in sodium, which helps fight against high blood pressure and prevent strokes.

Bananas can soothe heartburn because of the natural antacid effect it has on the body.

Bananas are high in fiber. This can help regulate bowel movements without resorting to laxatives.

The potassium in bananas helps you stay focused and alert.

The inside of banana peels can soothe mosquito bites. *Bananas also taste good.*

Types of Tea

Black Tea, Green Tea, Oolong Tea, White Tea - Both black and green tea is harvested from an evergreen, tree-like shrub known as camellia sinensis. Most likely originating in China, the camellia sinensis is thought to have first been used to brew a medicinal drink during the Shang Dynasty (1600 BC to 1046 BC). By the third century BC, it had become a relatively popular drink using only the leaves from this plant, rather than mixed with other things as was common when used medicinally.

Leaves that are going to be used for black tea are allowed to ferment, or oxidize, completely. The general process is to roll, tear, or crush the leaves to help the oxidation process (similar to why the inside of an apple turns brown when exposed to air). The leaves are then dried out, sometimes in the sun or using machines. As the leaves oxidize, they gradually turn from green to black.

Manufacturers create green tea by picking the leaves off the plant and then heating them immediately. This is commonly done by pan firing the leaves or steaming them. Heat stops the leaves from oxidizing and allows them to maintain their green color.

Oolong tea is initially generally processed in the same way as black tea, but is not allowed to oxidize for as long. Once the desired oxidation level has been reached, which varies by type and manufacturer (some oolong tea is closer to green tea, while others are closer to black), the leaves are fired similar to green tea to stop the oxidation process at that point.

White tea is made by picking the leaves and buds early in the year while the bud is still closed. The leaves may be placed out to dry in the sun or mechanically, and minimizing oxidation.

Tea leaves are full of healthy antioxidants and contain substances that lower the risk for cancer, diabetes, and heart disease. In addition, consuming tea can help reduce joint inflammation due to the presence of polyphenols. Tea helps lower cholesterol, encourages weight loss, and sharpens mental alertness. *A cup of tea is generally six ounces.*

Highest tea consumption per person per year, as of 2014:

1 Turkey 6.87 kg (242 oz)
2 Morocco 4.34 kg (153 oz)
3 Ireland 3.22 kg (114 oz)
4 Mauritania (Africa) 3.22 kg (114 oz)
5 United Kingdom 2.74 kg (97 oz).

Seven Super Brain Foods

Whether it is a new dance or a foreign language, the older you get the harder it is to learn new things. Some foods have been found to be beneficial to keeping the brain sharp. Alzheimer's researchers like to say what is good for your heart is good for your brain.

Blackberries can get the conversation flowing again. They provide potent antioxidants known as polyphenols that zap inflammation and encourage communication between neurons, improving our ability to soak up new information according to a Tufts University study.

A recent Finnish study of 1,400 longtime *coffee* drinkers reveals that people who drank between three to five cups of coffee a day in their

40s and 50s reduced their odds of developing Alzheimer's disease by 65 percent compared with those who downed fewer than two cups a day. Researchers believe that coffee's caffeine and antioxidants are the keys to its protective affects.

Apples are a leading source of quercetin, an antioxidant plant chemical that keeps your mental juices flowing by protecting your brain cells. According to researchers at Cornell University, quercetin defends your brain cells from free radical attacks which can damage the outer lining of delicate neurons and eventually lead to cognitive decline. To get the most quercetin bang for your buck, eat apples with the skins on.

Chocolate can lower blood pressure and it can also keep your mind sharp. A Journal of Nutrition study found that eating as little as one-third of an ounce of chocolate a day (the size of about two Hersey's kisses) helps protect against age-related memory loss. They credit polyphenols in cocoa with increasing blood flow to the brain.

Cinnamon research from the University of California at Santa Barbara reveals that two compounds in cinnamon, proanthocyanidins and cinnamaldehyde may inactivate tau proteins that can cause brain cells to die.

Spinach is packed with nutrients that prevent dementia, such as folate, vitamin E, and vitamin K. Just one-half cup of cooked spinach packs a third of the folate and five times the amount of vitamin K you need in a day. A 2006 Neurology study revealed that eating three servings of leafy green, yellow, and cruciferous vegetables a day can delay cognitive decline by 40 percent. Of these three, leafy greens were found to be the most protective. Try spinach drizzled with a little olive oil. Its healthy fats boost absorption of fat-soluble vitamins E and K.

Scientists found the heart-healthy polyphenols in red wine and *Concord grape juice* can also give your brain a boost. When researchers at the University of Cincinnati College of Medicine gave twelve older adults with declining memory a daily drink of Concord grape juice or a placebo drink for three months, they found that the volunteers who drank the grape juice significantly improved their spatial memory and verbal learning skills. Researchers believe that, just like blackberries, grape juice polyphenols improve communication between brain cells.

Types of Potato Chips

The United Kingdom and Ireland, crisps are potato chips which are eaten cold, while chips are similar to French fries and are served hot. Americans, Canadians, Australians, Indians, New Zealanders, many Europeans, and those in the West Indies use chips. Many other countries also call them chips. People in Austria, Germany, and Switzerland call them Kartoffelchips. The Japanese call them chippu.

In Ireland, the word Tayto is synonymous with potato chips after the Tayto brand and can be used to describe all varieties of chips, including those not produced by Tayto. In fact, the word has become a genericized trademark.

Seasonings have come into vogue around the world and now potato chips have such flavorings as dill pickle, ketchup, barbecue, salt and vinegar, sour cream and onion, and ranch dressing. There are wasabi chips, poutine, maple bacon, Jamaican jerk chicken, cheddar and lemon-lime, Greek feta and olive, Ballpark hot dog, and barbeque baby back ribs, among others.

In Germany they have red paprika and ready salted along with sour cream and onion, cheese, oriental, chakalaka, currywurst, red and white with tomato ketchup and mayonnaise. The Japanese have pizza-flavored chips along with nori and shiyo, consommé, wasabi, soy sauce and butter, garlic, plum, barbecue, pizza, mayonnaise, and black pepper. Chili, scallop with butter, teriyaki, takoyaki and yakitorie.

There are prawn cocktail, Worcester sauce, roast chicken, steak and onion, smoky bacon, lamb and mint, ham and mustard, barbecue rib, tomato ketchup, sausage and ketchup, pickled onion, Branston pickle, and Marmite.

You can also find Thai sweet chili, roast pork and creamy mustard sauce, lime and Thai spices, chicken with Italian herbs, sea salt and cracked black pepper, turkey and bacon, caramelized onion and sweet balsamic vinegar, stilton and cranberry, mango chili, and American Cheeseburger, English roast beef and Yorkshire pudding.

If you like them hot, you can find Mexican limes with chili, salsa with mesquite, Buffalo mozzarella tomato and basil, mature cheddar with Adnams broadside beer, Soulmate cheeses and onion, crawtator, Cajun dill, voodoo, and Creole onion.

Cheese Harms the Environment?

Cheese of any type, made from the milk of cows, or goats, or sheep has a significant impact on the environment compared with other food products according to some 'researchers'. According to them, sheep cheese is especially bad.

Environmentalists are saying cheese may do as much harm to the environment as some kinds of meat. Based on figures from Sweden, the production of a 1.5 ounce serving of cheese might be expected to produce around 16 ounces of carbon dioxide equivalent. Depending on which study you consult, a 2 - 3 ounce serving of cooked, boneless chicken meat should yield between 4.3 and 31 ounces of CO2-equivalent, although you get about the same number of calories from each.

According to them, raising a milk-bearing animal puts out a significant amount of greenhouse gases, thanks in large part to the methane the animals emit. Feed production also contributes to global warming, and animal waste has implications for both water and air quality.

A dairy researcher at Langston University says feta cheese is one of the best options in terms of processing impacts and notes that Chèvre, Brie, and Camembert are also pretty green. Mozzarella is also on the 'green' list, since it doesn't require aging.

Sheep cheese is going to be worse for the planet than cow or goat varieties according to researchers from MTT Agrifood Research, Finland. They estimated that greenhouse gas emissions per unit of cheese would be roughly the same for cows and goats, but sheep might emit twice the amount of methane as a cow or a goat, per unit of milk produced. *Am amazed someone actually paid to study this.*

Calories are Calories

A few years ago, for a class project of ten weeks, Mark Haub, a professor of human nutrition at Kansas State University, ate sugary foods for his meals. To add variety in his stream of Hostess and Little Debbie snacks, he munched on Doritos chips, sugary cereals, Oreos, Twinkies, Nutty bars, and powdered donuts.

His daily intake included : Doritos Cool Ranch: 75 calories; 4 grams of fat,
Kellogg's Corn Pops: 220 calories; 0 grams of fat,

whole milk: 150 calories; 8 grams of fat,
baby carrots: 18 calories; 0 grams of fat,
Duncan Hines Family Style Brownie Chewy Fudge: 270 calories; 14 grams of fat,
Little Debbie Zebra Cake: 160 calories; 8 grams of fat,
Hostess Twinkies Golden Sponge Cake: 150 calories; 5 grams of fat,
Centrum Advanced Formula From A To Zinc vitamin: 0 calories; 0 grams of fat,
Little Debbie Star Crunch: 150 calories; 6 grams of fat,
Hostess Twinkies Golden Sponge Cake: 150 calories; 5 grams of fat, and
Diet Mountain Dew: 0 calories; 0 grams of fat.

His premise was, "In weight loss, pure calorie counting is what matters most - not the nutritional value of the food." (*Not the best for lifelong intake, but an easy diet.*)

A man of Haub's pre-dieting size usually consumes about 2,600 calories daily. So he followed a basic principle of weight loss and consumed less than 1,800 calories a day.

The result - Haub's 'bad' cholesterol, or LDL, dropped 20 percent and his 'good' cholesterol, or HDL, increased by 20 percent. He reduced the level of triglycerides, which are a form of fat, by 39 percent. In addition, the premise held up as he dropped 27 pounds during the course of his diet.

What's in a Name, Pineapple - Pine cones used to be called pineapples and pineapples got the name because they resembled pine cones. Originally, the word pineapple in English was first recorded in 1398, when it was used to describe the reproductive organs of conifer trees (now called pine cones).

When European explorers discovered the tropical fruit in the Americas, they called them pineapples, because they resembled pine cones (with the original name). Most European countries eventually adapted, and still use the name ananas, which came from the Tupi word nanas (also meaning pineapple).

Incidentally, The pineapple "fruit" is not really a fruit, but is a mass of individual berries fused to the central stalk. This is why the "fruit" has leaves on top. They are actually the continued growth of the stalk beyond where the berries are attached. Pineapples are not grown from seed.

Coffee Ground Uses - Coffee grounds serve a dual purpose when it comes to cleaning pots and pans. Grounds attract and absorb grease and oil, making them an ideal candidate, with dish soap for removing excess grease from a pan.

Coffee attracts worms and their presence means a healthy garden. Also, the acidity in the grounds keeps snails and slugs away. The grounds alter the pH level of soil, which can result in new colors for flowers.

Sprinkling grounds over wood before setting a fire can stop ashes from flying around.

After rinsing your hands, scrub them with used grounds, and then wash to remove the smell of garlic or fish from them. The grounds exfoliate your skin and remove dead tissue, which is where much of the smell resides.

Coffee grounds as a skin scrub can help revitalize your face and reduce cellulite.

Put a bowl of grounds in the back of the fridge, and another in the freezer. Some people argue that raw grounds work as the best deodorizer, while others claim used grounds are best. Try a half-and-half mixture.

Spring Cleaning with Beer - Wash wooden furniture to get the winter grime off, then pour a bit of flat beer onto a microfiber or soft cloth and rub it onto the surface of your favorite outdoor wood furniture. It works like a traditional furniture polish product, removing the dullness of years of wear and tear and instilling a shining, rich color. Works indoors, also.

Nutella - Many people use Nutella as an alternative to peanut butter. Its main ingredient is sugar, followed by palm oil, then hazelnuts. The label says that jars contain "over 50 hazelnuts per 13 oz. jar."

It is manufactured by the Italian company Ferrero that was first introduced in 1964, although its first iteration dates to 1946. It was originally sold as a solid block, but Ferrero started to sell a creamy version during 1951. Its composition was again modified and it was renamed Nutella in 1964.

Ads highlight the fact that Nutella has no artificial colors or preservatives and it contains, sugar, modified palm oil, and hazelnut, followed by cocoa solids, skimmed milk powder, whey powder, lecithin, and vanillin flavor. In the US, it also contains soy products.

According to its nutritional label, Nutella contains 58% of processed sugar by weight and 10.4 percent of saturated fat. A two-tablespoon (37 gram) serving of Nutella contains 200 calories including 99 calories from 11 grams of fat (3.5g of which are saturated) and 80 calories from 21 grams of sugar. The spread also contains 15 mg of sodium and 2g of protein per serving.

Incidentally, Nutella is marketed as "hazelnut cream" in many countries.

Calendar and Holiday Facts

HOLIDAYS AND FESTIVALS

Forty Celebrations - There are about 40 time zones, so New Years Eve can be celebrated 40 different times.

New Year Census - The US population is at 326.47 million people as of 2017. During January 2015, the US was expected to have one birth every eight seconds and one death every 12 seconds. Net migration was expected to add one person to the US population every 33 seconds, according to the Census Bureau.

The combination of births, deaths, and net migration adds at least one person to the US population every 16 seconds.

New Year Resolution - Here is a good resolution for the new year. Consider reviewing your will. The Internet has complicated things for family and executors of wills. Many of us have multiple online accounts spread across the web and they should be dealt with if something unforeseen happens. If you have multiple online accounts, make sure your online friends are notified of your death and your accounts and email accounts are handled the way you want them to be handled. The best way to do that is to update your will and provide information about your multiple accounts and how you would like them dealt with.

There are many online services now that allow people to register an account, and safely store all their passwords, account information and more so that when they die, a copy of a death certificate to that company will allow all the information to be released to the next of kin or estate executor.

Facebook allows three methods. The first is easy, if you have the account name and password, you can log in and delete it. Second, you can have the account memorialized, meaning it will not change, but specific information will be removed. Third, you can have the account removed by sending a copy of the death certificate to Facebook and ask that the account be deleted.

Most other online services offer the same types of options. Too many to get into here, but check the 'Help' files and you can find what you need. Let's hope none of us need to use this info for a long time.

Wow, I thought the holidays were over, but here are a few more. Jan 19 was National Popcorn Day, Jan 20 is National Cheese Day and Jan 21 is National Hug Day. Also, January 24 is Global Belly Laugh Day - Smile, throw your arms in the air and laugh out loud.

Peanut Butter Day - Peanuts are native to the Americas and since Aztec times have been made into a paste to be eaten. Modern peanut butter originated in the late 1800's with the first patent dating back to 1884, but it was much runnier than modern versions.

Dr. John Harvey Kellogg patented another paste in 1895 that is much more similar to what we see today and served it to patients at the Battle Creek Sanitarium as a health supplement. It was originally so expensive that it became a staple of luxury in the early 1900's and was commonly served in upper class tearooms that populated New York and was paired with a wide array of foods such as cheese, celery, watercress, pimento, and crackers.

The first reference of peanut butter paired with jelly is from a recipe by Julia Davis in 1901, and by 1920 the sandwich caught the attention of less wealthy members of society and spread peanut butter around the nation.

As the price of peanut butter lowered, it became extremely popular with children and today it is one of the most widespread food items in America. In fact, the spread is so popular there is even a National Peanut Butter Day.

National Peanut Butter Day - January 24 is National Peanut Butter Day, an unfortunate choice, because it is also Global Belly Laugh Day, but extremely difficult to laugh out loud with a mouth full of peanut butter. One quickie, it takes 550 peanuts to make a 12 ounce jar of peanut butter. Peanuts are cholesterol free and an excellent source of protein. It is the high protein content that causes peanut butter to stick to the roof of your mouth.

The king, Elvis knew how to use it with his famous peanut butter, banana, bacon sandwiches and his Fool's Gold Loaf, with a loaf of Italian bread filled with a pound of bacon, peanut butter, and grape jelly.

Americans eat 500 million pounds of peanut butter a year, enough to coat the floor of the Grand Canyon.

National Weatherperson's Day - Every February 5th, the world collectively expresses their appreciation for meteorologists everywhere, mostly with tongue firmly in cheek.

National Weatherperson's Day commemorates the birth of John Jeffries in 1744. He was one of America's first weather observers, began taking daily weather observations in Boston in 1774, and he took the first balloon observation in 1784. This is a day to recognize the men and women who collectively provide Americans with weather, water, and climate forecasts, and warning services.

World Cancer Day - Celebrated on February 4 to raise awareness of cancer and to encourage its prevention, detection, and treatment. World Cancer Day was founded by the Union for International Cancer Control to support the goals of the World Cancer Declaration, written in 2008. The primary goal of the World Cancer Day is to significantly reduce illness and death caused by cancer by 2020.

Valentine's Day - February 14 is Valentine's Day; the second most celebrated holiday around the world, after New Year's Day.

Also celebrated on Feb 14 is National Condom Day, originally started on campus at the University of California, Berkeley. It is celebrated every year in California and is designed to raise awareness of safe sex practices and encourage the use of condoms in a humorous, educated way, and to educate people about the serious risks from having unprotected sex.

For the interested few, there are J&D's Bacon-Flavored Condoms that look like and taste like bacon.

National Flag Day of Canada - Since 1996, February 15 is the day it is celebrated. The day commemorates the inauguration of the Flag of Canada on that date in 1965. The day is marked by flying the flag, occasional public ceremonies, and educational programs in schools. It is not a public holiday, although there has been discussion about creating one.

The Maple Leaf flag replaced the Canadian Red Ensign, which had been in conventional use as the Canadian national flag since 1868. *Canada is the second largest country in the world.*

Punxsutawney Phil's Prediction - The tradition comes from the German legend and Catholic feast day of Candlemas. "If Candlemas be fair and bright, Winter has another flight. If Candlemas brings clouds and rain, Winter will not come again."

This year, "It is agreed, there will be early Spring." The Groundhog Club emcee proclaimed, "There is no shadow to be cast. An early spring is my forecast." He added, "Take your jackets off, you are not going to need them." During the past 28 years, Phil was correct 13 times and incorrect 15 times. New Iberia's Pierre C. Shaddeaux (a nutria) agrees with Phil. Staten Island Chuck in New York and General Beauregard Lee in Georgia both concur with Phil that spring is coming soon.

The findings were independently verified by a groundhog in Canada, where Shubenacadie Sam, groundhog at Nova Scotia's Shubenacadie Wildlife Park also saw no shadow. According to a Canadian study looking at 13 different cities' groundhogs used for their respective festivals, the net accuracy was only 37%.

Ontario's Wiarton Willie predicted six more weeks of winter after spotting his shadow. Ohio's Buckeye Chuck agrees. Alabama's Sand Mountain Sam, who has been making appearances since 1993 also agrees and has only been wrong one year. West Virginia's French Creek Freddie also predicts six more weeks of winter.

In Manitoba, Groundhog Day celebrations had been cancelled following the death of Winnipeg Willow, who recently died at the Prairie Wildlife Rehabilitation Centre.

No word yet from North Carolina's Sir Wally Wally (wrong 7 out of the last 10 years), Louisiana's T-boy, the Cajun Groundhog (actually a nutria), or Alabama's Smith Lake Jake.

It appears these groundhogs are about equally as accurate as local weatherpersons.

Chinese New Year - Like other lunar dates, the Chinese New Year does not fall on the same date each year, although it is always in January or February. In 2018 it is February 16.

The Chinese New Year is an important celebration all over the world including Canada. There are similar New Year celebrations in Japan, Korea, and Vietnam known as the Lunar New Year or the Spring Festival.

Celebrations today are both literal and symbolic. Spring cleaning is started about a month prior to the Chinese New Year and must be completed before the celebrations begin.

Pancake Day - In the United Kingdom, Pancake Day, or Shrove Tuesday is the day before lent. During lent, one is supposed to fast, so a day of eating prior to 40 days of deprivation. Pancake day varies in line with Easter. In 2018, it is February 13.

Pancake day is the last chance to indulge yourself, and to use up the foods that were not allowed during Lent. Pancakes are eaten on this day, because they contain fat, butter, and eggs which were forbidden during Lent. Eating meat was also forbidden.

Pancake races and tossing the pancakes are two traditions that have stayed with us. Women race with pancakes in frying-pans, tossing them as they run. This was one of many merry-making games played at this time.

Shrove Tuesday gets its name from the ritual of shriving, when the faithful confessed their sins to the local priest and received forgiveness before the Lenten season began.

As far back as 1000 AD, "to shrive" meant to hear confessions. 'Short shrift' is derived from this and means giving little attention to someone's explanations.

Today, the Shrove Tuesday pancake tradition lives on throughout Western Europe, the United States, Canada, and Australia, but is most associated with the UK where it is simply known as Pancake Day, with a traditional recipe.

In France, as well as in New Orleans, US it is known as Fat Tuesday which kicks off the Mardi Gras festival with wild celebrations just before the austere Lenten season. Mardi Gras means Grease or Fat Tuesday.

In Poland, pączki and faworki are traditionally eaten on Fat Thursday, the one before Shrove Tuesday. However, in areas of Detroit, like Hamtramck with a large Polish population, they are eaten on "Fat Tuesday" due to French influence. Shrove Tuesday itself is sometimes referred to as "śledzik" ("little herring") and it is customary to have some pickled herring with Polish vodka that day.

International Battery Day - It is celebrated February 18 and a day to acknowledge the device that makes it possible for the smallest household items to the largest heavy-duty equipment to work smoothly. The unofficial holiday of unknown origins is also known as National Battery Day in the US. The battery has changed much over the years, but the core principle is still the same. The battery was invented during 1800, by Alessandro Volta (an Italian). He called it the Voltaic Pile and was combined layers of copper, zinc, and cardboard soaked in saltwater.

Almost early every stage in the evolution of the battery has come from a different country. An Englishman improved on Volta's battery, a Frenchman developed the first rechargeable battery, and a Swede invented the nickel-cadmium battery. The only American influence came from Benjamin Franklin, who was the first person to use the word battery.

Texas Independence Day - March 2 is the celebration of the adoption of the Texas Declaration of Independence on March 2, 1836. With this document signed by 59 people, settlers in Mexican Texas officially declared independence from Mexico and created the Republic of Texas.

National Potato Chip Day -March 14 every year marks the day we celebrate a thin and crispy snack, the awesome potato chip.

Potatoes were originally cultivated in South America, probably in Bolivia, Chile, and Peru. More than 400 years ago, the Inca Indians in those countries grew potatoes in their mountain valleys.

During the Alaskan Klondike gold rush, (1897-1898) potatoes were so valued for their vitamin C content that miners traded gold for potatoes.

Legend has it that potato chips were first made in 1853 while Commodore Cornelius Vanderbilt was on vacation in Saratoga Springs, New York. At one restaurant, he kept sending his fried potatoes back to the kitchen because he said they were "too thick". The chef, George Crum, decided that he would cut them into paper-thin slices, boil them in oil, fry them, and salt them as a joke to the Commodore. It backfired. They became an instant success and the restaurant became well known for them.

It was the invention of the mechanical potato peeler in the 1920s that paved the way for potato chips to soar from a small specialty item to a top-selling snack food. For several decades after their creation, potato chips were largely a Northern dinner dish. *I can still make a dinner of nothing but chips.*

Of course, I am partial to Detroit's Better Made Potato Chips. Detroiters eat an average of 7 pounds of chips per year, vs. 4 pounds in the rest of the country. Better Made has even sent chips to US troops in Iraq. Detroit, Michigan, US leads the way in potato chip consumption and is the potato chip consumption capital of the country.

Chips in other countries are also called crisps and Saratoga chips. The thickness of an ordinary potato chip is 55/1000 of an inch. Ridged chips are 4 times thicker, 210/1000 of an inch. Over fifty percent of US potatoes come from Idaho. The potato was the first vegetable to be grown in space.

Americans consume 1.2 billion pounds (over 17 billion US dollars) of potato chips each year. It remains the nation's favorite snack food. A recent survey showed 86% of US and France consume potato crisps/potato chips followed by 84% of Brits and 72% of Egyptians. Bottom of the scale is China with 28% consumption.

Have some fun, eat more chips and rest assured that all calories have been removed from all potato chips in the world for one day only. I have eaten hundreds of brands of chips from around the world, including the original Saratoga chips, but still prefer Better Made Potato Chips. Celebrity chef Rachael Ray named the Better Made's salt-and-vinegar chips the best in the nation.

For those who have been wondering, yes, there are bacon potato chips. Who's Your Daddy makes handmade bacon potato chips. They are available on the web and in stores around San Francisco.

St. Patrick's Day - St. Patrick's Day, March 17 is celebrated globally and is a time to get your green on and celebrate the many major parades, wear green, drink green beer, have a party, and remember the patron saint of Ireland. Why not save a few potato chips to savor with your favorite green beer. *Erin go Bragh!*

Pi Approximation Day - Yes, 3/14/16 is Rounded Pi Day, because it is closer to 3.1416 (not just 3/14), usually rounded for Pi. Traditional

Pi Day activities include eating pizza, fruit pies, doughnuts, pancakes, and other circular food.

Pi (not to be confused with Pi approximation day celebrated July 22) day - On 3/14/15 at 9:26:53 in the morning was a once in a century happening and we all got to celebrate it.

Pi Day was invented by physicist Larry Shaw and the first Pi Day celebration was held at the San Francisco Exploratorium in 1988. In 2009 the US Congress officially recognized March 14 as Pi Day in the United States.

International Day of Happiness - It is typical for politicians to take such a subject as happiness and make it serious. In 2012 the first ever UN conference on happiness took place and the UN General Assembly adopted a resolution which decreed that the International Day of Happiness would be observed every year on 20 March. It was celebrated for the first time in 2013.

The UN General Assembly adopted a resolution which recognized happiness as a "fundamental human goal" and called for "a more inclusive, equitable and balanced approach to economic growth that promotes the happiness and well-being of all peoples." "We need a new economic paradigm that recognizes the parity between the three pillars of sustainable development. Social, economic, and environmental well-being are indivisible. Together they define gross global happiness," the Secretary-General told the meeting's participants.

Norway jumped from 4th place in 2016 to 1st place in 2017, followed by Denmark, Iceland, and Switzerland in a tightly packed bunch, according to the World Happiness Report Update 2017, released by the Sustainable Development Solutions Network for the United Nations. The US came in nineteenth.

March 20 is the day to share videos, happy photos, and thoughts celebrating International Day of Happiness. *I will be passing out free smiles and hugs - all welcome.*

Washing the White Lions - During the middle ages, lions really were kept in the Tower of London. By Victoria's reign in 1837 all the lions had been moved to safer accommodation in Regents Park. In 1860 April Fool's day fell on a Sunday, so a prankster had an idea to invite 'all and sundry' to the Tower of London to see the annual washing of the white lions.

The invitation said: Admit the bearer and friend to view the annual ceremony of 'Washing the white lions' on Sunday, April 1st, 1860. Thousands of people turned up and waited, until one-by-one, it dawned on them that they had been hoaxed.

Color TV Hoax - Another April Fool's Day joke was played in 1962 when there was only one TV channel in Sweden, and it broadcast in black and white. The station's technical expert, Kjell Stensson, appeared on the news to announce that, thanks to a new technology, viewers could convert their existing sets to display color reception. All they had to do was pull a nylon stocking over their TV screen. Stensson proceeded to demonstrate the process. Thousands of people were taken in. Regular color broadcasts only commenced in Sweden on April 1, 1970.

Cheese Weasel Day - April 3rd is Cheese Weasel Day, the holiday where the Cheese Weasel brings dairy goodness to all the boys and girls in the tech industry. It seems to have started about 1992 when a weasel was spotted carrying a Kraft Cheese Single. They assumed it must be the Cheese Weasel and therefore, that it must be Cheese Weasel Day. He was off to put it under the keyboards of good tech workers everywhere and that is what many techies do today. Some offices put out a spread of exotic cheeses for all to enjoy. Some still hide cheese slices under keyboards of the unsuspecting.

Talk Like Shakespeare Day - To be or not to be a fun day, that is the question. It will be William Shakespeare's 454th birthday on April 23, 2018. Talk Like Shakespeare Day is a day on which all citizens are encouraged to incorporate Shakespearean lines into everyday conversation. It was started in 2009 in Chicago. *Make someone smile. "I would give all my fame for a pot of ale, and safety." ~Shakespeare*

Buddha Birthday - Buddha's official birthday April 8, 2018. It changes every year in the Gregorian Calendar. It is a national Holiday in some far East countries. He was estimated to be born about 400 BCE. *Happy Birthday Buddha!*

National Pretzel Day - April 26 was declared as National Pretzel Day by then-Pennsylvania Governor Ed Rendell in 2003.

World Tai Chi and Qigong Day - The last Saturday of April each year in hundreds of cities, spanning 80 nations, people come together to provide a healing vision for our world.

Tai chi (tie chee) and Qigong (chee gung) combine deep breathing techniques, gentle body movement, and visualization techniques. Tai chi is a form of Qigong and is an ancient Chinese tradition that is practiced as a graceful form of exercise. It involves a series of movements performed in a slow, focused manner and accompanied by deep breathing.

Tai chi is a noncompetitive, self-paced system of physical exercise and stretching. Each posture flows into the next without pause, ensuring that the body is in constant motion. It has many different styles. Each style may have its own subtle emphasis on various principles and methods. There are also variations within each style. Some may focus on health maintenance, while others focus on the martial arts aspect of tai chi. *I was learning/practiced tai chi locally for the a few years and, although some call it gentle, it is still a workout.*

International Dance Day - April 29 is International Dance Day. It was introduced in 1982 by the International Dance Council (Conseil International de la Danse). The main purpose of Dance Day events is to attract the attention of the wider public to the art of dance. Emphasis should be given to addressing a new public, people who do not follow dance events during the course of the year. Every year, the president of the CID sends the official message for Dance Day which circulates in every country of the world.

US National Dance Day was created by Nigel Lythgoe and takes place in the United States on the last Saturday in July. It was founded and officially recognized in 2010 when American congresswoman Eleanor Holmes Norton introduced a National Dance Day resolution to promote dance education and physical fitness.

National Humor Month - Hope you enjoyed National Humor Month in April. It was launched in 1976 by humorist Larry Wilde, Director of the Carmel Institute of Humor. He says, "Since April is often bleak and grim and taxes are due on the 15th, it can be one of the most stressful times of the year. Besides, it is the only month that begins with All Fool's Day - a day which has sanctioned frivolity and pranks ever since the 1500s." *That reminds me of a joke. . .*

Mother's Day - Sunday, May 13, 2018 is Mother's Day. *Be nice to your mother for a change.*

Mother's Day is celebrated on various days in many parts of the world, most commonly in May, but also in February, March, and April in some places. In the United States it was nationally recognized as a holiday (on the second Sunday in May) in 1914 after a multi-year campaign by Anna Jarvis (she died in 1905 and her daughter Anna Marie carried on the campaign). We use the singular (mother's) as opposed to the plural (mothers') to commemorate family mothers vs. all the mothers in the world.

As the US holiday was adopted by other countries and cultures, the date was changed to fit already existing celebrations honoring motherhood, like Mothering Sunday in the UK, or the Orthodox celebration of Jesus in the temple in Greece. In some countries it was changed to dates that were significant to the majority religion, such as the Virgin Mary day in Catholic countries, or the birthday of the daughter of the Prophet Muhammad in Islamic countries. Bolivia uses the date of a certain battle where women participated. Many Arab countries celebrate on March 21, the day of the vernal Equinox.

Traditionally, carnations represent Mother's Day. Many religious services copied the custom of giving away carnations or wearing a carnation on Mother's Day. Florists promoted wearing a red carnation if your mother was living or a white one if she was dead and this has remained popular.

Obscura Day - May 30 is Obscura Day and the day to celebrate the hidden wonders of the world. There are more than 150 events in 39 states and 25 countries, all on a single day, and all designed to celebrate the world's most curious and awe-inspiring places.

It is an international celebration of wondrous, curious, and esoteric places in cities and towns all over the world. You can see and experience such things as musical rocks, a worry bead museum, a European pyramid, unusual cemeteries, a hash museum, a 19th century landfill, a gasometer town, a giant lemon, and many more unusual and wonderful things.

The folks behind Atlas Obscura, 'a compendium of the world's wonders, curiosities, and esoterica' are putting it on. Here is the http://atlasobscura.com/ *Go on, get up, get out of the house, and see something truly amazing.*

Bermuda Day - May 24, on the Island of Bermuda is an official holiday celebrating their famous Bermuda shorts and a day anyone can wear them to work.

National Wine Day - Monday, May 25, 2015. Drink more wine.

National Tap Dance Day - In 1989, a joint US Senate/House resolution declared "National Tap Dance Day" to be May 25, the anniversary of Bill Robinson's (Mr. Bojangles) birth.

Pinch Bum Day, Oak Apple Day, Shick Shack Day - Monarchists would wear oak leaves on May 29 for Pinch-Bum Day, and 'Oak Apple Day' in memory of the time when the king hid in an oak tree following the Battle of Worcester.

"Parliament had ordered the 29 of May, the King's birthday, to be forever kept as a day of thanksgiving for our redemption from tyranny and the King's return to his Government, he entering London that day." The official holiday was abolished in 1859, but continues to be fondly celebrated in many parts of the commonwealth.

In parts of England where oak-apples are known as shick-shacks, the day is also known as Shick-Shack Day. It is traditional for monarchists to decorate the house with oak branches or wear a sprig of oak on 29th May. The oak is the national tree of England. It is also traditional to drink beer, dance, and eat plum pudding. (An oak apple is also known as an oak gall. It is caused by the larvae of a cynipid wasp. The gall look like an apple.)

Those who do not participate can have their bum pinched. Since few recognize or celebrate this holiday, have some fun by finding your favorite person and pinch their bum today - men and women can participate.

Incidentally, Everest, the world's tallest mountain was conquered at 11:30 a.m. on 29 May 1953. Edmund Hillary of New Zealand and

Tenzing Norgay, a Sherpa of Nepal, become the first explorers to reach the summit of Mount Everest, which at 29,028 feet above sea level is the highest point on earth.

Memorial Day - Memorial Day, originally called Decoration Day, is a day of remembrance for those who died in US service. The preferred name for the holiday gradually changed from "Decoration Day" to "Memorial Day," which was first used in 1882.

Decoration Day was officially proclaimed on 5 May 1868 to honor Union and Confederate soldiers by General John Logan, national commander of the Grand Army of the Republic, in his General Order No. 11, and was first observed on 30 May 1868, when flowers were placed on the graves of Union and Confederate soldiers at Arlington National Cemetery. The date was chosen because it was <u>not</u> the anniversary of a battle.

The holiday changed after World War 1 from honoring just those who died fighting in the Civil War to honoring Americans who died fighting in any war. In 1971, Memorial Day was declared a federal national holiday by an act of Congress, and its observance was set on the last Monday in May.

Memorial Day Poppies - Moina Michael conceived of an idea in 1918 after reading a poem, to wear red poppies on Memorial Day in honor of those who died serving the nation during war and sold poppies to her friends and co-workers with the money going to benefit servicemen in need. Later, Madam Guerin from France was visiting the United States and learned of this new custom. When she returned to France, she made artificial red poppies to raise money for war orphaned children and widowed women. This tradition spread to other countries.

In 1921, the practice of selling poppies was taken up by the American Legion Auxiliary and in 1922 by the VFW. Two years later their "Buddy" Poppy program was selling artificial poppies made by disabled veterans. The practice continues today.

Several southern states have an additional separate day for honoring the Confederate war dead: January 19 in Texas, April 26 in Alabama, Florida, Georgia, and Mississippi; May 10 in South Carolina; and June 3, Jefferson Davis' birthday, in Louisiana and Tennessee.

Happy National Doughnut Day - National Doughnut Day is celebrated on the first Friday of June each year. (Doughnut is the dictionary spelling, but donut is becoming more acceptable each year.)

National Doughnut Day started on June 7, 1938 when a young military doctor by the name of Morgan Pett was sent to a military base. On his way there he stopped at a bakery and picked up eight dozen doughnuts. When he arrived at the base he started helping many wounded soldiers, and would give them a free doughnut. One man he helped was a Lieutenant General by the name of Samuel Geary. Samuel Geary decided to make a fund raiser with Morgan Pett to give every wounded soldier, and the needy a doughnut. This fund raiser was later joined with the Salvation Army. Many donut shops still give out free donuts on this day.

In honor of the day Krispy Kreme, with no purchase necessary, will hand out a free donut of choice to each customer. Dunkin Donuts (which began the new spelling) will give out one free donut with the purchase of any beverage.

Incidentally, International Jelly-Filled Doughnut Day is widely recognized as June 8.

The Real D-Day - When Allied troops stormed the beaches at Normandy, it was a turning point of WWII. According to the National WWII Museum, June 6th, 1944 was not the only "D-Day." The term was used for any important operation. "D-Day" was the day of the operation itself, and the days leading up to and after the operation were indicated with "+" and "-". So the "D" is a variable. If June 6th, 1944 was "D-Day" then June 1st, 1944 was "D-5", and June 8th was "D+2." Since the variable references a specific day, "D" in "D-Day" essentially stands for "Day."

The Encyclopedia of Word and Phrase Origins says the French meaning of the D is "disembarkation," and it also quotes a letter from Eisenhower's executive assistant, Brigadier General Robert Schultz, in 1964 who responded to a letter to Eisenhower asking to clarify the meaning of "D-Day." Schultz wrote, "Be advised that any amphibious operation has a 'departed date'; therefore the shortened term 'D-Day' is used."

D-Day has become synonymous with June 6th, 1944 because of the significant impact that particular operation had on World War II and world history.

Flag Facts for Fourth of July - The historic photo and film footage of the American flag being raised at Iwo Jima actually shows the second flag erected on the Japanese island. The US had suffered more than 4,500 casualties during its 1,000 yard advance to capture Mt. Suribachi. Lt. Col. Chandler Johnson ordered a patrol up the mountain and handed Lt. George Schrier a 54" x 26" flag, saying "If you get to the top, put it up." Schrier's 40-man patrol snaked its way up to the mountain's summit and propped up Old Glory with an abandoned piece of drain pipe and some rocks.

Sensing a historic moment, the colonel sent an assistant to fetch a larger (96" x 54") flag that had flown on one of the ships bombed at Pearl Harbor and handed it to Pfc. Rene Gagnon. He ordered him to replace the smaller flag, "So every son of a bitch on this whole cruddy island can see it." AP photographer Joe Rosenthal snapped the Pulitzer Prize-winning photo of the second flag being raised.

The flag patch on the right sleeves of some U.S. military uniforms may appear to be backwards, as do the decals on the right side of U.S. aircraft and other vehicles. The reason for this: flag protocol dictates that the Stars and Stripes should always be displayed as if the flag is flying in a breeze.

This practice dates back to the earliest days of the US Army, when one soldier was designated as the "standard bearer."

As the standard bearer marched forward into battle, the flag would naturally unfurl behind him, away from the staff. The canton, or the area with the stars, should always be depicted facing forward.

The Parade of Nations, now a traditional part of the Olympic opening ceremonies, was first added to the program at the 1908 Games in London. As the teams passed the Royal Box, each nation's flag-bearer was expected to dip his nation's banner to King Edward VII. Ralph Rose, who was carrying the US flag, refused to do so and when questioned about keeping his nation's flag vertical, his reply was, "This flag dips for no earthly king."

The US flag bearers at the 1912, 1924, and 1932 Games were not so staunch in their patriotism, and lowered Old Glory when passing the head of state, even though the "no dip" rule was part of the official Flag Code adopted in 1923. The United States was the only nation to not dip its flag while passing Adolf Hitler in the stands during the Parade of Nations at the 1936 Games in Berlin, and the tradition has remained steadfast since then.

July 4th Revisited - Imagine how you would feel if someone, maybe a sister or brother, or someone else kept telling you what to do all of the time and kept taking more and more of your allowance. That is how the colonists felt in the years leading up to 1776. Great Britain kept trying to make the colonists follow more rules and pay higher taxes. People started getting angry and began making plans to be able to make their own rules. They no longer wanted Great Britain to be able to tell them what to do, so they decided to tell Great Britain that they wanted to be independent. *To be independent means to take care of yourself, make your own rules, and provide for your own needs. . . How soon we forget what our ancestors gave their lives for.*

St. Swithin's Day - Happy St. Swithin's (or Swithun's) Day, July 15. Legend says that if it rains today, it will rain for the next forty days. If it is dry, it will be dry for the next forty days.

Bologna Festival - It is July, 2018 in Yale, Michigan and over twenty thousand people are expected to join the fun. Yale bologna is said to be some of the best in the world. It is bit more course and strongly seasoned than Oscar Mayer slices. This bologna has been rumored to help people live to be 120 years old and I will let you know when I reach it. Every year, well over a thousand pounds of bologna are served either fried in sandwiches, stuck between a bun as a hot dog or placed on a stick for quick consumption. Bologna is also great barbecued.

The Bologna Queen crown is quite prestigious in Yale. Contestants must declare their intention to run up to six weeks in advance and be willing to raise tens of thousands of dollars for charity. The lucky lady who captures the title receives a crown of ring bologna and a King for her arm. Of course, there is also the outhouse race where people build interesting 'houses' on wheels to push around town as fast as they can. They must include a Sears catalog and somebody riding inside. *Mmmm, wish I was there; ring bologna is one of my favorites. Yes, bologna is the proper spelling even though most pronounce it baloney.*

National Hot Dog Day - You can renew that bad breath with some of your favorite toppings on a hot dog, wiener, or frankfurter. July 23, Americans celebrate National Hot Dog day.

Hot dogs were originally culturally imported from Germany. The word frankfurter comes from Frankfurt, Germany, where pork sausages similar to hot dogs originated. Wiener refers to Vienna, Austria, whose German name is 'Wien', home to a sausage made of a mixture of pork and beef.

Americans eat seven billion hot dogs from Memorial Day to Labor Day. That amounts to about 818 hot dogs consumed every second, according to the National Hot Dog and Sausage Council.

Hot dogs are made with a simple mixture of ground meats and spices, such as salt, garlic, and paprika. Some commercial makers include binders and fillers. Preservatives from curing typically include sodium erythorbate and sodium nitrite. Skinless dogs have the casing removed after cooking and before packaging. *I love the natural casing dogs that crunch with every bite.*

National Ice Cream Month - July is National Ice Cream Month, so here are a few ice cream facts.

In 1984, President Ronald Reagan declared the third Sunday in July to be National Ice Cream Day and the month of July to be National Ice Cream Month.

Per capita ice cream consumption in the US is about 5 1/2 gallons.

It takes about twelve pounds of whole milk to make one gallon of ice cream. One gallon of milk weighs 8.6 pounds.

French Ice Cream is enriched with egg yolks.

More ice cream is sold on Sunday than any other day of the week.

It takes 50 licks to finish a single scoop of ice cream.

The top five most popular ice cream flavors are: vanilla, chocolate, Neapolitan, strawberry, and cookies n' cream.

Vanilla makes up about twenty five percent of all ice cream sales

Neapolitan ice cream is ice cream made up of blocks of chocolate, vanilla, and strawberry ice cream side by side in the same container. Giuseppe Tortoni, a Neapolitan (living in Paris) created many layered ice cream cakes and the term Neapolitan was named in his honor.

Testicle Festival - Speaking of gaudy, this festival runs from August 3 - 7 at the Rock Creek Lodge, Montana. Obviously for adults only, it is also known as the "Testy Festy" or the "Breasticle Festival," this four-day drunken jamboree is filled with wet t-shirt contests, pig wrestling, stripping, mooning, bull riding, and fried bull testicle consumption.

Rocky Mountain Oysters or bull testicles are considered delicious by a select group of fine diners. In a showcase of masculine virility, there is even a bull testicle eating contest. One year, Matt Powers took the title after consuming over 40 bull testicles in four minutes. Mentioned in Playboy as one of the top things to do in the summer, they advertise "Come out and have a ball."

Just Because Day - We celebrate the unofficial holiday each year on August 27. You can celebrate this day any way you choose, just because. It started during the 1950s and has been growing in celebrations since then.

Every day we all do things that are expected or required of us. On National Just Because Day, that does not apply. The day is a chance to do something without reason. How about that person you have secretly been wanting to kiss; do it, just because.

August 27 is also National Burger Day in the UK. They probably chose that day, just because.

Possibly you want to sing really loud while in your car by yourself with your windows rolled down; do it, just because. I may walk around the block backward, just because.

Thanksgiving - It is hard to find the actual 'first thanksgiving' in the US. Of course Texas, never one to miss an opportunity, claims to be first with the story of the first Thanksgiving feast celebrated in 1598 in El Paso, Texas by Don Juan de Oñate – 22 years before the English colonial Thanksgiving.

By early March 1598, Oñate's expedition of 500 people, including soldiers, colonists, wives and children and 7,000 head of livestock, was ready to cross the treacherous Chihuahuan Desert. Almost from the beginning of the 50-day march, nature challenged the Spaniards. First, seven consecutive days of rain made travel miserable. Then the hardship was reversed, and the travelers suffered greatly from the dry weather. On one occasion, a chance rain shower saved the parched colonists.

Finally, for the last five days of the march, before reaching the Rio Grande the expedition ran out of both food and water, forcing the men, women, and children to seek roots and other scarce desert vegetation to eat. Both animals and humans almost went mad with thirst before the party reached water. Two horses drank until their stomachs burst, and two others drowned in the river in their haste to consume as much water as possible.

The Rio Grande was the salvation of the expedition. After recuperating for 10 days, Oñate ordered a day of thanksgiving for the survival of the expedition. Included in the event was a feast, supplied with game by the Spaniards and with fish by the natives of the region. A mass was said by the Franciscan missionaries traveling with the expedition. Finally, Oñate read La Toma - the taking - declaring the land drained by the Great River to be the possession of King Philip II of Spain.

Some historians call this one of the truly important dates in the history of the continent, marking the beginning of Spanish colonization in the American Southwest.

There is no doubt that today's Thanksgiving tradition is New England born and bred. It is not a single tradition, but a combination of traditions, according to a researcher for Plimoth Plantation Inc., which operates a model 17th century village at Plymouth, Mass.

He says today's celebration is a cross between a British harvest festival and a special day of religious thanksgiving, both originally observed by pilgrims in New England.

In 1621, just months after their arrival from England, residents of Plymouth celebrated a harvest festival, which was indistinguishable from those observed throughout Britain at the time. It was a secular event with feasting and games. The only religious observance was the saying of grace before the meal.

Two years later, the governor of Plymouth colony called for a special day of religious thanksgiving for the end of a drought that plagued the colony. This was an extra day of prayer and religious observance. Special days of religious thanksgiving were called throughout the colonial period.

Connecticut is given credit for initially adopting an annual day of general thanksgiving. The first for which a proclamation exists was called for Sept. 18, 1639, although some may have been held earlier. Another on record was held in 1644, and from 1649 onward, these special days of general thanksgiving were held annually. Massachusetts Bay Colony began annual observances in 1660.

Several other states also claim the first thanksgiving. Puritans who arrived to establish Massachusetts Bay Colony in 1630 observed a special day of prayer that is often called the 'first Thanksgiving'. Even earlier in Florida, a small colony of French Huguenots living near present-day Jacksonville noted a special thanksgiving prayer. The colony soon was wiped out by the Spanish.

Maine stakes its claim to the first Thanksgiving on the basis of a service held by colonists on August 9, 1607, to give thanks for a safe voyage.

Virginians are convinced their ancestors celebrated the first Thanksgiving when Jamestown settlers in 1610 held a service of thanksgiving for their survival of a harsh winter.

Detroit Lions Started Thanksgiving Football - In 1934, radio executive G.A. Richards bought the Portsmouth, Ohio Spartans NFL team, moved them to Detroit, and renamed them the Lions. Unfortunately for him, nobody in Detroit cared much for watching the Lions.

Despite winning all their games but one before Thanksgiving, having several stars of the day, and one super star in Earl "Dutch" Clark, the average turn out for each game was only about 12,000 people.

At the time, it was fairly traditional for various football programs in high schools and colleges to hold particularly significant games on Thanksgiving. So Richards decided to try to bring this same tradition to the NFL, convincing the NFL to allow the Lions and the defending World Champion Chicago Bears to play for the Western Division championship on Thanksgiving.

Richards then used his considerable influence in radio to convince NBC that they should broadcast this game on the radio all across the United States, something that had never been done before for an NFL game. The game ended up being a huge success, being played at the University of Detroit Stadium in front of a sold out crowd of 26,000 fans and broadcast across the nation on over 94 different radio stations. In the end, the Bears won 19-16, but the game was such a success, as far as ratings and fan turn-out went, that Richards fought to be allowed to continue having the Lions play on Thanksgiving going forward and to continue to have that games broadcast out on the radio nationwide.

* The Dallas Cowboys have played their traditional Thanksgiving Day game since 1966, missing games in 1975 and 1977.

* The first televised Thanksgiving Day game was in 1956 the Green Bay Packers with the Lions losing 24-20.

* In order to appease fans of other teams who also wanted their favorite team to take part in Thanksgiving NFL games, in 2006, the NFL instituted a third game, on top of the Detroit Lions and Dallas Cowboy traditional games. This third game has no fixed teams, as in the previous two.

Happy Constitution Day - Constitution Day (or Citizenship Day) is an American federal observance that recognizes the ratification of the United States Constitution and those who have become U.S. citizens. It is observed on September 17, the day the US Constitutional Convention signed the Constitution in 1787. *Australia also observes a Citizenship Day on this date.*

PARK(ing) Day - Couldn't resist adding International PARK(ing) Day, celebrated around the globe on the third Friday in September. It started in 2005 when a company paid the meter for a parking spot for 24 hours. Each year it gets bigger as people grab a spot and decorate it for a day. In 2011 it was celebrated in 975 parks, 162 cities, 35 countries, and on 6 continents. It is celebrated on the third Friday in September.

Ten Happy Halloween Facts - It is actually supposed to be spelled Hallowe'en.

1. It has been celebrated for over 2,000 years as pagan traditions.
2. Wearing masks comes from the Welsh and Celtic traditions that the dead visit the living on that day.
3. During the 1800s in America, the end of harvest was celebrated by wearing costumes, eating sweets, and playing tricks on each other.
4. Jack O' Lanterns started out in Ireland as hollowed out turnips with candles in them to ward off evil spirits.
   Over ninety percent of pumpkins are sold for Halloween for carving.
5. Orange and black are the traditional colors, because they represent the harvest and evil.

6. If you see a spider on Halloween, it is said to be the spirit of a loved one watching over you.
7. Eighty six percent of Americans decorate their house for Halloween, but the number is dwindling.
8. Halloween costume sales reached six billion dollars in 2009. Adults were 62% of that number.
9. Annually, about two billion dollars is spent on Halloween candy.

Day of the Geese - Antzar Eguna, is a Spanish tradition in which a greased goose is suspended over water and young men jump from boats and attempt to rip off the head of the goose. It is celebrated on September 5 and serves as a way for young men to prove their strength and eligibility to females.

The winner also gets to keep the goose. Although this tradition was once practiced all over Spain with live geese, it is now only held during the San Antolin festival in Lekeitio, with a dead goose.

Ginger (Redhead) Day – The ginger festival, where thousands of redheads come together for a gathering and bonding experience.

The celebrations for the annual Redhead Day, which has spilled across a weekend to mark all things ginger is paid for by the local government in Breda, a city in the south east Netherlands. It has been celebrated for years and has grown into a huge festival of ginger self-affirmation, overtaking the city center for one weekend every September. It now hosts over eighty countries.

The initiative is all for the redheads and there is much common ground for the members of one of the most genetically distinctive, yet disparate groups in the world. Men and women sporting a spectrum of ginger, from strawberry blonde to rich ochre, swap stories of being picked on in the playground and discrimination in the wider world. Here they just enjoy the fun and camaraderie.

Roadkill Festival - September, Marlinton, WV - With taglines like "You kill it we grill it; featuring some of the highway's finest" and "Eating food is more fun when you know it was hit on the run." Marlinton, West Virginia, knows how to bring a little humor into a good food festival. The annual event generates tens of thousands of dollars for the small town of 1,000. Although rarely practiced today, cooking roadkill has roots to the state's rugged culture, when wasting food and resources was unthinkable — why shouldn't a critter's highway misfortune turn in to a great family meal? Featuring any animal often, but in this case, not actually, roadkill, contestants cook up recipes using possum, beaver, raccoon, snake, deer, or armadillo. Care to try some "Deer Smear Quesadillas" or "Bumper Bruised Barbecued Bear"?

International Talk like a Pirate Day - Arrgh! It be celebrated every year on September 19. There is even a Facebook group dedicated to it.

A group, Pirates for Parkinsons, is using the day to march for Parkinsons Disease. To date there are 39 Pirates for Parkinson's walks or events, mostly in the UK, but others include: Amsterdam, The Netherlands; Dayton, Ohio, US; French Pyrenees, France; Ghana; Glasgow, UK; Hong Kong; Johannesburg, SA; Ketchikan, Alaska; Luxembourg; Plano, TX, USA; Stockholm, Sweden; Sydney, Australia; Tokyo, Japan; Wellington, NZ;   West Bank, Middle East. Avast, mateys, have fun for a good cause. *Let me know if you see any blonde pirates - They are the ones with patches over both eyes.*

In case you forgot, **World Alzheimer's Day** was September 21.

September 24 is **National Punctuation Day** (sic)

National Health IT Week, October 2-6, 2017 - National Health IT Week is a collaborative forum of assembling key healthcare constituents, vendors, provider organizations, payers, government agencies, pharmaceutical/biotech companies, industry/professional associations, research foundations, and consumer protection groups, working together to elevate national attention to the necessity of advancing health information technology.

Columbus Day - Don't forget Columbus Day, or Día de la Raza (Day of the Race) as they call it in many countries in Latin America, is observed on Oct 12.

OK - Nina, Pinta, and Santa Maria - The Pinta and Nina were nicknames and their real names were Santa Barbara and Santa Clara.

The other one was nicknamed La Gallega. *If Chris really looked like that, can you imagine what Queen Isabella looked like?*

Above is the emblem of the Knights of Columbus. You probably didn't know it, but this organization began a movement in 1953 to recommend the addition of "under God" to the US Pledge of Allegiance. It changed in 1954.

Casmir Pulaski Memorial Day - General Pulaski Memorial Day is a United States holiday in honor of General Kazimierz Pułaski, a Polish hero of the American Revolution. This holiday is held every year on October 11 by Presidential Proclamation, to commemorate his death from wounds suffered at the Siege of Savannah on October 9, 1779 and to honor the heritage of Polish Americans.

It is also celebrated as a legal holiday in Illinois on the first Monday of March with street parades and celebrations. Illinois has a large Polish population.

The observance was established in 1929 when Congress passed Public Resolution 16 of 1929 designating October 11 as General Pulaski Memorial Day. Every President has issued a proclamation for the observance annually since (except in 1930). His death was October 11, 1779 and he was buried at sea.

United Nations Day - October 24 - The United Nations is an international organization founded in 1945 after the Second World War by 51 countries (now 192) committed to maintaining international peace and security, developing friendly relations among nations and promoting social progress, better living standards and human rights.

Veterans Day - November 11 is Veterans Day. *Kiss a vet, it will make you both happy.* Other countries also still recognize November 11th as Armistice Day or Remembrance Day in honor of the Armistice treaty which ended World War I. The war officially ended when the Treaty of Versailles was signed on June 28, 1919, in the Palace of Versailles. However, fighting ceased seven months earlier when an armistice, or temporary cessation of hostilities, between the Allied nations and Germany went into effect on the eleventh hour of the eleventh day of the eleventh month.

In November 1919, President Wilson proclaimed November 11 as the first commemoration of Armistice Day with the following words: "To us in America, the reflections of Armistice Day will be filled with solemn pride in the heroism of those who died in the country's service and with gratitude for the victory, both because of the thing from which it has freed us and because of the opportunity it has given America to show her sympathy with peace and justice in the councils of the nations..." In 1938 Armistice Day was enacted as an official American holiday. In 1954 Congress changed the name from Armistice Day to Veterans Day to honor all veterans.

Recognized spelling - Veteran's Day, Veterans' Day, and Veterans Day. Veteran (from Latin vetus, meaning "old") is a person who has had long service or experience in an occupation or field.

Calendar Facts

If we lived in the 1500s, we would have skipped this October week. October is when the calendars changed from Julian to Gregorian. The ten days between Oct. 4 and Oct. 15, 1582 had been declared out of existence by the pope.

By the mid-1570s, the Julian calendar established in 45 B.C. was ten days behind the real seasons of the year. The spring equinox was actually occurring about March 12 and Easter was falling too late in spring. All this happened because the Earth year is about 11 minutes short of the 365¼ days set by Julius Caesar. It's really 365 days, 5 hours, 48 minutes, 46 seconds. If the drift kept up, Easter would eventually have been observed in the summer, and Christmas in the spring.

Pope Gregory XIII appointed a commission to tweak the Julian calendar. Under the leadership of physician Aloysius Lilius and Jesuit astronomer Christopher Clavius, the commission consulted with scientists and clergy. After wrestling with various ideas for half a decade, the commission proposed eliminating three leap years in every 400 (years ending in 00, unless they are divisible by 400).

That would prevent further creep of the calendar against the seasons (except for a minuscule under-correction). Resetting the calendar so the equinox would come in late March needed a more drastic solution: ten days would have to be wiped out of existence.

The commission sent its report to the pope Sept. 14, 1580. He issued a papal bull (formal proclamation issued by the pope, usually written in antiquated characters and sealed with a leaden bulla (seal)) on Feb. 24, 1582, declaring that the new calendar would go into force in October (when there were few holy days), and that ten days would be skipped. The day after October 4 would be called October 15.

Only Italy, Spain, and Portugal were fully ready by October.

Everyone's birthday moved to a calendar date 10 days later too, so 365 days would pass between one birthday and the next. Rents, interest, and wages had to be recalculated for a month that had only 21 days.

Most of Catholic Europe adopted the new, Gregorian calendar by 1584, but the old Julian calendar held on until 1752 in Britain and its colonies, and through 1918 in Russia, which used to celebrate its own October Revolution, in November. *My, how time flies.*

Speaking of BCE - My son told me about the new designations for BC and AD, so I had to go look it up. - There really is no difference between an AD/BC and BCE/CE system when it comes to historical dates. The year 23 AD is exactly the same as the year 23 CE, and 4004 BC is also 4004 BCE.

References to historical dates under either classification should not create confusion. Major historical dates such as 1492 AD is now 1492 CE and 1776 AD is 1776 CE.

CE is for Common Era and BCE is for Before Common Era. One way to relate to the old designations is to think of CE as Christ Existed and BCE as Before Christ Existed.

The AD/BC method of identifying historical dates is traced back to Catholic historians working in the early Middle Ages. Identifying historical dates until that point was often a complicated proposition, since different historians worked under different calendars.

Converting historical dates to the standard Gregorian calendar would not have been easy, so they began using the birth of Jesus Christ as a central point.

The term BC is short for "Before Christ.. Historical dates before the birth of Christ become smaller as they approach the theoretical Year Zero.

Historical dates after the birth of Christ are classified as AD, short for the Latin phrase Anno Domini, or "in the year of our Lord". Alas, *another goodie that we learned in school has become useless - and that was one of the few things I actually remembered.*

Week Day Name Origins - *Sunday* has been set aside as the "day of the sun" since ancient Egyptian times in honor of the sun-god Ra. The Egyptians passed their idea of a 7-day week onto the Romans, who also started their week with the Sun's day, dies solis. When translated into early German, the first day was called sunnon-dagaz, which made its way into Middle English as sone day.

For some in the Christian tradition, the first day of the week is named in accordance with the creation tale in the first book of the Bible, Genesis, where one of the first things God did was say, "Let there be light, and there was light."

Not every culture has Sunday as its first day, and notable exceptions are found in the Slavic languages, where Sunday is the last day of the week and is not named in honor of the sun. For example, in Hungary, Sunday is called Vasárnap and means market day, and in Old Russian, where Sunday was sometimes called free day.

Monday was named after the moon. In Latin, it was known as dies lunae (day of the moon), and this made its way into Old English as mon(an)dæg and the monday in Middle English. In early pagan traditions, Monday was dedicated to the goddess of the moon, although in some Christian traditions, assigning the moon to the second day also follows the story of Genesis, where in between the first and second days, darkness was separated from light and "evening came."

Tuesday has always been dedicated to a war god, and in ancient Greek, it was known as hemera Areos (day of Ares), modified only slightly by the Roman dies Martis (day of Mars), and later in Old English Tiwesdæg, in honor of a Norse god of war and law, Tiwaz or Tiw.

Wednesday was dedicated to the messenger of the gods, and for the Greeks, it was known as hemera Hermu (day of Hermes), then to the Romans as dies Mercurii (day of Mercury). When it was adopted by the Anglo-Saxons, as Mercury's areas of expertise overlapped with his, they dedicated the day to Odin, Woden in Old English (calling the day wodnesdæg).

Thursday assigned to Jupiter for the fifth day, dies Jovis, by the Romans, and it was assigned to Thor by the Norse, where it was originally called thorsdgr, later modified by Old English into thurresdæg, and then into Middle English's thur(e)sday.

Friday was assigned to Aphrodite and Venus, in Latin dies Veneris. In Old Norse and English, Venus was associated with Frigg, a goddess of knowledge and wisdom. By Old English, the day's name had been modified into frigedæg (Frigg's day) and by Middle English, to fridai. Incidentally, *TGIF, for Thank God It's Friday, dates back to 1946.*

Saturday historically was dedicated to Saturn, or Cronus to the Greeks, Jupiter's father and a god associated with dissolution, renewal, generation, agriculture and wealth. In Latin, the day was originally called dies Saturni, which was transformed into sæter(nes)dæg in Old English and saterday in Middle English. For some religions, Saturday is celebrated as the weekly day of rest, known as the Shabbat in Judaism and Sabbath for Seventh Day Adventists.

Russia and DST - Russia turns back its clocks for the last time March 8 to permanently adopt winter hours. It will also increased its time zones from nine to eleven, from the Pacific to the borders of the European Union. The Soviet Union introduced Daylight Saving Time in 1981. In 2011, then President Dmitry Medvedev introduced measures to reduce Russia's time zones to nine, and to keep summer time all year round. Russians put their clocks forward one hour, but did not put them back in winter time. For the past few years, Russia kept permanent summer time, but it proved to be highly unpopular with many Russians. When Crimea was annexed by Russia from Ukraine, Crimea's time was adjusted to match Moscow time.

Russian President Vladimir Putin announced during 2014 that the country permanently switch its eleven time zones to winter time on 26 October, 2014. Russia will not observe DST during 2017.

Longer Days - The earth is gradually slowing down. Every few years, an extra second is added to make up for lost time. Millions of years ago, a day on Earth would have been only 20 hours long. It is believed that, in another million years time, a day on Earth will be 27 hours long.

March Equinox, Spring, Easter - March Equinox in Plano, Texas, U.S.A. was on Saturday, March 19, 2016 at 11:30 PM CDT. The March equinox or Northward equinox is the equinox on the earth when the Sun appears to leave the southern hemisphere and cross the celestial equator, heading northward as seen from earth. In the northern hemisphere the March equinox is known as the vernal equinox, and in the southern hemisphere as the autumnal equinox. On the equinoxes the Sun shines directly on the equator and the length of day and night is nearly equal. This also signals the first day of Spring for the Northern Hemisphere or the first day of Fall in the Southern Hemisphere.

In 325CE (AD) the Council of Nicaea established that Easter would be held on the first Sunday after the first full moon occurring on or after the vernal equinox.

Spring Sunshine - The Sun's light reaches the surface of Earth about 8 minutes after it left the surface of the Sun. It takes 3 minutes to reach Mercury and about 4 hours to reach Neptune.

Famous Days in History

Happy Pheidippides Day - Legend has it that, on September 3 in the year 490 BCE (BC), a trained runner by the name of Pheidippides (or Phidippides or Philippides) of Athens, was dispatched to seek help against the invading Persian army. He ran for two days and two nights to the city of Sparta, about 125 miles away. Because of a religious festival, he could not get the needed help until after the next full moon, so he ran back without reinforcements.

Fortunately, they won the battle against the Persians at Marathon. After the battle and victory, Pheidippides ran 26 miles from Marathon to Athens to carry the news of the victory. His last words before he collapsed and died, were something like, "We have won."

In honor of Pheidippides, the 26-mile marathon became part of the Olympic Games held in Athens in 1896. Seventeen runners began, but only nine finished the race. Hamilton Ontario's 30k Around the Bay Road Race is the oldest long-distance race in North America. It was first run in 1894 – two years before the first Olympics and three years before Boston.

At the Olympic games in London in 1908, King Edward VII asked to have the race begin near Queen Victoria's statue at Windsor Castle. The revised distance of 26 miles to the stadium, plus a 385-yard lap of the track was established. This is the distance each race honors today.

Black Tot Day - For hundreds of years, Royal Navy seamen lined up in galleys from the poles to the tropics to receive their regulation lunchtime tot (about eighth to half pint) of rum but, years ago, the tradition was ended. On 31 July 1970, known in the navy as Black Tot Day, free rum was retired from navy life.

By 1970, the rum bosun's daily doling out of rum at midday, diluted with water (grog) for junior ratings, neat for senior - was a reasonably gentlemanly affair. A grog was a mixture of two pints water and a half pint rum. The Admiralty took away the rum, because it was concerned it would hinder sailors' ability to operate increasingly complex weapons systems and navigational tools.

Beer had been the staple beverage of the Royal Navy until the 17th Century, used as a self-preserving replacement for water, which became undrinkable when kept in casks for long periods. As the horizons of the British Empire expanded, the sheer bulk of beer, the ration for which was a gallon per day per seaman, and its liability to go sour in warmer climates, made it impractical to take on long voyages. Wine and spirits started to take the place of beer place until 1655, after the capture of the island of Jamaica from Spain, the navy introduced rum.

Until 1740 the daily ration was half a pint of neat rum, twice a day. Sailors would check their rum had not been watered down by pouring it onto gunpowder and setting light to it, from where the term "proof" originates. By volume, 57.15% alcohol has been calculated as the minimum required for it to pass the test.

Alcoholic proof in the United States is defined as twice the percentage of alcohol by volume. Consequently, 100-proof whiskey contains 50% alcohol by volume; 86-proof whiskey contains 43% alcohol, etc.

Happy Pi Approximation Day - Even though March 14 is the official Pi Day, July 22 or 22/7 in the more common day/month format, is an ancient approximation of pi, so we celebrate Pi Approximation. *Hey, who needs an excuse to have a holiday.*

Decembers Past - In 1942, US President Franklin D. Roosevelt ordered liquidation of the Works Progress Administration, created during the Great Depression to provide work for the unemployed. *Seems to me that worked better than unemployment checks.*

* In 1768, Encyclopedia Britannica was first published.
* In 1954, the first Burger King fast-food restaurant opened in Miami.
* In 1975, the US Senate authorized a $2.3 billion emergency loan to save New York City from bankruptcy.
* In 2009, the US unemployment rate fell to 10 percent in November, down from its peak of 10.2 percent in October.
* In 2010, the US unemployment rate went up to 9.8% in November, from 9.6% in October.
* In 1929, the Ford Motor Co. raised the pay of its employees from $5 to $7 a day despite the collapse of the US stock market.
* In 1967, Dr. Christiaan Barnard performed the first successful heart transplant at Cape Town, South Africa.

Yuletide Holidays

Saint Nicholas Day - St Nicholas died on December 6, 343 and is remembered every year on the 6th of December. It continues in many places, and some cultures still use this occasion to give gifts to children. There are still celebrations in Germany, the Netherlands, Belgium, and Milwaukee also has a strong tradition of celebrating "St Nick's Day," due to its large immigrant German community.

The Dutch celebrate the 'Feast of Sinterklaas', (Santa Claus is a variation of the name), as we celebrate Christmas. Some celebrate on December 5 (like Christmas Eve). The myth involving Sinterklaas is that he rides on his white horse across the roofs of houses, and that his helpers, who are entirely black and called Zwarte Piet (Black Pete), climb down the chimneys and put presents in people's shoes. Children leave a carrot in the shoes for his horse.

St Nicholas (or St Nickolas) was Bishop of Myra (Turkey) and remains the Patron Saint of sailors, fishermen, the falsely accused, pawnbrokers, thieves, and a number of cities.

Now you can understand why old pictures of Santa Claus show the bishop's miter (hat) and staff.

Many miracles and good deeds are attributed to St Nicholas. One relates how a father, who could not afford a dowry for his three daughters (which would mean they were unable to marry, and might have been sold), would find little bags of gold coins thrown through his window, under cover of night. The bags landed on stockings left to dry before the fire. *This is why people hang stockings on the fireplace at Christmas, hoping for them to be filled with goodies.*

Growing up, we celebrated St. Nicholas day by throwing small bags of candy on neighbor's porches at dusk, then running away. We were always home in time to enjoy the candy treats thrown on our porch.

Old Saint Nicholas - During 1823 in the Troy NY Sentinel published the poem we know as "A Visit from St. Nicholas" by Clement C. Moore. It was published anonymously under the newspaper editor's title, Account of a Visit from St. Nicholas. Moore wrote it a year earlier and read it to his children, who saved it.

He was a professor of Oriental and Greek literature and never sought to do any more than read the story to his children that one time. Clement referred to the poem "a mere trifle." Some have questioned whether he was the author, but proof has been elusive.

It is known that Donner and Blitzen were originally from Dunder and Blixem, Dutch for thunder and lightning. Rudolph did not come along until 1939.

Prior to the poem, American ideas about St. Nicholas and other Christmas visitors varied considerably. The poem has influenced ideas about St. Nicholas and Santa Claus beyond the United States to the rest of the world. He was the first to describe eight tiny reindeer. Oh, and it ended with 'Happy Christmas to all'.

Santa and Saint Nick - What's the difference between Santa Claus and Saint Nicholas?
Santa Claus belongs to childhood;
St. Nicholas models for all of life.

Santa Claus was developed to boost Christmas sales, the commercial
Christmas message;
St. Nicholas told the story of Christ and peace, goodwill toward all, the
hope-filled Christmas message.

Santa Claus encourages consumption;
St. Nicholas encourages compassion.

Santa Claus appears each year to be seen and heard for a short time;
St. Nicholas surrounds us always.

Santa Claus flies through the air from the North Pole;
St. Nicholas walked the earth caring for those in need.

Santa Claus isn't bad;
St. Nicholas is just better.

Saint Nikolaus and Santa Claus - Though they have similar
outfits, Nikolaus is not to be confused with Santa Claus, who Germans
call the Weihnachtsmann, or Father Christmas. They are two different
people.

In fact, many religious families try to focus more on Nikolaus earlier
in December to insure that Christmas is actually about Jesus' birth,
and not presents from an Americanized and commercialized Santa.

Each year on December 6, Germans remember the death of Nikolas of
Myra (now part of modern Turkey), who died on that day in 346. He
was a Greek Christian bishop known for miracles and giving gifts
secretly, and is now the patron saint of little children, sailors,
merchants, and students. Known as Nikolas the Wonderworker for his
miracles, he is also identified with Santa Claus. Beliefs and traditions
about Nikolaus were probably combined with German mythology,
particularly regarding stories about the bearded pagan god Odin, who
also had a beard and a bag to capture naughty children.

The custom of leaving shoes out began because the historical St.
Nicholaus had a reputation for leaving secret gifts, such as coins, in
people's shoes or stockings overnight. Kids traditionally put out their
boots, though shoes or stockings will suffice for those without boots.
Dirty boots are unacceptable. Children polish their boots to show they
have been good. They usually place just one boot outside their door so
they do not appear too greedy.

Lord of Misrule - In ancient Roman times, December 17 was the beginning of the festival of Saturnalia, in honor of the god Saturn (of agriculture). It was originally just a day event, but eventually grew into a seven day orgy of revelry, feasting, and merrymaking.

The Saturnalia was a holiday period for all, including the slaves, who changed places with their masters for the duration. Presents were exchanged, especially candles, informal clothes worn, and gambling games permitted. It was also customary to appoint a master of the revels (Saturnalicius princeps), a character that reappeared in England as the Lord of Misrule. The Lord of Misrule formally presided over the Christmas celebrations, or over the entire period from All-Hallows Eve (Oct 31) to Candlemas (Feb 2).

It is commonly believed that the church chose this time (Pope Julius I chose December 25) in an effort to adopt and absorb the traditions of the pagan Saturnalia festival. It was first called the Feast of the Nativity, the custom spread to Egypt by 432, and to England by the end of the sixth century. By the end of the eighth century, the celebration of Christmas had spread to Scandinavia. Today, in the Greek and Russian orthodox churches, Christmas is celebrated 13 days after the 25th, which is also referred to as the Epiphany or Three Kings Day, as it is believed then the three wise men finally found Jesus in the manger.

Winter Solstice - In the Northern Hemisphere, the Winter Solstice marks the first day of the season of winter. It falls on or near December 21.

The Pagan celebration of Winter Solstice (also known as Yule) is one of the oldest winter celebrations in the world. It is a celebration of the shortest day and longest night of the year in the Northern Hemisphere, when the North Pole is at its furthest point away from the sun.

The Druids (Celtic priests) would cut the mistletoe that grew on the oak tree and give it as a blessing. Oaks were seen as sacred and the winter fruit of the mistletoe was a symbol of life in the dark winter months.

Yule logs are traditionally lit on the first day of the Solstice and are burned throughout the Solstice night for 12 hours as a symbol of hope and belief that the sun will return. The Celts thought that the sun stood still for twelve days in the middle of winter and during this time, a log was lit to conquer the darkness, banish evil spirits, and bring luck for the coming year.

Holiday Town Names - Place names associated with the holiday season include North Pole, Alaska (population 2,212); Santa Claus, IN (2,314); Santa Claus, GA (250); Noel, MO (1,608); the village of Rudolph, WI (412) and Dasher, GA (849). There is Snowflake, AZ (5,673) and a dozen places named Holly, including Holly Springs, MS, Mount Holly, NC, and Holly, MI.

Christmas Thoughts - "On Christmas Eve all animals can speak." However, it is bad luck to test this superstition.

"The child born on Christmas Day will have a special fortune." *One of my Aunts was born on Christmas, 1908. She was special. Also, 25th December 1642, Sir Isaac Newton was born. He found white light could be split into the colors of the Rainbow.*

Wearing new shoes on Christmas Day will bring bad luck.

Good luck will come to the home where a fire is kept burning throughout the Christmas season.

If a girl raps at the hen house door on Christmas Eve and a rooster crows, she will marry within the year.

A mild December precedes a cold snap later in the winter.

A green December fills the graveyard.

A clear star-filled sky on Christmas Eve will bring good crops in the summer.

If sun shines through the apple trees upon a Christmas Day, when autumn comes they will a load of fruit display.

White (snow) on Christmas means Easter will be green.

A green Christmas; a white Easter.

If Christmas day be bright and clear there will be two winters in the year.

The nearer the New Moon to Christmas Day, the harder the winter.

Christmas Facts - $1.3 billion in sales by US Christmas tree farmers during 2015. During 2015, people purchased 25.9 million real Christmas trees, and fake trees at 12.5 million for $854 million.

The US Census Bureau estimates that $1.1 billion worth of Christmas tree ornaments and $346 million of Christmas tree lights were imported from China between January and September 2016. China accounted for 92% of the total US ornament imports and 87% of the total US tree light imports.

$470.3 million in imports of Christmas tree ornaments from China between January and August 2009. China was the leading country of origin for such items.

Kissing Under the Mistletoe - The Ancient Celts used mistletoe as an animal aphrodisiac, or more specifically, to increase the fertility of sheep. Such became the mythic power of mistletoe that in addition to bringing a lamb-ful spring, mistletoe was hung over doorways to ward off fire, lightning, and evil spirits. Despite its protective properties, mistletoe could not throw off its fertile past, and even though it was hung in people's doorways, it seemed as if something romantic should occur in its presence. Thus the kissing.

Did you know that mistletoe's power runs out? Every time a man steals a kiss under the mistletoe, he must pay by plucking one of its berries. When the berries are gone, no more kissing.

New Year's Eve - The last day of the year is New Year's Eve. Many people see the old year out with a party, welcoming in the New Year with toasts of champagne, and exchanging good wishes for a 'Happy New Year'. This celebration is particularly dear to the Scots. They call it Big Ben Hogmanay. All over Britain there are parties, fireworks, singing, and dancing, to ring out the old year and ring in the new. As the clock Big Ben strikes midnight, people link arms and sing a song called 'Auld Lang Syne' to remind them of old and new friends.

A New Year superstition in Yorkshire, England - people say 'Black rabbits, black rabbits, black rabbits' during the closing seconds of the old year. Then they say, 'White rabbits, white rabbits, white rabbits,' as their first utterance of the New Year. This is supposed to bring good luck.

What the Heck is an Auld Lang Syne - On New Year's Eve at least a few of us will be singing about Robert Burns 1788 poem put to music.

The song is also sung at funerals, graduations, and other occasions of farewell.

Literally translated, it means "old long since," but usually interpreted as "days gone by." Now we sing it loosely meaning "for the sake of old times."

It begins asking if it is right that old times be forgotten, and asks to remember long time relationships.

Should auld acquaintance be forgot,
And never brought to mind?
Should auld acquaintance be forgot,
And auld lang syne? (*and days gone by*)

For auld lang syne, my dear,
For auld lang syne,
We'll tak a cup o' kindness yet,
For auld lang syne.

And surely ye'll be your pint-stowp, (*You'll buy your pint* cup)
And surely I'll be mine! (*and I'll buy mine*)
And we'll tak a cup o' kindness yet,
For auld lang syne.

Boxing Day - Boxing Day is a holiday in the United Kingdom, Canada, and many other Commonwealth nations. It is a time for family and friends to gather for food and fun. Outdoor sports, such as soccer, horse racing, and hunting are popular on this holiday. Retailers offer huge savings on many items on this day, making it the biggest shopping day of the year in Canada. It is celebrated on December 26th and is a statutory holiday in the federal jurisdiction and Ontario. If it falls on a Saturday or a Sunday, the working day immediately preceding or following Boxing Day is considered a legal holiday.

Boxing Day, also known as the Feast of St. Stephen, after the first Christian martyr. It originated in England in the middle of the nineteenth century under Queen Victoria. It began as a holiday for members of the merchant class to give boxes containing food and fruit, clothing, and/or money to trades people and servants.

Many workers were required to work on Christmas Day and took the following day off to visit their families. As they prepared to leave, their employers would present them with Christmas boxes. The gifts were an expression of gratitude similar to the bonuses many employers offer their employees today. These gifts, usually given in wood or clay boxes, gave the holiday it's name, "Boxing Day".

Also related to the origin of Boxing Day is the tradition of opening the alms boxes placed in churches during the Christmas season. The contents of these boxes were distributed amongst the poor by the clergy on the day after Christmas.

When great sailing ships were setting off to discover new land, a Christmas Box was used as a good luck device. It was a small container placed on each ship while it was still in port. It was put there by a priest, and those crewmen who wanted to ensure a safe return would drop money into the box. It was then sealed up and kept on board for the entire voyage. If the ship came home safely, the box was handed over to the priest in the exchange for celebrating a Mass of thanks for the success of the voyage. The Priest would keep the box sealed until Christmas when he would open it to share the contents with the poor.

During the late 18th century, Lords and Ladies of the manor would "box up" their leftover food, and sometimes gifts and distribute them the day after Christmas to tenants who lived and worked on their lands.

Kwanzaa - The relatively new holiday Kwanza was created in 1966 by Dr. Maulana Karenga, professor and chairman of Black Studies at California State University, Long Beach. He saw it as a way to bring African-Americans together as a community. He combined aspects of several different harvest celebrations, such as those of the Ashanti and those of the Zulu. The name was derived from a phrase that means 'first fruits.' Later the second "A" was later added to make 7 letters to coincide with the seven candles he decided should be lit for the holidays.

Kwanzaa is a non-religious African-American holiday which celebrates family, community, and culture. Celebrations often include songs and dances, African drums, storytelling, poetry reading, and a large traditional meal. On each of the seven nights, the family gathers and a child lights one of the candles. It is celebrated for seven days: December 26 - January 1.

Christmas Carols - "Carol" is a derivative of the French word caroller, the interpretation of which means dancing around in a circle. Carol and carols, eventually came to mean not only to dance, but included music and lyrics - hence Christmas Caroling.

Christmas carols are based on Christian lyrics and relate mostly to the Nativity. Christmas carols were introduced in to church services by St. Francis of Assisi in the 12th century.

The joyous themes for many traditional Christmas carols were banned in England by the staunch Protestant Oliver Cromwell and many of the very old Christmas carols and songs were subsequently lost for all time. They were only fully popularized again during the Victorian era when they again expressed joyful and merry themes in their carol lyrics as opposed to the normal somber, Christian lyrics found in hymns. As religious observances in the United States and England were closely linked, the popularity of Christmas carols grew in both countries during the 19th century. Many Christmas songs are relatively recent, and bear no relation to Christmas carols, such as the famous, *'Grandma got run over by a reindeer'*.

Christmas Tree Lights - Some sources credit Edison with being the first to use electric lights as Christmas decorations, when he strung multiple lights attached to a single cord around his laboratory in 1880. It was three years after Edison had demonstrated that light bulbs were practical.

Ten Things Not to Get Her for Christmas - Electronics, any jewelry on sale, picture of yourself, cleaning stuff, kitchen stuff, lingerie, exercise equipment, beauty supplies, and a stripper pole.

Four Christmas Song Authors - Interesting that four popular Christmas songs were actually written by Jewish authors. "White Christmas" was written by Irving Berlin in 1940. "Silver Bells" was written by Jay Livingston and Ray Evans in 1951. "Let it Snow. Let it Snow. Let it Snow" was written by Jule Styne with lyrics by Sammy Cahn in 1945. "Rudolph, the Red-Nosed Reindeer" was written by Johnny Marks in 1949.

Companies Against Christmas - True - According to the American Family Association, the following companies "may use 'Christmas' sparingly in a single or unique product description, but as a company, does not recognize it". As of November 2010

Barnes & Noble
CVS Pharmacy
Office Depot
Radio Shack
Staples
SUPERVALU
Victoria's Secret

Rudolph, the Red-Nosed Reindeer - The most famous reindeer of them all. The song is one of the best selling of all time as sung by the singing cowboy, Gene Autry. It is also on albums by the Supremes and the Jackson 5.

Rudolph was created ten years before the song in 1939, by Johnny Marks' brother-in-law Robert L. May for Montgomery Ward. The store wanted something to bring in holiday shoppers and the story/poem was given out to children as an advertising gimmick.

A parent complained about the song's religious reference and got it pulled from her child's kindergarten Christmas show at Murrayville Elementary School. The song was pulled "because it had the word Christmas in it," said Rick Holliday, assistant school superintendent.

A Jewish mother, who didn't want her name published, objected to what she called "religious overtones" in the song. So the principal agreed to pull it from the program. Luckily the board and attorneys reviewed it and decided the song was not religious and had it reinstated into the kindergarten program.

Modern reaction to this song about a reindeer, "Rudolph the Red-Nosed Reindeer" caused a stir at a New Hanover County school at Christmas time during 2008.

Mistletoe - There are many stories about Mistletoe and the origins of use, dating back to Pliny the Elder, but this is the one I like. According to Norse/Germanic legend, Frigga got all the plants and animals of the Earth to promise not to harm her son - except mistletoe.

Loki, the god of mischief, took that opportunity to kill Baldur with a

Karen
McCormick
likes this
one.

spear made of mistletoe. Frigga's tears then turned into mistletoe berries, which brought Baldur back to life, prompting Frigga to declare mistletoe a symbol of love. It is appropriate that we speak of Frigga on Friday as some references show this as the early etymology of the word Friday. *Last chance to use the mistletoe to kiss your favorite this season.*

New Year's Eve - The last day of the year is New Year's Eve. Many people see the old year out with a party, welcoming in the New Year with toasts of champagne, and exchanging good wishes for a 'Happy New Year'. This celebration is particularly dear to the Scots. They call it Big Ben Hogmanay. All over Britain there are parties, fireworks, singing and dancing, to ring out the old year and ring in the new. As the clock Big Ben strikes midnight, people link arms and sing a song called 'Auld Lang Syne' to remind them of old and new friends.

A New Year superstition in Yorkshire, England - people say 'Black rabbits, black rabbits, black rabbits' during the closing seconds of the old year. Then they say, 'White rabbits, white rabbits, white rabbits,' as their first utterance of the New Year. This is suppose to bring good luck.

Hogmanay - Hogmanay is the Scots word for the last day of the year and is synonymous with the celebration of the New Year in the Scottish manner. It is normally only the start of a celebration which lasts through the night until the morning of New Year's Day, or, in some cases, 2 January which is a Scottish Bank Holiday. Literally translated it means "gift."

There are many customs associated with Hogmanay. The most widespread is the practice of 'first-footing' which starts immediately after midnight. This involves being the first person to cross the threshold of a friend or neighbor and often involved the giving of symbolic gifts such as salt, coal, shortbread, whiskey, and fruit cake intended to bring different kinds of luck to the householder. Food and drink are then given to the guests. This may go on throughout the early hours of the morning and well into the next day. The first-foot is supposed to set the luck for the rest of the year.

Christmas 1864 - After his Civil War march across Georgia, Union General William T. Sherman sent U.S. President Abraham Lincoln this message, "I beg to present you as a Christmas present the city of Savannah."

Christmas, 1876 - "Christmas and New Year are a very merry time for some people; but for cabmen and cabmen's horses it is no holiday, though it may be a harvest. There are so many parties, balls, and places of amusement open, that the work is hard and often late.

Sometimes driver and horse have to wait hours in the rain or frost, shivering with cold, while the merry people within are dancing away to the music. I wonder if the beautiful ladies ever think of the weary cabman waiting on his box, and his patient beast standing till his legs get stiff with cold."

From Black Beauty: The Autobiography of a Horse by Anna Sewell, published in November, 1877. She never wrote another book. She died on April 25, 1878, five months after the publication of her classic horse story.

Christmas 1882 - Edward Johnson, who worked at Edison Illumination Company, finds an application for electric lights and becomes the first person to use them as Christmas tree decorations. (Edison decorated his office with lights prior to this, but not a tree.)

Johnson used 80 small red, white and blue electric bulbs, strung together along a single power cord, to light the Christmas tree in his New York home.

Musical Interlude - I couldn't share Christmas without my favorite Christmas music, Mario Lanza's 'O Holy Night'. Celine Dione also absolutely rocks with 'O Holy Night'.

On December 24, 1818, "Silent Night, Holy Night" was first sung. The words were written by Joseph Franz Mohr, a young priest, and the music by Herr Gruber in Oberndorf, Austria.

Horology

The science of timekeeping is known as horology.

Nanosecond and Picosecond - A nanosecond is one billionth of a second, and a picosecond is one trillionth or 0.000 000 000 001 of a second.

Planck time - Planck time is the shortest known time span. It is the time it takes for light to travel a Planck length or 1.616199 × 10-35 meters in vacuum.

Easter celebration date - Easter is normally celebrated on the first Sunday after the first full moon that occurs on or after the Spring Equinox.

Light year - A light year is not a unit of time, but a unit of distance. The International Astronomical Union defines a light year as the distance light travels in vacuum in one Julian Year. In astronomy, a Julian Year corresponds to exactly 365.25 days.

Fortnight - A fortnight is a unit of time that refers to 14 days. It comes from an old English word, fēowertȳne niht, meaning fourteen night. It is commonly used in the UK, Ireland, and many commonwealth countries. People in the US and most parts of Canada use the term biweekly to refer to the time period of two weeks.

New York minute - The phrase in a New York minute refers to a very short period of time or an instant. Legend has it that the phrase originated in Texas in the late 1960s. The phrase was popularized by TV personality Johnny Carson who joked that a New York minute was the time between a traffic light turning green and the car behind one's car honking.

Jiffy - Jiffy is usually used to indicate a very short period of time, but it is formally defined in the fields of Physics and Chemistry as the time required for light to travel a centimeter. Also known as a light centimeter, a jiffy is equal to about 33.3564 picoseconds.

Friday 13th - Any month in the Gregorian Calendar that begins on a Sunday will have a Friday, the 13th, and there is at least one Friday the 13th in every year. A single calendar year can have up to 3 Friday the 13ths.

Geography Facts

NEW AND OLD SEVEN WONDERS OF THE WORLD

A global poll determined the new seven wonders of the world. They are:
'Christ the Redeemer' statue in Rio de Janeiro;

Coliseum in Rome;

Taj Mahal in India;

Great Wall of China;

Ancient city of Petra, in Jordan;

Inca ruins of Machu Picchu in Peru;

Ancient Mayan city of Chichén Itzá, in Mexico.

Interesting how our tastes have changed, such as the Coliseum in its glory was not considered good enough for the old list, but now that it is ruins, it is a 'wonder'.

The old Seven Wonders of the World:
Great Pyramid of Egypt, Giza;

Colossus of Rhodes, Greece;

Lighthouse of Alexandria, Egypt;

Statue of Zeus at Olympia, Greece;

Hanging Gardens of Babylon, Iraq;

Mausoleum of Halicarnassus, Turkey,

Temple of Artemis, Turkey.

AMAZING WORLD FACTS

Blue Roses - In some cultures, blue roses traditionally signify a mystery, or attaining the impossible, or never ending quest for the impossible. They are believed to be able to grant the owner youth or grant wishes. Historically, this symbolism derives from the rose's meaning in the language of flowers common in Victorian times.

The color blue is also traditionally associated with royal blood, and thus the blue rose can also denote regal majesty and splendor. In Chinese folklore, the blue rose signifies hope against unattainable love.

Due to the absence in nature of blue roses they have come to symbolize mystery and longing to attain the impossible with some cultures believing that the holder of a blue rose will have his wishes granted. In 2004, researchers used genetic modification to create blue pigmented roses, but they were a bit dark and leaned more to lavender. Recent work using cloned pigments from Irises, along with depressing the production of cyanidin has produced a mauve colored flower, with only trace amounts of cyanidin. Genetically modified blue roses are patented and currently being grown by Suntory Ltd., Japan

----

Bottled Water - The smug greenies have done it to themselves again. Many folks are back to opting for tap water or filtered tap water, because of the nasty environmental effects of producing and shipping bottled waters and the cleanup of the bottles themselves.

An increasing number of restaurants are offering only filtered tap water to customers these days. Mario Batali (from TV fame) stopped selling bottled water at his New York City restaurants in 2009, and eateries in Florida and Massachusetts are also serving only tap.

New York is the 11th state to require a bottled-water deposit, and the list is expected to grow. Americans toss away 35 billion water bottles a year. Of those, about 12 percent are recycled. In one year, Americans threw away an estimated 2.5 million bottles an hour, according to data provided by the US Clean Air Council.

US landfills are overflowing with 2 million tons of discarded water bottles. Because plastics are produced with fossil fuels, that makes them an environmental hazard and an enormous waste of valuable resources.

The US Conference of Mayors voted in June, 2009 to recommend that City Halls stop serving bottled water even at special functions. *I always said bottled water was the pet rock of the decade, now it looks like some folks are beginning to agree with me.*

Bottled Water Ban - A rural town in Australia has voted overwhelmingly to ban the sale of bottled water over concerns about its environmental impact. They say huge amounts of resources are used to extract, package, and transport bottled water.

Only one resident voted against the ban, along with a representative from the bottled water industry, ABC news reported.

Campaigner John Dee said local opinion had been incensed when a drinks company announced plans to tap an underground reservoir in the town. "The company has been looking to extract water locally, bottle it in Sydney, and bring it back here to sell it," he said.

New South Wales Premier Nathan Rees backed the cause, ordering government departments to stop buying bottled water and use tap water instead.

Population Disparity - Rhode Island, the smallest US state has a larger population than the largest US state, Alaska. Rhode Island has 1.056 million and Alaska has 741,894 people.

How to Move a Mountain - Mother Nature can do in seconds what mankind has never been able to do. Geologists in China announced the 7.8-magnitude earthquake that struck Nepal caused Mount Everest to move three centimeters (1.2 inches) to the southwest.

The world's highest peak had been moving northeast at a pace of four centimeters (1.6 inches) per year during the past decade and China's national surveying administration said the height of the mountain has risen by three centimeters (1.2 inches) from 2005 to 2015.

The April 25, 2015 earthquake, which triggered an avalanche on Mount Everest, was one of two major quakes that struck Nepal that year, leaving more than 8,700 people dead.

Masdar - We have seen the new city of Masdar in the Saudi desert, described to be the first city with no 'carbon footprint'.

The US did it first in 1970. Arcosanti, the model city conceived by the Italian-born architect Paolo Soleri as an 'urban laboratory' for experiments in sustainable living. Founded in 1970, this precursor to Masdar, was an attempt to combine innovative architecture with the clean technologies then at hand to conserve energy and minimize waste.

It is a demonstration of Soleri's vision for how society could lessen its destructive impact on the environment. It grows its own food, recycles its waste for agricultural nutrients, and has its own mostly self-contained economic system. *Arcosanti is near Phoenix. Have been there and had one of the beautiful Soleri bells on my patio. Great full sound. They are made on-site and sold to tourists to help fund the city.*

Millions of Lakes - There are 117 million lakes on Earth, covering 3.7 percent of the continental land surface. This does not include Antarctica, Greenland, or the Caspian Sea. About 90 million of these lakes are less than two football fields in size, or 0.5 to 2.5 acres (0.2 to 1 hectares).

Language Facts - There are a bit over 6,900 languages spoken in the world today. About 6% of them have more than a million speakers each, and collectively account for 94% of the world population. The top three are Chinese: 1,197 million native speakers, Spanish: 399 million, and English: 335 million (with 1.5 billion overall English speakers). The most widely spoken by number of countries/dependencies where the language has official or de facto status is English (101).

Research shows that one language vanishes every 14 days when its last speaker dies. In a hundred years, predictions are that half will disappear.

In Brazil, less than 8,000 people are left who speak Kayapo. Their language distinguishes between 56 types of bees. Of the 231 languages spoken in Australia, at least 50 have never been written.

Forty languages are still spoken in Oklahoma, Texas, and New Mexico, many of them originally used by Indian tribes and others introduced by Eastern tribes that were forced to resettle on reservations.

83 languages with "global" influence are spoken and written by 80 percent of the world population. Lesser used languages will fall by the

wayside, while English has become the most used form of communication around the world. More people in China speak English than in the whole United States. English is the official language of more countries than any other language.

There are 292 spoken languages in China. I thought the US had many at 175. *That's not even counting local dialects, Y'all.*

Tidbits - The Main Library at Indiana University sinks over an inch every year because when it was built engineers failed to take into account the weight of all the books that would occupy the building.

Erosion at the base of Niagara Falls, US undermines the shale cliffs and as a result, the falls have receded approximately 7 miles over the last 10,000 years.

Hawaii is moving toward Japan 4 inches every year.

Ninety percent of Canada's 36,000,000 citizens live within 100 miles of the US border. (California, US has 39 million citizens)

The Eiffel Tower shrinks 6 inches in winter.

La Paz, Bolivia is the world's most fireproof city. At 12,000 feet about sea level, the amount of oxygen in the air barely supports a flame.

Plano, Texas - Plano, based on its population, is the ninth-largest city in the state (69th largest in US), bigger than Midland, Waco, or Amarillo. Nationally, it outsizes Salt Lake City, Little Rock, Providence, Orlando, and Fort Lauderdale.

Venus Rising - The Soviets successfully landed several spacecraft on Venus, beginning in 1975. Seven of the landers conducted chemical analysis of rocks, which indicate a composition similar to that of terrestrial basaltic volcanic rocks. In 1981, the Venera 13 lander provided the first color images of the surface of Venus. The US sent Pioneer to Venus in 1979 and Magellan in 1989 to continue the work of mapping the surface of the planet. Neither landed on the surface of the planet.

At the surface, the atmospheric pressure is 92 times that of the Earth's at sea-level. Venus has a surface temperature of about 900° F.

It is about 84% of the size of earth and a Venusian day is 243 Earth days. Venus rotates from east to west, so the Sun rises in the west and sets in the east.

League of Nations, **United Nations, NATO, SCO** - The **League of Nations** was formed after World War I (1914-1919) and was dissolved by the beginning of World War II (1939).

It was an intergovernmental organization founded as a result of the Paris Peace Conference that ended World War I, and it was the precursor to the United Nations.

The League was the first permanent international security organization whose principal mission was to maintain world peace. It had 58 members. The League's primary goals included preventing war through collective security, disarmament, and settling international disputes through negotiation and arbitration. Germany, under Hitler withdrew from the League and was followed by other nations. WWII showed that the League had failed its primary purpose, which was to avoid a future world war.

The name **United Nations** was devised by US president Franklin D. Roosevelt following World War II and set up as another world organization for preventing future wars. The United Nations officially came into existence in October 1945, when the Atlantic Charter had been ratified by China, France, USSR, UK, and a majority of other signatories. It has 193 members. The main purposes of the United Nations are to *facilitate cooperation in international law, international security, human rights, social progress, and accomplish world peace.*

North Atlantic Treaty Organization or NATO, also called the North Atlantic Alliance, is an intergovernmental military alliance based on the North Atlantic Treaty which was signed on 4 April 1949. The organization constitutes a system of collective defense where its members agree to mutual defense in response to an attack by any external party. It has 29 members. The Korean War galvanized the member states, and an integrated military structure was built up under the direction of two US supreme commanders.

The combined military spending of all NATO members constitutes over 70% of the world's defense spending. The United States accounts for 37% of the total military spending of the world and the United Kingdom, France, Germany, and Italy account for another 15%.

The six-member **Shanghai Cooperation Organization (SCO)** was set up in 2001 by China, Kazakhstan, Kyrgyzstan, Russia, Tajikistan, and Uzbekistan to address religious extremism and border security in Central Asia, and as a security counterweight to NATO that would allow Russia and China to rival US influence in Asia. It is now also looking to cooperate at an economic level. Its membership now includes: Kyrgyzstan, Tajikistan, Uzbekistan, China, Kazakhstan, Russia, India, and Pakistan, with Iran, and Mongolia attending meetings.

Its summits bring together an eclectic gathering of world leaders. In a recent summit declaration signed by all the member states, the organization also attacked missile defense programs in another apparent dig at the United States.

Smallest Country - The smallest country in the world is the Vatican. It is less than two tenths of a square mile. Its population is less than 451, as of 2012. Vatican City is about the size of a golf course. It is basically a walled enclave inside of Rome, Italy. The entire country does not have a single street address.

It may be small, but it is very powerful. It is the sovereign territory of the Holy See, or the seat of the Catholic Church, which has over one billion people as constituents.

The Vatican was created in 1929 by the Lateran Treaty (signed by Dictator Benito Mussolini) and is ruled by the Pope, a non-hereditary, elected monarch who rules with absolute authority. The Pope is the only absolute monarch in Europe.

Another unique thing about the smallest country in the world is that it has no permanent citizens. Citizenship of Vatican City is conferred upon those who work at the Vatican (as well as spouses and children) and is revoked when they stop working there.

It is guarded by the smallest and oldest regular army in the world, the Swiss Guard, originally made up of Swiss mercenaries in 1506. The army, who are also personal bodyguards of the Pope, number about 100 Catholic, unmarried, male Swiss citizens. The Swiss Guard's Renaissance-style uniform was commonly attributed as to have been designed by Michelangelo, but that is not true. It was a common style during the Renaissance. Most of the Swiss Guards carry pistols and automatic rifles.

The official languages of the Vatican are Latin and Italian and its ATMs are the only ones in the world that offer services in Latin.

It has a country code top level domain for the web of .va and currently there are few publicly known .va domains. It also has a radio broadcasting service, called Vatican Radio, which was set up by Guglielmo Marconi, the Father of Radio.

The country is the only non-commercial economy in the world. It is supported financially by contributions of Catholics worldwide (called Peter's Pence), the sale of postage stamps and publications, and tourism. It has no tax.

Survey Says - In Scotland, 13% of the population have red hair, according to the first online dating service exclusively for people with red hair, Redhedd.com. This is the highest proportion of any country in the world.

> *Less than two percent of the world's population has red hair.*

Five Lake Superior Facts - Lake Superior contains ten percent of all the fresh water on earth.

It has enough water to cover all of North and South America with water a foot deep.

Lake Superior is, by surface area, the largest lake in the world.

It contains as much water as all the other Great Lakes combined, plus three extra Lake Eries.

In the summer, the sun sets more than 35 minutes later on the western shore of Lake Superior than at its southeastern edge. *(Lake Superior is the lake at the top of Michigan's upper peninsula and also touches Wisconsin, Minnesota, and Ontario.)*

China becomes more monolithic - China completed its own satellite navigation system, BeiDou Navigation Satellite System, making it independent of foreign technology such as the US Global Positioning System (GPS) by 2020.

The Beidou Navigation System will enable military and civilian users from China to find their way anywhere in the world. "The system will shake off the dependence on foreign systems," said Zhang Xiaojin, director of astronautics at the China Aerospace Science and Technology Corp.

China aims to launch 30 more satellites into space. The system currently in place only provides regional navigation services within China's own territory.

The Beidou Navigation System is seen as a rival not just of the GPS, but also the European Union's Galileo Positioning System and Russia's Global Navigation Satellite System. *Just what we need, more space garbage flying around.*

China Consumes - China consumes over 59% of the world's cement. It consumes 48% of the world's iron ore and consumes 47% of the world's coal (more than the rest of the world combined). China is well ahead of the US in the consumption of television sets, refrigerators, and mobile phones. China has become the world's second largest luxury goods consumer with 27.5% of the world's luxury goods. It also consumes 25% of the world's beer.

China is the world's largest cigarette producer, with a growing market of about 320 million (more than the total US population). Chinese cigarettes are also among the cheapest in the world - a pack can cost as little as 8 US cents.

China has 1.3 billion population and that is a bit over 20% of the world's population. India's population is 1.1 billion, a bit over 1/6th of the world population, and is younger and growing faster than China.

Chinese Inventions - Did you know the Chinese invented making silk from the cocoons of certain caterpillars? They also invented the compass, gunpowder, porcelain, wheelbarrow, paper, and early computer called an abacus. This was a simple calculator using beads which were moved along wires.

Others, including the Egyptians, Greeks, Romans, and Japanese also used it to perform arithmetic calculations. It can be used to add, subtract, multiply, and divide, and to calculate square roots and cube root. The abacus is still in use today.

Recycled Glass - Thai monks from the Sisaket province have used over one million recycled glass bottle to construct a Buddhist temple. They used the recycled bottles to build everything from the toilets to their crematorium.

The Wat Pa Maha Chedi Kaew temple, also referred to as "Wat Lan Kuad" or "Temple of Million Bottles" is about 400 miles northeast of Bangkok in the city of Khun Han close to the Cambodian border. Using green Heineken bottles and brown Chang Beer bottles, the monks were able to clean up local pollution and create a useful structure. The water tower and tourist bathrooms are also made from recycled beer bottles. The temple also has large intricately crafted mosaics made entirely from the left over bottle caps.

Can You Hear Me Now - Remember the old adage, if a tree falls in the forest and no one is there to hear it. . . Have you ever thought about space? Sound is vibrations of air particles, and it only can travel through a solid, liquid, or gas, so there is no sound in space. Sound travels fastest through solids, a bit less fast through liquids, and slowest through gases.

Light waves and radio waves, which are a part of the electromagnetic spectrum, can be interpreted by radio equipment and then be translated into sound, but not the sound itself.

Even though explosion of stars, collision of asteroids, etc., can cause sound, it does not travel to be detected as we hear sound on Earth. Space, as an almost perfect vacuum, is not an efficient medium for sound to travel and be heard by us, but extremely sensitive instruments can pick up sound (*almost* perfect vacuum is the key). Astronauts talk to each other when space walking, by using radio waves. Sounds can travel by air in the spacecraft and through the metal.

If something exploded outside the craft, you would not hear it until something hit your craft, then the sound would travel from the metal, through the air inside to your ears. *Hollywood doesn't care, so you only hear sounds from space in movies and TV. . . as well as a many other unnatural things emanating from CA.*

Did You Know - The city of Roma (not Rome) is found on every continent, except Antarctica.

Trees - A mature tree can produce as much oxygen in a season as 10 people inhale in a year. It takes 12 trees to produce a ton of printing paper, 24 trees for higher grade writing paper. *Emails are treeless.*

Rainbows - A rainbow is not the flat two-dimensional arc it appears to be. It appears flat for the same reason a spherical burst of fireworks high in the sky appears as a disk-because of a lack of distance cues. The rainbow you see is actually a three-dimensional cone with the tip at your eye.

Consider a glass cone, the shape of those paper cones you sometimes see at drinking fountains. If you held the tip of such a glass cone against your eye, you would see the glass as a circle. All the drops that disperse the rainbow's light toward you lie in the shape of a cone of different layers with drops that deflect red to your eye on the outside, orange beneath the red, yellow beneath the orange, and so on all the way to violet on the inner conical surface. The thicker the region containing the water drops, the thicker conical edge that you look through.

Your cone of vision that intersects the cloud of drops that creates your rainbow is different from that of a person next to you. Everybody sees his or her own personal rainbow.

If the Earth were not in the way, a rainbow would be a complete circle. *This is why you will never find the golden pot at the end of the rainbow.*

Death Valley - In July 1913, the highest temperature ever recorded in the continental United States was 134 degrees which melted thermometers that day in Death Valley, California. *I thought it was cooler before global warming started.*

English is spoken by 334 million people in:
Akrotiri, American Samoa, Anguilla, Antigua and Barbuda, Argentina, Aruba, Australia, Bahamas, The, Bahrain, Bangladesh, Barbados, Belize, Bermuda, Botswana, Brazil, British Virgin Islands, Brunei, Cambodia, Cameroon, Canada, Cayman Islands, Christmas Island, Cocos (Keeling) Islands, Cook Islands, Costa Rica, Cyprus, Denmark, Dhekelia, Dominica, Egypt, Ethiopia, Falkland Islands (Islas Malvinas), Fiji, Gambia, The, Gaza Strip, Ghana, Gibraltar, Greece, Greenland, Grenada, Guam, Guernsey, Guyana, Hong Kong, Iceland,

India, Indonesia, Ireland, Isle of Man, Israel, Jamaica, Jersey, Jordan, Kenya, Kiribati, Korea, South, Kuwait, Laos, Lebanon, Lesotho, Liberia, Libya, Madagascar, Malaysia, Maldives, Malta, Marshall Islands, Mauritius, Micronesia, Federated States of, Monaco, Montserrat, Namibia, Nauru, Nepal, Netherlands Antilles, New Zealand, Nicaragua, Nigeria, Niue, Norfolk Island, Northern Mariana Islands, Oman, Pakistan, Palau, Panama, Papua New Guinea, Philippines, Pitcairn Islands, Puerto Rico, Qatar, Rwanda, Saint Barthelemy, Saint Helena, Saint Kitts and Nevis, Saint Lucia, Saint Martin, Saint Vincent and the Grenadines, Samoa, Seychelles, Sierra Leone, Singapore, Solomon Islands, Somalia, South Africa, Sri Lanka, Sudan, Suriname, Swaziland, Switzerland, Syria, Tanzania, Thailand, Timor-Leste, Tokelau, Tonga, Trinidad and Tobago, Turks and Caicos Islands, Tuvalu, Uganda, United Arab Emirates, United Kingdom, United States, Vanuatu, Vietnam, Virgin Islands, West Bank, Zambia, and Zimbabwe.

Spanish or Castillian Spanish is spoken in Argentina, Aruba, Belize, Bolivia, Brazil, Chile, Colombia, Costa Rica, Cuba, Dominican Republic, Ecuador, El Salvador, Equatorial Guinea, Gibraltar, Guatemala, Honduras, Mexico, Netherlands Antilles, Nicaragua, Panama, Paraguay, Peru, Puerto Rico, Saint Martin, Spain, Switzerland, Trinidad and Tobago, United States, Uruguay, Venezuela, and Virgin Islands.

Satellite Orbits - The reason we do not hear about satellites bumping into each other is because they each have their own protected orbit, kind of like a one lane highway. Orbits are not patented, but "useful systems which incorporate particular orbits, such as technological solutions for providing telecommunications which utilize equipment in those orbits, are patent-eligible."

So while a company could not attempt to patent a specific set of gravitational dynamics, it could exert control over an orbit by patenting the specific set of innovations needed to keep a satellite in that orbit.

US Patent No. 5,410,728, was issued to Motorola, and outlines how a formation of several satellites can optimize cellular coverage. The satellite orbit is not subject to this patent, but the process of deploying them into those orbits for some use as telecommunications is patented.

Incidentally, Sci-Fi author Arthur C. Clarke wrote about patenting orbits way back in 1945. The geostationary orbit he proposed that year is now home to hundreds of satellites, and has been officially designated the Clarke orbit by the International Astronomical Union.

Beach Fact - It appears, New Zealand might be stretching the facts a bit. New Zealand's 90-Mile Beach is only 55 miles long. Back when missionaries traveled on horseback a horse could travel on average about 30 miles (50 km) in a day before needing to be rested. The beach took three days to travel therefore earning its name. However, the missionaries did not take into account the slower pace of the horses walking in the sand, thus thinking they had traveled about 90 miles (140 km) when in fact they had traveled just 55 (88km).

Moon and Earth Names - Translations of the Bible into English was one of the earliest recorded uses of the name Earth – "God called the dry land Earth, and the waters that were gathered together he called Seas. And God saw that it was good."

It is called 'terra' in Portuguese, 'dünya' in Turkish and 'aarde' in Dutch. The common thread in all languages is that they were all derived from the same meaning in their origins, which is 'ground' or 'soil'.

The modern English word and name for our planet Earth goes back at least 1,000 years. Just as the English language evolved from 'Anglo-Saxon' (English-German) with the migration of certain Germanic tribes from the continent to Britain in the fifth century AD, the word 'Earth' came from the Anglo-Saxon word 'erda' and its Germanic equivalent 'erde' which means ground or soil. In Old English, the word became 'eor(th)e' or 'ertha'.

The Moon did have other names, including the name of an ancient deity, Luna, the Roman Goddess of the Moon. The word Luna is still associated with the Moon. For instance, Luna is the root of words like lunar.

When humanity first learned of other moons orbiting the planets in our solar system, one of the primary reasons they were given names was to differentiate them from the Moon, which is still the official name of our moon in English. The word "moon" can be traced back to Old English, where it is said to have derived from the Proto-Germanic word "menon", which in turn derived from the Latin "menses", meaning "month, moon".

With few exceptions, the Moon has long been associated with women, fertility, and a whole host of other female attributes. In most cases, menstrual cycles more or less coincide with the phases of the Moon. It should then come as no surprise that across many languages, the words for "moon", "month", and the name for a woman's menstrual cycle often has the same root word.

Canada U.S. War of Pork and Beans - Canada and the United States have not fought a war against each other officially since 1814, but in 1839, there was a 'war' of sorts fought mainly with fists and axe handles. It was along the New Brunswick–Maine border and the warriors were lumbermen. It is known as 'the war of pork and beans', or the 'Aroostook Controversy'.

Logging along both sides of the border was controlled by powerful lumber barons who were not always careful about the areas into which they sent their lumberjacks. Most of the trouble was in the rich Aroostook Valley pines. The worst battle broke out on February 8, 1839. Under normal circumstances, the fighting among loggers might not have caused much alarm, but the situation was dangerous, because of the dispute about the location of the border.

Maine and New Brunswick called out the militia. Nova Scotia passed an appropriation for defense, and British troops were rushed from Halifax to guard the border along St. Croix River. The United States Congress voted $10,000,000 to raise a force of 50,000 men if required.

London and Washington realized the seriousness of the situation and President Van Buren persuaded the Governors of Maine and New Brunswick to arrange a truce. Britain and the United States finally agreed on a border. The Ashburton-Webster Treaty provided a settlement in 1842.

Canadian Inventions - Did you know the following were all invented in Canada: peanut butter, wonderbra, Trivial Pursuit, the car odometer, Imax, egg cartons, McIntosh apples, discovery of insulin, sports instant replay, luggage bag tags, electric wheelchair, and more.

New New Zealand Flag - New Zealand decided not to change its national flag. The silver fern will not replace the status quo in the second round of voting between March 3 and March 24. 2016.

Australia is Moving - Australia's national GPS coordinates were recalculated and adjusted to keep pace with changing navigation technology. The continent moves north by seven centimeters (2.76 inches) every year due to its position on the world's fastest moving continental tectonic plate, according to Geoscience Australia. The country's coordinates were off by 1.5 meters (4.9 feet) due to years of natural shifting.

Satellite navigation systems on smartphones align with digital map information and autonomous vehicles could show you are in the middle of the road or you are in another lane. The Geocentric Datum of Australia, the nation's local coordinate system, was last updated during 1994.

Incidentally, the Indian Subcontinent in the past was moving towards Asia at a speed of about 6 inches per year. When they collided, the Himalayas came into being. They are still growing, but since then, India is only pushing into Asia proper at about 2 inches per year.

Languages - According to Ethnologue, there are over 7,000 distinct languages in the world and about 40,000 dialects. Some languages, like Russian and Hindi, are written from left-to-right, while others, like Hebrew and Persian, are written right-to-left.

The nation of Papua New Guinea has the highest language diversity in the world. There are 820 languages spoken in an area the size of Spain.

There are logographic languages, like Japanese and Korean, where symbols represent words, and there are Dongba and Nsibidi which are pictographic languages where symbols represent ideas.

Incidentally, there are over 1.5 billion speakers of English globally. In 2015, out of the total 195 countries in the world, 67 nations have English as the primary language of 'official status'. Plus there are 27 countries where English is spoken as a secondary 'official' language.

Ten German Inventions

MP3 - A German inventor, Karlheinz Brandenburg is responsible for an invention that has revolutionized how we listen to music.

Ring binder, ink eraser, hole punch, glue stick - Confirming the stereotype that Germans like to keep orderly records of everything, some of the most useful office supplies have been invented by Germans. Friedrich Soennecken invented ring binders and hole punches in the late 19th Century. Another German, Louis Leitz, then improved on the invention by putting a finger hole in the binder to make it easier to remove from a crowded shelf.

Aspirin - The world's favorite painkiller made from willow bark was developed by Felix Hoffmann in August 1897 for pharmaceutical giant Bayer, and although a US company claimed the patent for the drug after the First World War, 12,000 of the 50,000 tons of aspirin produced each year are still made by Bayer.

Carabiners - The most important piece of gear in any climber's equipment was invented by Otto Herzog, a Bavarian climber and inventor. The carabiner has many uses, but this metal loop with a spring-loaded gate is most commonly used to allow a climber to safely scale or descend a steep cliff with the aid of a rope.

Lithography - Invented by Alois Senefelder in Bavaria in 1796, lithography has given the world some of its finest art. Most famously, Edvard (sic) Munch used the printing technique, but Picasso, Monet, Manet and more have also used the technique.

Accordion - When asked to think of Germany, one often thinks of a portly man wearing lederhosen and a green hat, playing folk tunes on a huge accordion. In fact, early versions of the instrument date back to third century BC China. But the first 'true' accordion was invented by a German, Christian Friedrich Buschmann, who in 1822 attached bellows to a portable keyboard with vibrating reeds, naming it a 'hand-aeoline'.

X-ray machine - The first X-ray machine was invented by Wilhelm Conrad Röntgen, physics chair at the University of Würzburg. He apparently discovered the unknown radiation, which he marked with an x, while investigating cathode rays. He noticed that the radiation could pass through human tissue, but not bones.

Contact lens - Although Leonardo da Vinci is said to have been the first man to come up with the idea of a contact lens, it was a German by the name of Adolf Gaston Eugen Fick who first made a contact lens and successfully fitted it to the human eye. Fick's prototype could only be worn for an hour or two at a time due to its unwieldy size.

Playmobil - Playmobil was invented by Hans Beck in the 1970s with the idea to make a flexible toy that was still simple enough for young children to understand. With the original toys being an American Indian, a cowboy, and a builder, the little figures were a hit as soon as they came on the market.

Airbag - Walter Linderer came up with the idea of using compressed air in a bag which would inflate when the bumpers of two cars made contact. He patented it in 1951, although his design did not inflate fast enough and had little practical value at the time.

End Thoughts

I LIKE YOU

- At least five people in this world love you so much they would die for you.

- At least fifteen people in this world love you in some way.

- The only reason anyone would ever hate you is because they want to be just like you.

- A smile from you can bring happiness to anyone, even if they do not like you.

- Every night, someone thinks about you before they go to sleep.

- You mean the world to someone.

- If not for you, someone may not be living.

- When you make the biggest mistake ever, something good comes from it.

- When you think the world has turned its back on you, take a look: you most likely turned your back on the world.

- When you think you have no chance of getting what you want, you probably will not get it, but if you believe in yourself, sooner or later, you will get it.

- Always remember the compliments you received. Forget about the rude remarks.

- Always tell someone how you feel about them; you will feel much better when they know.

- If you have a great friend, take the time to let them know that they are great.

- You are special and unique.

- Someone that you do not even know exists loves you.

Index